the essenti
personnel
sourcebook

second edition

DAVID JAY

Series Editor
ROS JAY

FINANCIAL TIMES
PITMAN PUBLISHING

LONDON · HONG KONG · JOHANNESBURG
MELBOURNE · SINGAPORE · WASHINGTON DC

FINANCIAL TIMES MANAGEMENT
128 Long Acre, London WC2E 9AN
Tel: +44 (0)171 447 2000
Fax: +44 (0)171 240 5771
Website: www.ftmanagement.com

A Division of Financial Times Professional Limited

First published in Great Britain 1996
Second edition 1998

British Library Cataloguing in Publication Data
A CIP catalogue record for this book can be obtained from the British Library.

ISBN 0 273 63109 8

10 9 8 7 6 5 4 3 2 1

Typeset by Pantek Arts, Maidstone, Kent
Printed and bound in Great Britain by Bell and Bain Ltd, Glasgow

The Publishers' policy is to use paper manufactured from sustainable forests.

SURVEYS AND REPORTS, 1998

The following surveys, reports and publications are produced by the organisations which have contributed to this book. You will find listed many of the full reports from which we have reproduced extracts in this book, along with other relevant publications. If you would like to order any of the surveys, reports or other publications listed here, the full contact details of the organisations are in Appendix 2 on page 335. Prices may not include extras such as VAT, and postage and packing.

Recruitment

Employee Selection in The UK, Institute of Manpower Studies, 1988
Employers' Use of Flexible Labour, by Bernard Casey, Hilary Metcalf and Neil Millward, Policy Studies Institute, 1997. Available from Grantham Books, £16.95
Key Facts on Psychological Testing, IPD, September 1997
Maternity Rights in Britain, Policy Studies Institute, November 1991, £29.95
Employers' Recruitment Practices: The 1992 Survey, Social and Community Planning Research, 1993, £20.00
Recruitment, Lloyds Bank/SBRT Quarterly Small Business Management Survey Report, Vol. 5 No. 2, July 1997
Recruit, Retrain, Retain: Personnel Management and the Three R's, Personnel Management, November 1989
Skill Needs in Britain 1996, Public Attitude Surveys Ltd research for the Department for Education and Employment, £47.50
Temporary Work and the Labour Market, J. Atkinson, J. Rick, S. Morris and M. Williams, IES Report No. 311, 1997. Available from BEBC Distribution, £35.00
Training – the Business Case, CBI, 1993, free
Women's Employment During Family Formation, Policy Studies Institute, January 1996, £9.95

Staff relations

Compliance Costs, NatWest/SBRT Quarterly Survey of Small Businesses in Britain, Vol. 12, No.1, 1996
Consultation and Communication, ACAS, 1990
Employee Commitment and the Skills Revolution, Policy Studies Institute, June 1993, £9.95

'Employee Job Mobility and Relocation', *Personnel Review*, Vol. 19, No. 6.

Employee Morale during Downsizing, Institute for Employment Studies, 1995, £16.00

Employee Motivation and the Psychological Contract, IPD Employee Attitude Survey, 1997

Is Flatter Better? Delayering the Management Hierarchy, Institute for Employment Studies, 1995, £25.00

Managing Redundancy, IRS Employment Trends, 1995

New Agenda, IRPC Group Ltd, 1997

The 1992 Survey of Industrial Tribunal Applications, Department for Education and Employment (produced by SCPR), 1994, free

Staff effectiveness

Counting Costs to Keep Competitive, Confederation of British Industry, 1994

From Absence to Attendance, Alistair Evans and Steven Palmer, IPD, 1997, £15.95

Measuring and Monitoring Absence from Work, Institute for Employment Studies, 1995, £16.00

Sickness Absence Monitoring and Control – A Survey of Practice, IRS Employment Trends, September 1994

Team Working and Pay, Institute for Employment Studies, 1995, £16.00

Training

Careers in Organisations: Issues for the Future, Institute for Employment Studies, 1995, £25.00

Costs & Benefits of National Vocational Qualifications to Employers, Policy Studies Institute, November 1993, £14.95

Employers' Role in the Supply of Intermediate Skills, Policy Studies Institute, September 1994, £7.95

Education and Training For 16–18 Year Olds, Policy Studies Institute, May 1996, £14.95

Future Skill Demand and Supply, Policy Studies Institute, November 1995, £12.95

Individual Commitment to Lifetime Learning: Individuals' Attitudes, Department for Education and Employment (produced by SPCR), 1994, free

Individual Take-up Of N/SVQs – Stimuli and Obstacles, Policy Studies Institute research for the Department for Education and Employment, 1996

IT Training Survey, Benchmark Research Ltd, August 1996

Line Manager Training Survey, Benchmark Research Ltd, November 1996, £20.00

Personal Development Plans: Case Studies of Practice, Institute for Employment Studies, 1995, £30.00
Towing the Line: Helping Managers to Manage People, Institute for Employment Studies, 1994, £16.00
Training for Industry and Commerce Survey, Benchmark Research Ltd, November 1996, £60.00
Training for Recovery, Institute of Management, 1993
UK Training Video Survey, Benchmark Research Ltd, June 1996, £40.00

Health and safety

Attitudes towards Alcohol in the Workplace, MORI for the Health Education Authority, 1995
Survey of Health and Safety Management in the UK, Performance Support International, 1994
Health and Safety Statistics, The Health and Safety Executive
Working for your Health, Confederation of British Industry, 1993

Towards the millennium

Benchmark Research Ltd Survey for Hewlett Packard, IBM and Oracle, 1995
I.T. Answers to H.R. Questions, Peter Kingsbury, IPD, 1997
Information Technology, Barclays Review, 1996
People and Technology, Benchmark Research Ltd Survey for Coopers & Lybrand and Oracle, 1994
Survey of the UK's Top 100 Exporting Companies, LinguaTel, 1995

General

CBI Employment Affairs Report, including Databank Survey of Pay Settlements and Awards, Confederation of British Industry. Annual subscription: £100 CBI members: £160 non-members
Cleaner Production in Industry, Policy Studies Institute, October 1995, £19.95
Measuring the Personnel Function, Institute for Employment Studies, 1995, £30.00
Organisational Change, The Henley Centre, November 1994, £5.00

ACKNOWLEDGEMENTS

We would like to thank the following people and organisations for their help and contributions in putting together this book.

ACAS
Barclays Bank plc Small Business Services
The Basic Skills Agency
Benchmark Research Ltd
Capita Management Consultancy Ltd
The Chartered Institute of Purchasing and Supply
The Confederation of British Industry
Coutts Career Consultants
Dartmouth Publishing
The Department for Education and Employment
The Employment Gazette
The Equal Opportunities Commission
John Fenton International Training plc
The Health Education Authority
The Health and Safety Executive
IFF Research Ltd
Incomes Data Services Ltd
Industrial Relations Services
The Inland Revenue
The Institute of Directors
The Institute of Employment Studies
The Institute of Management

The Institute of Personnel and Development
IRPC Group Ltd
LinguaTel Ltd
Lloyds Bank Small Business Research Trust
London Business School
Marketing Week magazine
Media Monitoring Services
NatWest Small Business Research Trust
People Management magazine
Performance Support International
Personnel Review magazine
The Policy Studies Institute
Remuneration Economics Ltd, Romtec Plc
Small Business Research Trust
Social and Community Planning Research

Ken Burnett
Bob Garrett
Schuyler Henderson
Carolyn Highley
Paul West

We would also like to thank Alison Alsbury for her work in preparing the second edition.

CONTENTS

monitor levels of ethnic minority staff? ■ What problems are most often encountered when introducing positive action policies? ■ What proportion of small businesses are run by ethnic minorities?

Why do some companies make an effort to recruit older workers? ■ What are the most effective policies for increasing the number of older workers in the workforce?

What proportion of employers meet the legal quota of disabled employees? ■ Why are people with disabilities not employed? ■ What are the advantages and disadvantages of employing disabled workers? ■ To what extent do extra provisions need to be made for disabled employees? ■ How many companies have special facilities for disabled people? ■ What proportion of companies have an explicit policy with regard to recruiting disabled people? ■ What proportion of organisations actively seek to employ disabled people? ■ How do companies go about recruiting disabled people?

What is the average management salary? ■ What proportion of employees are satisfied with their salaries? ■ How many companies link human resources and payroll responsibilities? ■ How many companies have a formal remuneration policy? ■ What proportion of employees receive incentive payments? ■ What proportion of earnings do incentive payments represent? ■ How common, and how sizeable are premium payments? ■ What proportion of employees are paid in cash?

What effects do fringe benefits have on recruitment and retention? ■ What benefits are most commonly available? ■ What percentage of managers and company directors receive company cars?

What is the average level of pay awards? ■ What are the main pressures on pay settlements? ■ What are the main determinants of wage levels for new employees?

What proportion of pay are individual bonuses usually worth? ■ What proportion of directors and managers receive bonuses, and how much are these bonuses worth? ■ How much are management and directors' bonuses worth in cash terms?

encouraged or discouraged? ■ What areas of work do unions have the most influence over? ■ Does the presence of a trade union affect perceptions of employee–management relations?

Are union members more likely to apply to an industrial tribunal for unfair dismissal? ■ Do industrial tribunals normally involve companies who already have a record of applications against them? ■ What are the main reasons for dismissals which are appealed against? ■ How many industrial tribunal applicants have applied before? ■ How far do industrial tribunal applications usually go? ■ How many tribunals find in favour of the applicant, and what is the actual cost? ■ What other costs are associated with industrial tribunals?

How many organisations have union agreements on redundancy? ■ What factors influence decisions when selecting for redundancy? ■ How are skills assessed for redundancy selection? ■ How is performance assessed for redundancy selection? ■ How can you assess the ability to perform alternative jobs? ■ By what means are redundancies achieved? ■ To what extent is voluntary redundancy used? ■ To what extent is the principle of 'last in first out' used? ■ What are the arguments in favour of 'last in first out'? ■ What are the arguments against using 'last in first out'? ■ Do most companies stick to the statutory minimum severance payments? ■ What is a reasonable service qualification for severance pay? ■ What qualifies as 'length of service' in such calculations? ■ How many companies provide counselling for employees who are made redundant?

How many companies provide outplacement services? ■ For what grades of staff are outplacement services usually provided? ■ Are outplacement services usually provided in-house or by external companies?

What retraining do staff need when they relocate? ■ How stressful is relocation?

PENSIONS 107

Why should you provide pension plans for employees? ■ What are the most important issues with regard to planning pension schemes? ■ How appreciative of pension schemes are employees? ■ How can employee appreciation of pension schemes be improved? ■ What changes in the labour force have most impact on pension provision? ■ How long should you take to recover pension surpluses? ■ What is the best type of pension provision to make?

STAFF ATTITUDES 113

Employees 113

What aspects of their job are most employees satisfied, or dissatisfied, with? ■ What are the possible reasons for middle management resistance to employee involvement? ■ How can you increase employee involvement? ■ To what extent do staff have a say in the way that their company operates? ■ Are employees happy with the level of input they have into organisational decisions? ■ Does employee involvement affect employee perceptions of changes at work? ■ Does employee involvement affect perceptions of employee–management relations?

Leadership 116

Is there a change in leadership style? ■ Is there a change in leadership language? ■ How will leadership be benchmarked in the future?

Company culture 118

What effect does 'flattening' your organisation have on company culture? ■ Do staff like flatter structures? ■ How can you guarantee the success of a flatter organisation? ■ Do leaner organisations have better staff relations? ■ How do lean organisations make sure that they are efficient? ■ How many organisations treat manual workers the same as non-manual workers?

Promotions 121

What proportion of employees are aiming for a promotion? ■ Do employees feel that there are enough opportunities for promotion in their company?

STAFF BEHAVIOUR 122

Violence 122

How common is physical or verbal workplace violence? ■ How does this violence break down?

STAFF EFFECTIVNESS

IT solutions 295

Are the benefits of IT well understood? ■ How can you make sure that money spent on IT is well spent? ■ What are the benefits of electronic networks? ■ How do you use the Internet effectively? ■ How can you make the best use of your phone?

IT training 298

How many employers provide IT training? ■ What are the main reasons for providing IT training? ■ What organisational factors have most effect on IT training? ■ How important is IT training for different occupations? ■ How many companies have a formal IT training programme, and what time-frame does it cover? ■ Which functions does your business use computers for? ■ What are the main areas of IT training? ■ What are the best ways to select IT training suppliers? ■ What proportion of the IT budget is spent on training?

Small businesses 306

How important is IT to the small business?

HOMEWORKING 307

What are the main reasons for introducing homeworking?

FOREIGN LANGUAGE SKILLS 308

How well can companies handle calls in a foreign language? ■ How important is foreign business and therefore foreign languages to British companies? ■ Is it always necessary to speak your customer's language? ■ For what foreign clients are foreign language skills really needed? ■ Who needs to be able to speak a foreign language? ■ How are language needs most commonly met? ■ How do people cope with unmet language needs? ■ Which languages create a genuine barrier to business? ■ How many companies provide language training for staff who need to speak that language for their work? ■ What are the most popular methods of language training?

Appendix 1: How to read statistics 319

Appendix 2: Contact addresses 335

INTRODUCTION

This is a business reference book with a difference. The information it contains is directly useful to you and your business. There's a lot of statistical material currently available, but it tends to be industry-specific or whole industry figures. It's not terribly helpful to know what's going on in the baked bean industry if you run a chain of travel agencies. And knowing what the total UK training spend is each year tells you precious little about your own training budget.

This book will give you generic – not industry-specific – business data, so it will apply to you whatever business you're in. It starts with the questions you might reasonably ask, and tries to answer them.

All the information in this book is relevant to the UK. Businesses overseas do some things very differently, and building their research information into the results would dilute the accuracy of the figures. The book gives you average data for the individual organisation, so you can see how they compare with yours.

You can use *The Essential Personnel Sourcebook* for four main purposes:

- **Benchmarking:** you'll find plenty of information about how other businesses conduct various personnel activities, and you can measure your own performance against the average.

- **Planning:** before you launch into a new initiative, you can look through the relevant section to see what are the key factors to consider. For example, if you're thinking of installing a profit-related pay system, you'll find that the relevant section of this book will tell you what problems you might encounter, and what the main benefits are likely to be.

> The book gives you average data for the individual organisation, so you can see how it compares with yours.

- **Decision making:** you'll find the answers to all sorts of questions here, to help you reach decisions. Suppose you need to fill a vacant post in your organisation, and you need to do it quickly. The relevant section of this book will tell you which recruitment channels produce the fastest response from applicants.

- **Supporting proposals and presentations:** the information in this book comes from reliable and authoritative sources. Consequently you will find it invaluable for adding weight to your own arguments. Suppose you want to persuade the board of directors that they should set up briefing meetings to improve internal communication levels, rather than sending out more memos. After referring to this

> You'll find the answers to all sorts of questions here, to help you reach decisions.

book, you will be able to inform them that internal meetings will improve employees' satisfaction with internal communication significantly more than sending out more pieces of paper.

The *Essential Personnel Sourcebook* pulls together information on personnel topics from recruitment and staff turnover through to the need for foreign languages, calling in on training, unions, variable pay systems, outplacement, benefits packages, counselling and many others along the way. It should quickly become one of the most well-thumbed books on your shelf.

The series

This book is one of *The Essential Business Sourcebooks*. The other book in the series is *The Essential Marketing Sourcebook*. They cover two vital aspects of business, and have proved immensely popular. The second editions carry updated material where relevant, and extend their coverage to reflect new developments in the last few years. Gurus – leading industry specialists – have also kindly contributed to the second editions, so they include a wealth of practical advice from people in the know.

You may find that certain topics you are interested in are included in the other book. For example, presentations, which you might reasonably consider to be an aspect of personnel, has been included in *The Essential Marketing Sourcebook* since most of the information available on the subject relates to marketing.

However, where only one or two pieces of data overlap between the books, we have included them in both books to make it easier for you to find them. For instance, you will find that the section of this book on internal communication also appears in *The Essential Marketing Sourcebook*.

The data

In this series of books we have used only the most reliable data we could find. Clearly the methodology varies widely between studies, but if we included the full details of it each time, there would be no room to include the findings. Each piece of data is clearly sourced where it appears in the text, and you will find a complete list of contact details at the back of the book (Appendix 2) should you wish to find out more.

Includes a wealth of practical advice from people in the know.

We have studied the data ourselves, of course, and we have not included any material that we consider to be unreliable. In a few cases, we felt that the information available needed to be treated with a measure of caution. In these instances, we have made this view clear in the surrounding text. We took the view, however, that any information is more useful than no information, as long as you are aware of the possible risks in treating it as gospel. Where we felt that data were seriously flawed or biased, we excluded them.

The research findings included in the series are the most up-to-date we could find. In the vast majority of cases the research was published within the last three or four years. In a few cases the research is older than this, but often the reason no one has updated it is precisely because they do not expect it to have changed. We have not included any information that we considered to be unreliable because of its age.

The *Essential Business Sourcebooks* are a comprehensive guide to useful UK business data. But since the series is based on research data, we are obviously limited by the research that is available. We have found useful material on all the major areas of business, but it is possible that you may be interested in a particular aspect of one of these areas that you cannot find listed in the contents. If this happens, it will be because (after months of research, and contacts with hundreds of organisations) we have failed to track down any reliable data on the subject. If you know of any survey or other research data that are relevant to this series but which we have not included, we would be very pleased to hear from you so that we can include them in the next edition.

The contributors

The data in these books have been contributed by many of the most highly respected institutes and research organisations, by government departments, and by some of the top experts in various fields. We are very grateful to them for their co-operation.

Some of the reports that we have taken extracts from are publicly available from these organisations. In most cases, we have reproduced only a small part of the full research findings – the information we think will be of the widest interest. But if you have a special interest in any subject, you may well want to see the full report. A listing of surveys and reports that are published by our contributing organisations appears at the front of this book. This listing not only includes the reports from which we have taken extracts, but also gives details of any other reports and surveys that you might find interesting.

How to use the book

The book is divided into broad personnel categories (for example 'recruitment'), which are subdivided into more specific categories (such as 'selection'). These are then divided further into areas within this (for example 'selection procedures'). Finally, the data in these sections have been split into individual subject areas, each headed with a question (e.g. Which are the most commonly used selection procedures?). You will find a very comprehensive contents at the front of the book, to help you find your way around this system.

> The data have been contributed by many of the most highly respected institutes and research organisations.

We have presented each piece of data in the form which illustrates it most clearly. In many cases, this involves using charts, graphs, matrices and other things that make some people feel slightly unnerved and confused. If you're one of these people, you may find Appendix 1 helpful. It is a user-friendly guide to reading statistics which briefly explains each type of graph, chart and figure that you may come across while using the book. Let me reassure you, however, that we have not tried to be clever, but have used only those graphics which are in relatively common usage.

Although we have designed the books to be functional, we were surprised when we put them together to find just how fascinating much of the research material is, even when the subject matter is not immediately relevant to you. You should find it easy to track down the information you want; we hope, however, that you will find the book sufficiently

We were surprised to find just how fascinating much of the research material is.

interesting that you will not only use it for its primary purpose – as a reference book – but will also find it entertaining to browse through for general interest.

RECRUITMENT

STYLE

The data below come from the SCRP *Employers' Recruitment Practices Survey* 1992, one of a ten-yearly series; the next survey will be published in 2002. Details of this survey are on page 7, following the data given here.

Recruitment channels

■ *What are the most successfully used recruitment channels?*

If you are responsible for recruitment, then you will know how many options are open to you each time you want to advertise a vacancy. Naturally, then, you will want to know how effective each of these recruitment channels is. Below are the figures for the percentage of engagements by recruitment channel used for first contact. For example, 12.3% of employees recruited in the last 12 months were found through the Jobcentre. The top 8 channels in this respect were:

Direct application	16.8%
Local paid-for press	16.1%
Jobcentre	12.3%
Trade press	8.6%
Personal recommendation	7.5%
Internal notices	6.8%
National press	5.4%
Re-employed former employee	5.1%

But how much was each channel actually used? The survey also examined the number of establishments using each channel.

Most used channels	Percentage of companies using channel
Jobcentre	52%
Local paid-for press	48%
Personal recommendation	44%
Internal noticeboards	35%
Direct/speculative applications	28%

RECRUITMENT

■ What are the most popular recruitment channels for different occupations?

Of course, people recruit in different ways for different jobs. So which are the most commonly used channels for different posts? The figures below indicate, for several of the major recruitment channels, which posts were most often filled through this channel. This is expressed as the percentage of vacancies of each type filled through the channel in question.

Percentage of engagements by occupation where first contact was through Jobcentre:

Routine/unskilled	23.6%
Clerical/secretarial	16.0%
Operative and assembly	15.6%

Percentage of engagements by occupation where first contact was through paid-for local press:

Clerical/secretarial	22.3%
Personal services	22.0%
Routine/unskilled	21.1%

Percentage of engagements by occupation where first contact was through direct application:

Sales	27.5%
Craft/skilled service	25.1%
Operative/assembly	22.7%

Percentage of engagements by occupation where first contact was through fee-charging agency:

Managerial	11.9%
Clerical/secretarial	9.5%
Profession associate/technical	7.5%
Sales	6.9%
Professional	6.5%

■ *How effective are different recruitment channels?*

Of course, it may be that many new recruits are found through Jobcentres simply because these are used so much. If you really want to get an idea of how effective each channel is, then it helps to know how often it is successful relative to how often it was used. The way that this was rated in the SCPR survey was as a ratio of usage to success, in other words, the number of times that the channel was used divided by the number of times that the recruit was found through this channel. So a high number means that the channel was used a lot, but was not actually responsible for many recruitments.

The figures (given as x:1 ratio) were:

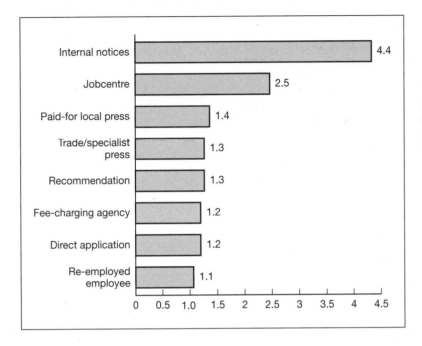

■ How long does it take to find your new recruit?

There are times when you need to find someone to take up a job as soon as possible, but how soon is this likely to be? This was gauged by how long it took from placing the advert, hiring the agency, or letting it be known that there was a vacancy, until the interview of the person who was finally recruited. Post-interview procedures are therefore not taken into account. The first factor that was considered was the level of the post that needed to be filled, and the findings for different occupational groups were as follows:

Professional	28.5 days
Managerial; Personal services; Professional associate/technical	25 days approx.
Other occupations	10–15 days

The time it takes to find your new recruit may also depend on the salary that the position offers. The survey found that:

- The time taken decreased as the hourly rate of pay decreased.
- So, it takes on average 27.3 days to fill a post which pays £7.50–£9.99 an hour.
- But it takes only 8.2 days for a post paying £2.50.
- The exception to this was posts which paid over £10 an hour; they took an average of 25.8 days to fill.

Of course, if you are in a hurry to fill a vacant post, the length of time the different recruitment channels that you might use will take can be crucial. If you want to be as quick as possible, you will not want to rely on internal notices, as the following chart of average time (in days) from use of successful channel to interview date shows.

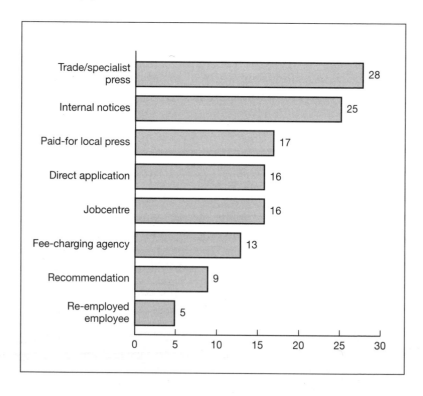

The SCPR *Employers' Recruitment Practices Survey* was conducted in 1992 by Social and Community Planning Research for the Employment Service. It is the latest in a series, the previous surveys having been conducted in 1982 and 1988. A total of 10,000 establishments were contacted with a 78% response rate. The figures are based on interviews conducted at 5,635 establishments, giving details of over 22,700 engagements.

Source: Employers' Recruitment Practices: The 1992 Survey, Social and Community Planning Research, 1992

RECRUITMENT

■ What are the advantages and disadvantages of the main recruitment channels?

Of course, speed will not always be your top priority when making recruitment decisions – your needs may vary quite considerably, even from case to case. So, what channel would suit you best if, for instance, price were your main concern? In the SCPR survey, respondents were asked to indicate which of the specified attributes they considered to be an advantage in each recruitment channel, and which they saw as a disadvantage. The attributes given were: speed of recruitment; cost; quality of applicants; number of applicants; service (convenience); PR/image consequences of using this channel. Respondents were allowed to indicate more than one attribute for each channel (advantage/disadvantage) and were also given the option of 'none' for each channel. In most cases, the three top scoring advantages are given (as the percentage of respondents who indicated them as an advantage), along with the percentage of respondents who indicated this as a disadvantage. The scores for 'none' are also given.

● Other attributes were rated fairly equally (8%–3% for advantages and 8%–0% for disadvantages), so cost is predictably included as the greatest disadvantage.

7

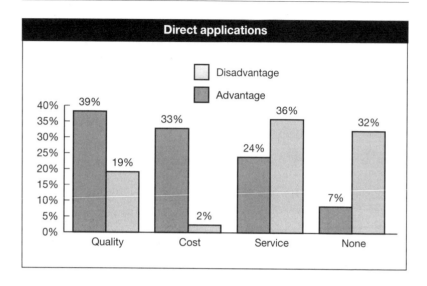

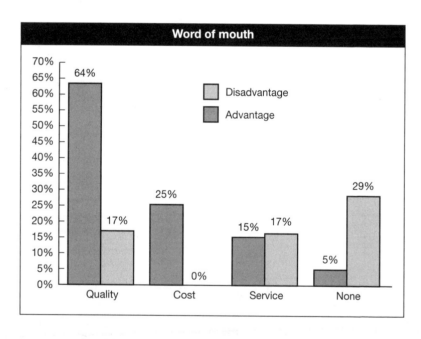

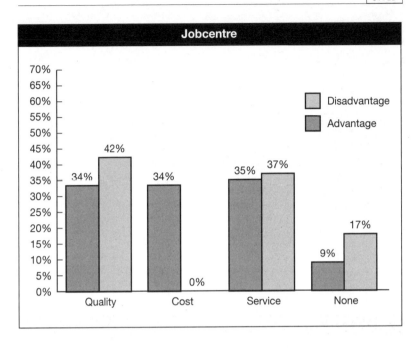

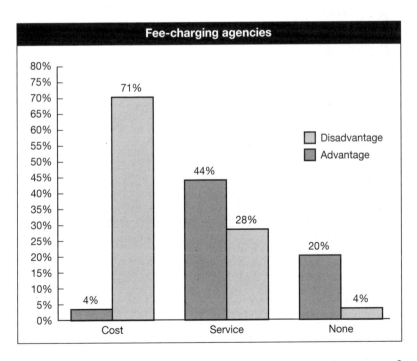

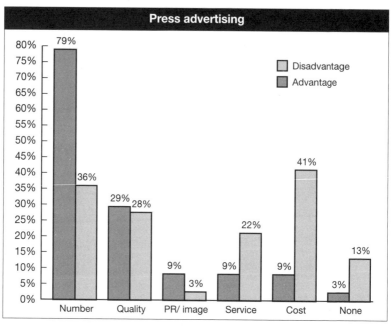

Source: Employers' Recruitment Practices: The 1992 Survey, Social and Community Planning Research, 1992

■ *When are vacancies most often advertised?*

As with many aspects of business, recruitment has its seasons. But what exactly are they? The figures below show the amount of recruitment advertising in the national press (in 100,000 column centimetres) for each month from September 1994 to August 1995.

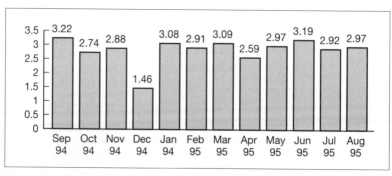

Source: Data from Media Monitoring Services Ltd

Small businesses

■ *Do small businesses have a different recruitment style?*

Much attention has been paid to the importance of local economic networks to small businesses. So is their recruitment style very different from the overall one?

- 62% of small businesses (under 50 employees) recruit by word of mouth.

- As firms grow in size, the use of Jobcentres, local press, agencies and national press grows.

- Preference for word of mouth was notably stronger in the South (71%) than in the Midlands and the North (57 and 53% respectively).

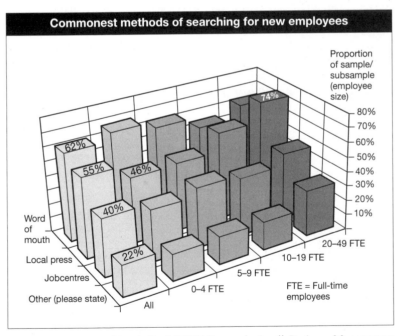

Source: Recruitment, Lloyds Bank/SBRT Quarterly Small Business Management Report Vol. 5 No. 2, July 1997

SELECTION

Assessing talent

■ Will future recruiters select recruits on different criteria?

Dr Robert McHenry, chairman of Oxford Psychologists' Press, maintains that in future:

> Jobs will be described in terms of what people are good at, rather than what the job requires as an output ... Organisations are aware of the need to adopt new ways of identifying and assessing the talent they'll require to succeed in the future.

Recruitment methods will therefore change. Future recruiters may look for potential, not existing, skills.

Source: 'The Latest in Recruitment and Selection', Dr Robert McHenry's speech to the Institute of Personnel and Development's national conference, Harrogate, 22 October 1997

■ What criteria will we use in the future?

Dr McHenry maintains that traditional tests measure what the applicant already knows. New methods of testing will be needed to measure what the applicant can potentially learn. He suggests structured learning exercises, designed to measure someone's ability to pick up a job by simulating it:

1. Give people fairly simple work samples, and tell them how they are doing.

2. Give them more complex work samples, and test them on how they perform.

If potential recruits are taught and tested, then the employer can assess how quickly the recruit can learn. It will also be a test of personal resources, because each individual will be free to exercise their individuality about how to perform the task.

Source: 'The Latest in Recruitment and Selection', Dr Robert McHenry's speech to the Institute of Personnel and Development's national conference, Harrogate, 22 October 1997

■ *Why do selection methods need to change?*

Dr McHenry reckons that frustration with the old methods of selection is the main reason. However, this change will also help employers respond to the new anti-discrimination laws. It will no longer be important to have specific knowledge, or to have been to a particular kind of school, or educated in a certain way. The only test will be in the ability to learn and perform the job.

Source: 'The Latest in Recruitment and Selection', Dr Robert McHenry's speech to the Institute of Personnel and Development's national conference, Harrogate, 22 October 1997

Selection procedures

■ *What are the factors that most affect companies' employment strategies?*

Many things have to be prioritised before an effective recruitment policy or strategy can be agreed. But what should come top of the priority list? The figures below show what percentage of companies rated which consideration as their number one priority.

Cost reductions	35%
Increased flexibility	14%
Increased productivity	13%
Competitive pressures	12%
Focus on core activities	8%
Increased demand	8%
Changing skill mix	4%
Increased use of IT	4%

Source: Survey of Long Term Employment Strategies, Institute of Management, 1994

■ Which are the most commonly used selection procedures?

The procedures for selecting your ideal candidate range from basic pre-selection through different forms of psychological testing to exotic arts such as graphology. But, in practice, which of these methods are really used to select the desired candidate? The figures that follow show the percentage of companies using the methods named.

Method	Percentage of companies
Pre-selection	75%
Panel interviews	61%
Personality testing	39%
Psychometric testing	37%
Assessment centres	18%
Inventories	2%
Graphology	0.5%
Other methods	8%

Source: 'Recruit, Retrain, Retain: Personnel Management and the Three Rs', *Personnel Management*, November 1989

■ Are more employers using psychometric tests?

If you are considering introducing psychometric tests as part of your selection procedures, you may well want to know how common they are, and how well they function.

● According to a recent Institute of Personnel and Development report, more companies are using tests to help decide the best person for the job.

Source: *Key Facts on Psychological Testing*, IPD, September 1997

■ Is feedback on psychological testing important, and how should it be handled?

The same survey stressed that 'feedback should always be given unless there are good reasons why this should not be the case'. Feedback can help unsuccessful candidates take a more positive view of a negative outcome. Angela Edward, IPD policy adviser, says:

Taking a series of tests and then finding out that you have not been successful can be highly demoralising. Candidates may feel that they have put in a lot of effort for no result. Feedback shows them that their application has been considered and evaluated; it can help them understand why they were unsuccessful and where their strengths lie. It turns the process into a learning experience.

Source: *Key Facts on Psychological Testing*, IPD, September 1997

■ How should feedback be given?

The same report warns that feedback is a delicate process – it should be conducted by people who are qualified in the use of tests and skilled in giving feedback.

Source: *Key Facts on Psychological Testing*, IPD, September 1997

CVs

■ How reliable are CVs considered to be?

As a recruiter, you will probably come into contact with many CVs, some of them more impressive than others. You may well be required to make a judgement of the candidate on this basis. But how reliable is that judgement likely to be if a CV is all you have to go on? One survey asked recruiters how reliable they thought CVs were. The respondents were given four possible responses (including 'don't know'). The percentage giving each response is shown below:

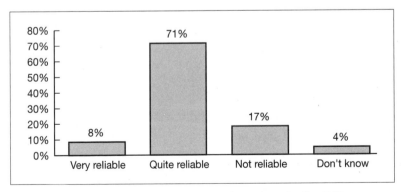

Source: *Employee Selection in the UK*, Institute of Manpower Studies 1988

Selection interviews

■ *What are the main reasons for using selection interviews?*

Many employers use selection interviews, but what are their reasons? The chart below shows what percentage of respondents felt that the given reason was a 'very important' one for conducting selection interviews. (Respondents were allowed to select more than one reason.)

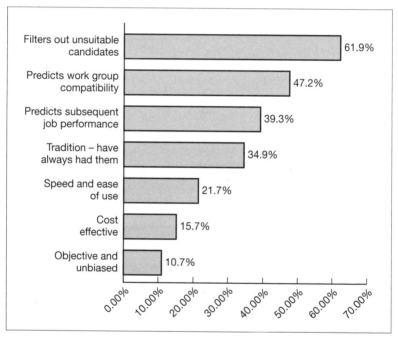

Source: *Employee Selection in the UK*, Institute of Manpower Studies, 1988

■ *How reliable are selection interviews considered to be?*

No selection method is 100% reliable, but some are obviously a better indication of how a candidate would fit the post than others. Selection interviews are, not surprisingly, considered one of the most reliable in this respect. If you think that they are the be all and end all of candidate assessment, are you being less cynical than most? One survey asked recruiters to rate the reliability of selection interviews according to four possible responses (including 'don't know'). The percentage giving each response is shown here:

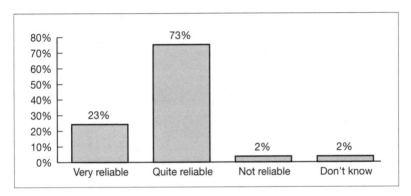

Source: Employee Selection in the UK, Institute of Manpower Studies, 1988

References

■ *What are the main reasons for using references?*

References can give many indications about a prospective recruit. But what information are they actually used to assess? The chart that follows shows what percentage of respondents felt that the given reason was a 'very important' one for using references. (Respondents were allowed to select more than one reason.)

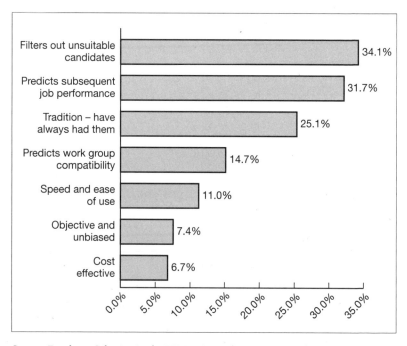

Source: Employee Selection in the UK, Institute of Manpower Studies, 1988

■ *How reliable are references considered to be?*

As an employer, the chances are that you have encountered quite a few references in your time. But how much should you actually trust the information that you receive through this source? The chart over-leaf shows how reliable they are perceived to be. Respondents were given four possible responses (including 'don't know').

The percentage giving each response is shown here:

Source: Employee Selection in the UK, Institute of Manpower Studies, 1988

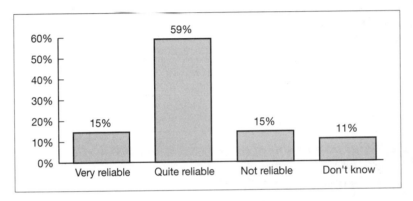

■ *How often are references checked out?*

You can only tell whether the wonderful references that your candidate has given you are genuine if you follow them up. But how necessary is it to check references?

- 59% of companies check all the references that their candidates give.
- A further 38% check some of the references they are given.
- Only 3% of companies do not check out any references from prospective employees.

Source: 'Recruit, Retrain, Retain: Personnel Management and the Three Rs', *Personnel Management*, November 1989

19

Qualifications

■ What level of qualifications do people have?

Naturally, if you want to select people with good qualifications, or train your staff well, you need to know what the average standard of qualifications is. Of course, it is impossible to give an overall assessment of this, but here are some helpful figures from the Confederation of British Industry:

- In 1992, 55% of young people were qualified to NVQ/SVQ level 2 or its academic equivalent.
- 33.5% were qualified to level 3 or its equivalent.
- 33% of adults were trained to level 3 or its equivalent.

Source: Training – The Business Case, CBI, 1993

■ What proportion of employers with hard-to-fill vacancies require a qualification or a particular level of experience?

Some vacancies can prove to be a real pain – no appropriate candidates seem to be applying. One factor that could restrict the number of applicants is having a particular requirement on qualifications or experience. But how often are hard-to-fill posts restricted in this way? If your hard-to-fill posts do not have such requirements, is this normal?

In a recent survey, recruitment difficulties were attributed to a number of reasons:

- 61% of employers cited a lack of suitably skilled people.
- 39% of employers cited a lack of interested applicants.
- 29% blamed problems on a lack of work experience.

The most common main reason for recruitment difficulties was a lack of suitably skilled people.

Source: Skill Needs in Britain 1996, Public Attitude Surveys Ltd research for the Department for Education and Employment

■ To what extent are S/NVQs used for selecting candidates?

The Scottish and National Vocational Qualifications have received quite a lot of publicity. When it comes to recruitment and selection, how much currency do they really have? One survey asked senior managers whether they or their companies use S/NVQs in the selection procedure.

- 53% of the senior managers surveyed did not use NVQs in their selection procedures, and this was also the case for 39% of companies.
- 29% of the respondents and 34% of their companies did use them for some jobs.
- Only 3% of individuals and 4% of companies used them for all job applications.

Source: Training For Recovery, Institute of Management, 1993

■ What proportion of employers check qualifications?

Of course, to be sure that your prospective employees really have the qualifications they claim, you would have to check. But how many employers really consider this necessary?

- Only 22% of employers check all the qualifications that candidates claim.
- 54% check some of these qualifications.
- That leaves 24% of organisations who do not check any qualifications claimed by their candidates.

Source: 'Recruit, Retrain, Retain: Personnel Management and the Three Rs', *Personnel Management*, November 1989

Shortlisting

■ *How many applicants normally make it to the shortlist?*

Shortlisting is often important in the recruitment process. But exactly how many applicants are you supposed to weed out at this stage of the process? If you are involved in shortlisting candidates, and are not sure how brutal or generous to be, then the figures below may interest you. Answers to this question were naturally restricted to cases where the respondent knew how many applicants there had been, and how many had been shortlisted.

• The mean average number of applicants in this survey was 58.

• The mean average number on the shortlist was 20 – just over a third of the applicants.

• These figures may, however, be misleading, and should be compared to the median average figures, which were 20 applications and 5 candidates on the shortlist – one quarter of applicants.

Source: Employers' Recruitment Practices: The 1992 Survey, Social and Community Planning Research, 1992

Graduates

■ *How reliable are graduate application forms considered to be, relative to campus interviews?*

If you are recruiting graduates, then one of the choices open to you is whether to use campus interviews or graduate application forms to select your graduate recruits. One survey aimed to find out the advantages (and disadvantages) of these two methods by asking both employers and graduates what they thought. Below is the ranking (most applicable 5 down to least applicable 1) that employers gave for the five descriptions provided for application forms. The ranking that graduates gave each quality is shown in parentheses.

1 Easy to fake	(1)
2 Fair to candidates	(3)
3 Preferred by employers	(4)
4 Preferred by candidates	(2)
5 Predictive of performance	(5)

And this is the ranking (most applicable down to least applicable) that employers gave for the five descriptions provided for campus interviews, with graduate ranking again in parentheses.

1 Preferred by employers	(1)
2 Preferred by candidates	(2)
3 Predictive of performance	(3)
4 Easy to fake	(4)
5 Fair to candidates	(5)

Source: Shortlisting the Best Graduates, Institute of Employment Studies, 1993

■ *What is the average graduate starting salary?*

Graduates are an important segment of the recruitment market. If you want to make use of this human resource, then you will certainly have to consider how much they are worth, and what sort of pay they are justified in expecting.

- In 1994 the median average graduate starting salary was £13,793.
- Actual figures varied from £9,000 to £20,000.

Source: IDS Management Pay Review, 1995

■ *What proportion of graduates are employed on a temporary basis?*

If you want to try out graduate recruits by taking them on as temporary workers, then you won't be alone. One survey found that just under 25% of organisations employing graduates recruited some or all of them on temporary contracts.

Source: IDS Management Pay Review, 1995

■ Are graduates more likely to be recruited than MBAs?

Different qualifications are treated in very different ways in the labour market. If you want to make the most of the recruitment options available to you, then perhaps you should consider recruiting MBAs as well as standard graduates. If you do so, will you be taking advantage of an untapped area of the market, or have many companies had this bright idea?

- 62% of companies said that they take on graduate recruits.
- Only 11% said that they recruit MBAs.

Source: 'Recruit, Retrain, Retain: Personnel Management and the Three Rs', *Personnel Management*, November 1989

RECRUITMENT DIFFICULTIES

Constraints

■ How many employers experience recruitment difficulties?

Some vacancies will always be harder to fill than others, but sometimes there are posts which cause particular problems. If you have encountered several of these recently, then you might be interested to know how common this problem is.

- At the time of the survey, one in six employers (17%) with at least 25 employees had a post that was proving hard to fill.
- A further 16% had had such a post in the previous 12 months.
- The South-East and London had the highest proportion of employers with hard-to-fill vacancies (22% and 18% respectively); this compares with 12% in Scotland and the North-West.

Source: Skill Needs in Britain 1996, Public Attitude Surveys Ltd research for the Department for Education and Employment

■ *What are the main effects of hard-to-fill vacancies?*

The main effects of hard-to-fill vacancies were:

Increased running costs	49%
Above average recruitment costs	48%
Loss of service quality	44%

Source: Skill Needs in Britain 1996, Public Attitude Surveys Ltd research for the Department for Education and Employment

■ *What are the greatest constraints on recruitment?*

The people you want to recruit may well be out there, but that is a long way from having them in your company. A lot can stand in the way of being able to find and recruit the staff that you would like to employ. But which of the many potential problems do recruiters consider to be the biggest reasons why their dream candidate doesn't want the job? Here are the main factors cited by recruiters:

Salary level	63%
Cost of housing	28%
Cost of living	24%
Job location	21%
Benefits package	18%

Source: 'Recruit, Retrain, Retain: Personnel Management and the Three Rs', *Personnel Management*, November 1989

■ *Which employee groups are hardest to recruit for?*

Some posts will cause more trouble than others. If your problems are often concerned with finding managers or administrators, is this the way that the cookie usually crumbles? The following chart shows the percentage of employers employing a particular group who said that they had had difficulties in recruiting for that group:

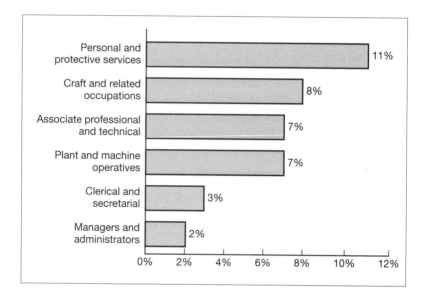

The same survey also tried to determine which minor occupational groups were the hardest to recruit for. Their top 5 (hardest first) were as follows:

- Miscellaneous occupations in sales and services
- Catering occupations
- Health associate professionals (mainly nurses)
- Health and related occupations
- Engineers and technologists.

Source: Skill Needs in Britain 1994, IFF research for Employment Department

■ What steps are being taken to overcome recruitment difficulties?

Many changes can be made to employment conditions to attract more and better recruits. These can be in terms of pay, perks, or working arrangements (e.g. holidays). So, which are the most popular changes that organisations make, and which are the least used?

The figures below show the percentage of companies which have improved certain employment conditions with the primary objective of improving recruitment.

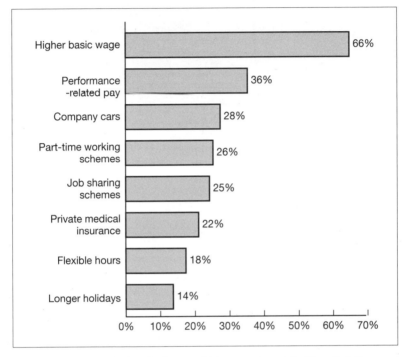

Source: 'Recruit, Retrain, Retain: Personnel Management and the Three Rs', *Personnel Management*, November 1989

■ *What other changes can be made to improve recruitment?*

Of course, you can also improve your recruitment situation in other ways. Changes can be made to the recruitment system itself, to increase the ease of finding the person you want to fill the vacancy. The figures below show what proportion of companies have made particular changes to their recruitment or induction system in order to make their recruitment task a little easier.

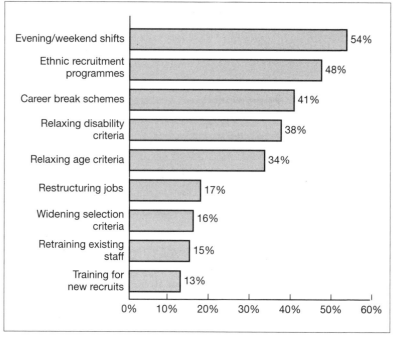

Source: 'Recruit, Retrain, Retain: Personnel Management and the Three Rs', *Personnel Management*, November 1989

■ *Are employers willing to recruit the long-term unemployed?*

One way to improve your chances of finding a suitable candidate for your vacancy is to increase the breadth of your search to include the long-term unemployed. But is this a rash and desperate measure, or are there many like-minded companies? One survey found that 96% of companies said that they were willing to do so.

Source: Skill Needs In Britain 1994, IFF research for Employment Department

■ *Is recruitment a growing concern, and how much work does it entail?*

At different times, each personnel manager will find that different issues take priority. Recruitment has always been an important area for every personnel manager. Is its importance growing? How important is it in terms of time spent?

- 54% of personnel managers said that recruitment was a growing concern.

- 41% indicated that it took up more than 25% of their time at work.

Source: 'Recruit, Retrain, Retain: Personnel Management and the Three Rs', *Personnel Management*, November 1989

■ *How many recruiters are experiencing increased recruitment difficulties and in what areas?*

Recruitment has never been easy, but has it ever been this hard? If you are finding it difficult to fill a post for a technical worker, then it seems you are not alone. A *Personnel Management* survey shows that many recruiters feel that recruiting is getting hard, and for some jobs more so than others. The graph below shows what percentage of recruiters felt that recruiting was more difficult, easier, or about the same as it used to be for what turned out to be the five hardest grades.

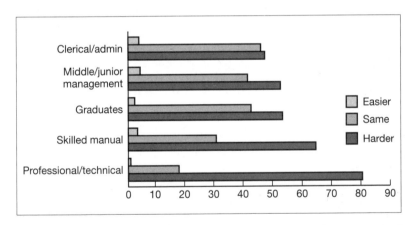

- The grade for which the highest number said that recruitment had become easier was top management, but even here only 7% went for the easy option.

Source: 'Recruit, Retrain, Retain: Personnel Management and the Three Rs', *Personnel Management*, November 1989

■ What are the most important qualities that employers look for in applicants, and which are the hardest to find?

Many people talk about a 'skills gap' – a situation where few candidates have the skills that are required for the post that must be filled. How bad is this skills gap in different areas? If you are having trouble finding someone with appropriate problem solving skills, is this bad luck, or are there many others like you? One survey asked employers to rate which of the skills listed they considered most important in a prospective employee, and which they felt had the largest skills gap. The figures below show overall rankings and are ranked here in order of the skills gap.

Quality	Ranking of skills gap	Ranking of importance
Attitude/motivation/ personality	1	1=
Problem solving skills	2	7
Flexibility/willingness to change	3=	3=
Information technology skills	3=	9
Relevant experience	5	1=
Relevant qualifications	6	3=
Industry-specific skills	7	8
Numeracy	8	6
Literacy	9	5
Foreign language ability	10	10

Source: Flexible Labour Markets; Who Pays For Training? Confederation of British Industry, 1994

Small businesses

■ *Are small firms at a disadvantage relative to larger firms when recruiting new staff?*

If you run a small business, and feel that the larger firms can cream off the better staff, are you alone? No – but 70% of small firms over-all claimed that they were not at a disadvantage. However, the majority of firms who felt they were least disadvantaged were in the South. The same firms made best use of word-of-mouth methods of attracting new staff.

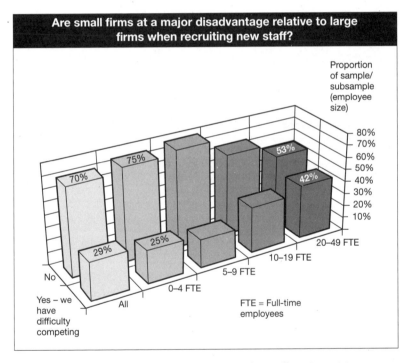

Source: Recruitment, Lloyds Bank/SBRT Quarterly Small Business Management Report Vol. 5 No. 2, July 1997

■ *Do small firms experience problems in recruiting new staff?*

If you are in the retail or distribution sectors, then you are likely to find recruitment easier. Overall, the firms which experienced fewest problems recruiting staff were using local networking strategies:

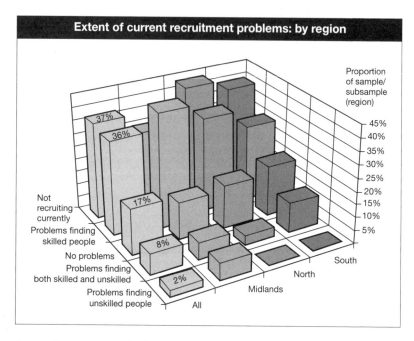

Source: Recruitment, Lloyds Bank/SBRT Quarterly Small Business Management Report Vol. 5 No. 2, July 1997

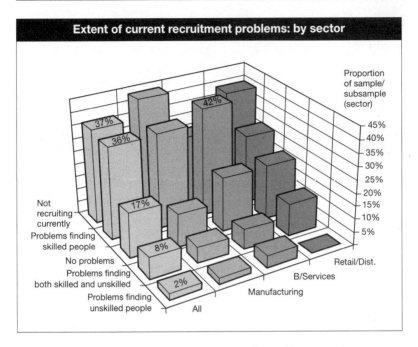

Source: Recruitment, Lloyds Bank/SBRT Quarterly Small Business Management Report Vol. 5 No. 2, July 1997

■ *Are small firms seriously affected by skill shortages?*

Small firms were asked about any major effects of skill shortages. The four main effects were, in order:

1. Having to settle for unsatisfactory employees

2. Missing business opportunities

3. Incurring extra training costs

4. Vacancies remaining unfilled.

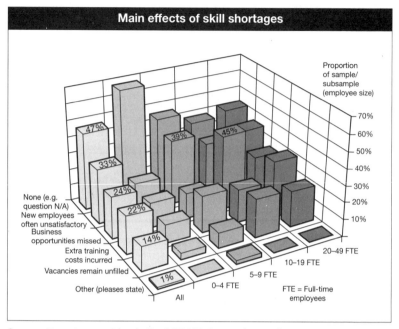

Main effects of skill shortages

Source: Recruitment, Lloyds Bank/SBRT Quarterly Small Business Management Report Vol. 5 No. 2, July 1997

■ *What are the reasons for skills shortages?*

No doubt each firm can lay the blame at a different door. The Small Business Research Trust highlighted 'schools', 'colleges' and 'other employers' as the main reasons for skills shortages. Individual statements about skills shortages indicated particular concerns:

> *Basic English needs full attention at all schooling levels. Even graduates lack spelling, grammar and focused reading skills.*

> *We are extremely worried about the quality of candidates. There is, no doubt, a decline in their educational standards and hence ability.*

> *We have a very unsatisfactory pool of 16 year olds to recruit every summer. [This is] not because 16 year olds are getting less able, but as a result of school keeping even mediocre students on into the sixth form, and then on to university.*

> *Most colleges in Graphic Design – our field – are out of date ... Probably the lecturers need regular in-trade refresher courses.*

Source: Recruitment, Lloyds Bank/SBRT Quarterly Small Business Management Report Vol. 5 No. 2, July 1997

FLEXIBLE WORKING

Use

■ What factors influence the use of flexible labour?

If you are considering using flexible labour, it may help to understand why other employers have made the same decision. Employers use widely differing patterns of flexible labour. Both the use of flexible labour and the precise form it takes are influenced by:

1. Variations in demand for the product.

2. The relative importance of labour costs.

3. External labour market constraints.

4. The wishes of employees.

5. The weight of past ways of working.

6. Management fads or inertia.

Source: Employers' Use of Flexible Labour, Bernard Casey, Hilary Metcalf and Neil Millward, Policy Studies Institute, 1997

■ What are the main reasons for introducing flexible labour?

Two out of three employers identified two main reasons for their use of temporary staff.

1. 'Matching staffing levels to peaks in demand' was cited by 40%.

2. 'Short-term cover whilst staff are away on holiday or sick-leave' was the second most popular reason – cited by 28%.

These two reasons were common across all industrial sectors. Very few employers cited reduced wage or training costs as reasons for taking on temporary workers.

Source: Temporary Work and the Labour Market, J. Atkinson, J. Rick, S. Morris and M. Williams, IES Report No. 311, 1997

■ Which flexible working practices are widely used?

There are many forms of flexible working, which are naturally used to different degrees. The chart below shows what percentage of companies use each of the flexible working styles named.

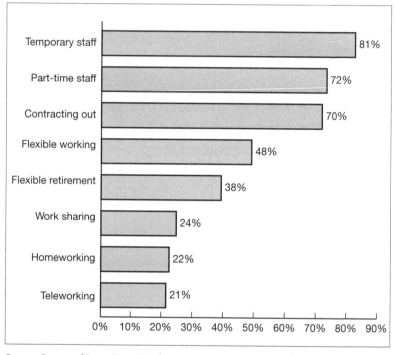

Source: *Survey of Long Term Employment Strategies*, Institute of Management, 1994

■ For what grades of staff are part-time or temporary employees most used?

Everyone knows how common it is to have a temp on your switchboard, but what about having a part-time manager? If this seems to be your best option, then you might like to know if others have also used this solution. The graph below shows what percentage of companies employ temps or part-timers in each occupational group.

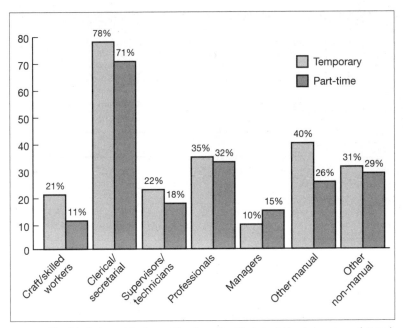

Source: *Flexible Labour Markets; Who Pays For Training?* Confederation of British Industry, 1994

■ What types of temporary staff are most commonly used?

Employing temporary staff seems to be the most common way of creating a more flexible workforce. But temporary workers can be employed in many ways. If you are employing a temp, you might like to know which kinds of temp companies most often choose, and which fall further down the list. The following chart shows what percentage of companies use each of the different types of temporary worker.

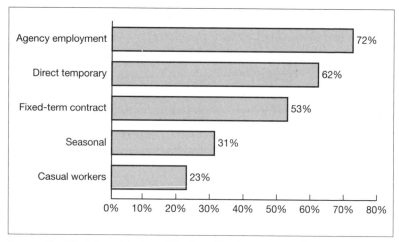

Source: *Flexible Labour Markets; Who Pays For Training?* Confederation of British Industry, 1994

■ *Is flexible working on the increase?*

The Policy Studies Institute has recently undertaken research into flexible working. It found that the traditional nine-to-five job is still the most common form of employment, but often in name only:

● More than half of all employees now work variable hours, although many are not required to do so by the terms of their contracts.

● This is more than double the proportion in the mid-1980s.

● The increase is mainly due to the growth in paid and unpaid over-time, rather than the growth of more flexible forms of employment contracts.

Source: *Employers' Use of Flexible Labour*, Bernard Casey, Hilary Metcalf and Neil Millward, Policy Studies Institute, 1997

■ *Are flexible working practices widely used?*

Is flexible working a useful and productive way to organise your workforce, or a short-term or undesirable option? The Department for Education and Employment conducted research into flexible working, and found that:

- Just less than 7% of employers said that temporary workers now formed more than half of their workforce.
- Over a third – 37% – of organisations have fewer than 5% of their employees on temporary contracts.
- Temporary workers constitute less than 10% of the workforce in well over half the employers surveyed.

Source: Temporary Work and the Labour Market, J. Atkinson, J. Rick, S. Morris and M. Williams, IES Report No. 311, 1997

■ What forms of flexible labour are on the increase?

Other forms of flexible labour are on the increase:

- Short-term contracts are increasing – but not in all sectors. In manufacturing, 93% of employers still do not use this form of employment at all; only 4% use this form of employment for more than 5% of their workforce.
- Yet in the public sector, 44% of schools have over 5% of their staff on short-term contracts.

Source: Employers' Use of Flexible Labour, Bernard Casey, Hilary Metcalf and Neil Millward, Policy Studies Institute, 1997

■ Are there any new forms of employment?

The zero-hours contract is still rare; few employers combine different forms of flexible labour. Only 4% of workforces, for example, use both short-term contracts and freelancers.

Source: Employers' Use of Flexible Labour, Bernard Casey, Hilary Metcalf and Neil Millward, Policy Studies Institute, 1997

■ Do large firms use more flexible labour than small ones?

The commonly held view is that small firms have been at the forefront of moves towards flexibility. Is this true in practice?

- No. The increase in flexible hours and temporary contracts has been greater in large and medium sized workplaces than smaller ones.
- The impetus towards flexible employment patterns has been provided by global competitive pressures and by policies within a public sector faced by budget constraints.

Source: Employers' Use of Flexible Labour, Bernard Casey, Hilary Metcalf and Neil Millward, Policy Studies Institute, 1997

■ *Is temporary working a strategic business tool?*

Temporary working has traditionally been seen as the main solution to holiday and absence cover, but attitudes towards it do seem to be changing:

- Some financial sector organisations described massive changes in their use of temporary workers as they introduced more telephone-based services to their clients.

- A national telephone service can be based in one location, with a core of permanent staff to meet minimum demand and a large-scale, fully trained temporary staff to be called in to meet highs in demand.

Source: Temporary Work and the Labour Market, J. Atkinson, J. Rick, S. Morris and M. Williams, IES Report No. 311, 1997

■ *What changes are to be expected in flexible working patterns?*

Flexible working, in one form or another, is used in many companies. To what extent will it continue to be used? The Institute of Management's 1994 survey asked companies whether they expected to be using various flexible working styles more in the next four years than they do now. The results show what percentage of companies thought that they would be using each style more in the next four years.

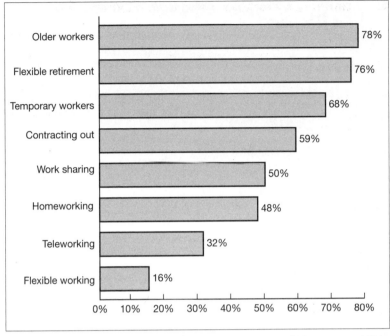

Source: *Survey of Long Term Employment Strategies*, Institute of Management, 1994

Different forms

■ *How many companies offer job sharing schemes?*

If you are thinking of introducing a scheme in your organisation, then you may want to know what kind of a precedent there is for this. Are job sharing schemes a good idea that is rarely put into practice? Or are they an up and coming formula for flexible working? As it turns out, some 23% of organisations offer job sharing schemes.

Source: *Skill Needs in Britain 1994*, IFF research for Employment Department

■ *How many companies offer term-time working arrangements?*

Some working mothers need special working arrangements to be able to cope with their domestic responsibilities. One possible solution is term-time working. But if you are considering this option, you might like to know how much of a precedent there is.

- In fact, it is a fairly limited practice, being operated by only 6% of companies.

- It is more often operated for manual, clerical, sales and administrative staff than for managers and professionals.

Source: Retaining Women Employees: Measures to Counteract Labour Shortages, Institute of Manpower Studies, 1990

■ *Why do companies introduce term-time working schemes?*

Precedent may well not be the only factor in your decision to adopt term-time working schemes for some employees, but how much weight should you give to other factors? It may be helpful to know the reasons that have led other companies to introduce such schemes. The following graph shows what percentage of companies currently running schemes consider each of the factors listed to be a reason why they introduced the scheme.

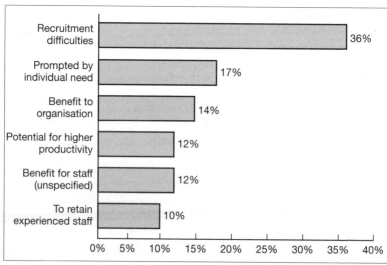

Source: Retaining Women Employees: Measures To Counteract Labour Shortages, Institute of Manpower Studies, 1990

■ What size companies are most likely to use temporary workers?

Perhaps you are more interested in temporary than part-time workers. Again, it helps to know what the usual company behaviour is. The following table gives the average proportions of the workforce who have temporary contracts in companies of different sizes.

Number of employees	Percentage temporary
1–99	5%
100–199	5%
200–499	3%
500–1999	5%
2000–4999	5%
5000+	4%

Source: Flexible Labour Markets; Who Pays for Training? Confederation of British Industry, 1994

■ What size companies are most likely to use part-time workers?

Is there an ideal number of part-time staff? It is hard to know where you should stand if you do not know how many other companies stand with you. Company size is, not surprisingly, one factor that can affect the number of employees who are on part-time contracts, but what effect does it actually have? These are the average proportions of the workforce who have part-time contracts in companies of different sizes.

Number of employees	Percentage part-time
1–99	6%
100–199	6%
200–499	5%
500–1999	5%
2000–4999	6%
5000+	18%

Source: Flexible Labour Markets; Who Pays for Training? Confederation of British Industry, 1994

■ What overtime payments are part-time employees usually entitled to?

Overtime payments for part-time workers can be a difficult area. It is often not possible to pay part-timers overtime as soon as they exceed their contracted hours. If you are responsible for dealing with overtime payments for part-timers, it might help to know what the general situation is.

- In 78% of companies, part-timers are only eligible for overtime after the standard full-time week has been worked.

- In only 9% of organisations do part-timers receive overtime for working longer than standard full-time daily hours.

- Only 7% of companies pay overtime to part-timers once they have worked more than their contracted hours.

Source: Part-Time Working 2: Changing Terms and Conditions of Employment, IRS Employment Trends, April 1993

■ How popular is the core/complementary pattern of employment?

Some companies choose to have full-time staff who are classed as the 'core' workforce, and to arrange for certain jobs to be done as and when they are needed by a 'complementary' workforce. The core/complementary workforce pattern seems popular, but to what extent is it actually used? How many companies are planning to adopt it? One survey asked respondents what proportion of their staff would be considered 'core' employees over the next year, and over the next four years.

- 70% of companies said that, over the next year, 90% of their staff would remain core employees.

- 22% of companies said that 75% of their staff would be core employees over this period.

- Only 50% predicted that their staff would be 90% core employees in four years' time.

- 54% said that, in four years, they were planning to have only 75% core employees.

- 14% said that they expected to retain just 50% core employees over this period.

Source: Survey of Long Term Employment Strategies, Institute of Management, 1994

EQUAL OPPORTUNITIES EMPLOYMENT

Procedures and policies

■ *What proportion of companies have special procedures for encouraging minority groups to apply for vacancies?*

Recruitment policies concerning people from minority groups vary. There is a big difference between simply giving them a chance if they apply, and actually encouraging applications. If you think that you could be taking more advantage of people from certain minority groups, then you might actually want to encourage them in this way. But how common is this, and for what groups is it most common? The following chart shows what proportion of companies have special procedures for encouraging people from each of the following groups to apply.

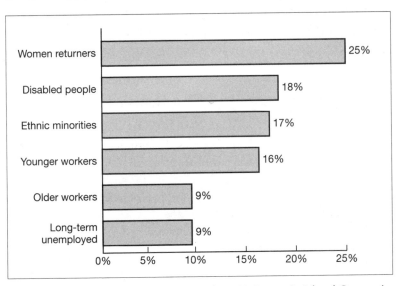

Source: Employers' Recruitment Practices: The 1992 Survey, Social and Community Planning Research, 1992

45

■ How many companies provide equal opportunities training on gender issues?

Providing training for your staff in equal opportunities issues improves the standing of equal opportunities in your organisation. But how realistic is this suggestion, and what proportion of companies actually operate such training on gender issues?

- 13% of companies operate an equal opportunities training scheme for either managerial or personnel staff, or both.
- Fewer companies (9%) operate such training for other employees.

Source: Retaining Women Employees: Measures to Counteract Labour Shortages, Institute of Manpower Studies, 1990

■ Can flexible working change gender attitudes?

Theoretically it can – but a Policy Studies Institute report warns that it can also work to reinforce gender stereotyping and pay differentials:

- Some employers assign all overtime, shift and night working to men, and all temporary and part-time work to women.
- There is still a tendency to address labour shortages by raising pay for men, but by changing working-time arrangements for women.

Source: Employers' Use of Flexible Labour, Bernard Casey, Hilary Metcalf and Neil Millward, Policy Studies Institute, 1997

■ How many companies have a standard procedure for dealing with complaints of discrimination?

Discrimination can be a very worrying issue if accusations are made at your workplace. You may well want to be prepared for such an eventuality by having a standard procedure for such occurrences. But is this really necessary, or can these problems simply be dealt with as and when they arise? Generally this does not seem to be considered sufficient – 76% of companies do have a procedure for handling complaints of discrimination.

Source: Skill Needs in Britain 1994, IFF research for Employment Department

Childcare

See also: **Maternity leave and career breaks** p. 148.

■ *How important is childcare provision?*

Before you make any decisions about whether to provide childcare, or what to provide, you will naturally want to assess whether the situation really warrants action on your part. So how big a problem is lack of company-provided childcare?

- 66% of company directors say that improved childcare arrangements would overcome skilled labour shortages.

Source: Institute of Directors survey

- Only 8% of companies offer assistance with childcare or provision of childcare services.

Source: Skill Needs in Britain 1994, IFF research for Employment Department

■ *How much does childcare cost?*

Of course, when an employee returns to work after a career break, certain things will be different. One of these is likely to be their outgoing expenses, since most working mothers have to make some financial arrangements for childcare. But how much does this actually cost? The chart that follows shows what percentage of working mothers spend which amount per week on childcare during term-time.

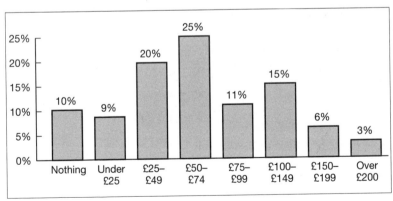

Source: Beyond the Career Break, Institute of Manpower Studies, 1992

■ *How helpful are childcare enhancements considered to be?*

Your company can make efforts to improve, directly or indirectly, a working mother's situation with regard to childcare arrangements – perhaps providing information or providing a crèche. But if you are thinking of providing some such enhancements, then you will want to provide something that is a genuine help to the staff concerned. The Institute of Manpower Studies survey asked women who had returned from a career break how helpful they thought various enhancements would be – 'very great help', 'significant help', 'limited help', or 'no help at all'. The figures below show the distribution of responses regarding helpfulness for some of the categories mentioned by the survey.

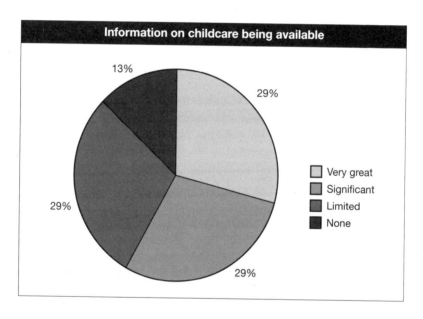

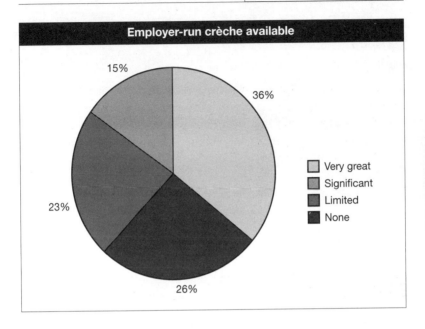

Employer-run crèche available

- 15%
- 36%
- 23%
- 26%

Very great
Significant
Limited
None

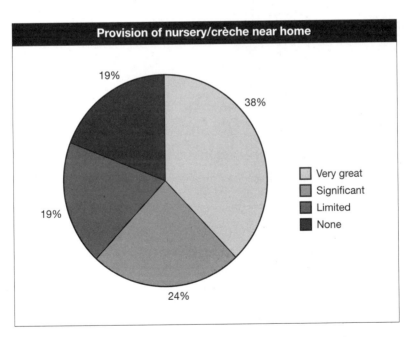

Provision of nursery/crèche near home

- 19%
- 38%
- 19%
- 24%

Very great
Significant
Limited
None

RECRUITMENT

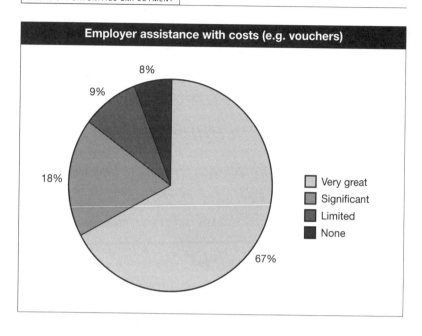

Employer assistance with costs (e.g. vouchers)

8%

9%

18%

67%

- Very great
- Significant
- Limited
- None

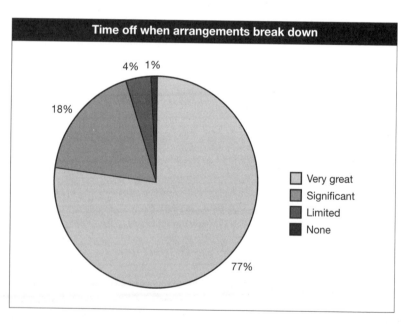

Time off when arrangements break down

4% 1%

18%

77%

- Very great
- Significant
- Limited
- None

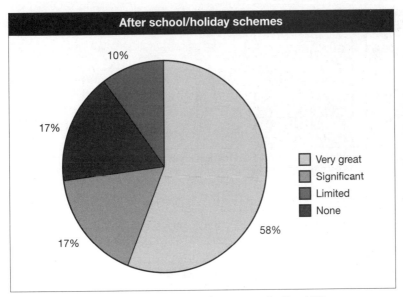

Source: Beyond the Career Break, Institute of Manpower Studies, 1992

■ *How many companies provide childcare enhancements?*

If you want to provide helpful childcare enhancements for working mothers in your organisation, you now know what are considered to be the most useful arrangements. But how often are such arrangements provided by other companies? In fact, even information on childcare, the most commonly available form of assistance, was available to less than a quarter of the women covered by the Institute of Manpower Studies survey. The chart below shows what percentage of women surveyed had access to each of the enhancements mentioned at their place of work.

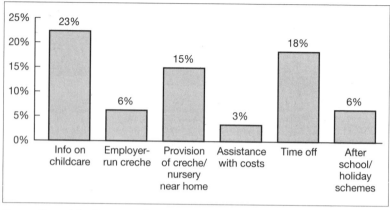

Source: Beyond the Career Break, Institute of Manpower Studies, 1992

Race issues

■ *What are the main symptoms of racial discrimination?*

Racial discrimination undeniably still exists, but it may not always be evident in obvious ways, such as verbal abuse. It will often come out in more subtle ways. Perhaps you are concerned about racial discrimination at your workplace. Or maybe you are just concerned about the possibility of industrial tribunal action being taken against your company on these grounds. Either way, you will probably be interested to know what the most common grounds are for industrial tribunals of this type. The figures given here are for the percentage of employers citing each ground as the one on which a case of racial discrimination was brought against them.

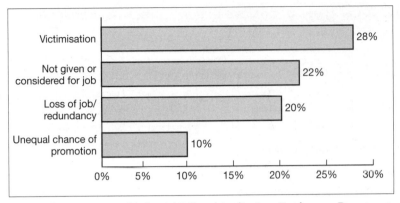

Source: The 1992 Survey of Industrial Tribunal Applications, Employment Department

■ *Why should you take positive action on race discrimination?*

Many companies, particularly large ones, take some form of positive action on race discrimination within their organisation. But if you are considering taking such action, what factors would justify this decision? The table below shows what percentage of organisations currently taking action consider each of the given reasons to be one that influenced their decision.

Demonstrating commitment to social justice	88%
Better use of human resources	87%
Better image in locality	80%
Better image among customers	71%
Addressing labour shortage	33%

Source: Acting Positively: Positive Action under The Race Relations Act 1976, Capita Management Consultancy, 1994, for the Department of Employment

■ What types of positive action on race discrimination are most often taken?

If you are deciding to take positive action on race discrimination issues, then you will naturally have to decide what kind of action to take. You may wish to take some cues from companies which are already operating schemes of this type. The graph below shows what proportion of companies take positive action for which reasons.

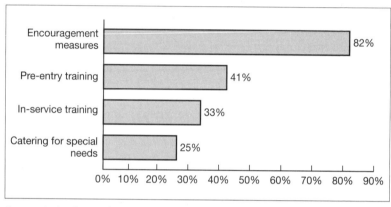

Source: *Acting Positively: Positive Action under The Race Relations Act 1976*, Capita Management Consultancy, 1994, for the Department of Employment

■ What type of encouragement measures are most commonly taken?

Encouragement measures, as we can see, are by far the most common type of positive action taken. What form do such measures take? The table below shows the most common encouragement measures taken, together with the proportion of companies taking such measures who use each method.

Method of encouragement	Percentage of companies
Advertising in ethnic minority areas	65%
Using job centres/agencies in ethnic minority areas	62%
Liaising with schools and careers officers in ethnic minority areas	61%
Advertising with community groups	23%

Source: Acting Positively: Positive Action under The Race Relations Act 1976, Capita Management Consultancy, 1994, for the Department of Employment

■ How are employees selected for in-service training?

Another widely used form of positive action is in-service training for ethnic minority workers, enabling them to compete for better jobs within the organisation. If you are considering taking this form of action, then you will have to select suitable trainees. How is this normally done?

- 40% of companies operating such schemes advertised training opportunities through company newsletters, magazines or noticeboards.
- Another 40% relied upon line managers to suggest suitable individuals.
- The remaining 20% used both of these methods in conjunction.

Source: Acting Positively: Positive Action under The Race Relations Act 1976, Capita Management Consultancy, 1994, for the Department of Employment

■ How are individuals selected for pre-entry training?

As with in-service training, if you are going to run a pre-entry training programme for people belonging to ethnic minorities, then you will have to adopt some method for selecting individuals for the programme. But what are your options for this, and which are the most commonly used? The table overleaf shows the most commonly used methods for selecting such individuals, together with the proportion of companies running pre-entry training programmes which use each method.

RECRUITMENT

Selection method	Percentage of companies
Press advertisements	52%
Careers offices	23%
Job centres	19%
Other	19%

Source: Acting Positively: Positive Action under The Race Relations Act 1976, Capita Management Consultancy, 1994, for the Department of Employment

■ How do employers monitor levels of ethnic minority staff?

If you are going to take positive action on ethnic minorities within your organisation, then you will probably want to keep track of your progress by monitoring the representation of ethnic minorities in your workforce. However, there are various ways of measuring these levels. Before deciding which one or ones you want to use, you may wish to know which are most commonly used. The table below shows, for each of the main methods, what proportion of companies which perform monitoring use this approach.

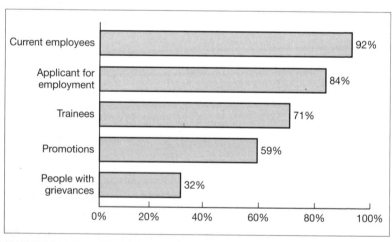

Source: Acting Positively: Positive Action under The Race Relations Act 1976, Capita Management Consultancy, 1994, for the Department of Employment

■ *What problems are most often encountered when introducing positive action policies?*

If you are going to take some form of positive action, then you will naturally want to know what sort of difficulties you can expect to encounter.

- Only 25% of companies covered by this survey said that they had encountered any problems in implementing positive action.

- The most common problem, mentioned by 33% of those who experienced difficulties, was concern that positive action was tantamount to reverse discrimination.

Source: Acting Positively: Positive Action under The Race Relations Act 1976, Capita Management Consultancy, 1994, for the Department of Employment

■ *What proportion of small businesses are run by ethnic minorities?*

Barclays recently commissioned research in recognition of the important role played by ethnic minority businesses within the small business sector. Ethnic minorities represent 5% of the UK population, yet around 9% of new business start-ups involve entrepreneurs from ethnic minority backgrounds. The research also found that:

- Asian small businesses continue to dominate the retail industry, and retailing accounts for 60% of all Asian-owned small businesses.

- Black small business owners are the most optimistic in the country: 84% are optimistic about the future; 79% believe that ethnic minority small businesses will have an increasingly important role to play in the economy.

Yet not all the findings were positive – discrimination still remains a major concern. Nearly half of black small businesses (46%) and 29% of Asian small businesses have experienced discrimination in some form.

Source: Cultural Change and the Small Firm, Barclays Review, 1997

Older workers

■ Why do some companies make an effort to recruit older workers?

Older workers are another minority group. They too may feel that they are somewhat left out of the job market. Some employers, however, are trying to redress this imbalance. If you are considering reviewing your policies towards older workers, then it might interest you to know why some companies have chosen to do this. In the following survey, employers who did have an older worker recruitment policy were given four factors which might have encouraged them to recruit older workers. They were asked to say which, if any, encouraged them to recruit such people. The number indicating that each of the suggestions had been a factor were as follows:

Reliability (of older employees)	51%
Ability (of older employees)	51%
Quantity (of older applicants)	36%
Price (of older employees)	16%

Source: Last in the Queue? Institute of Manpower Studies, 1991

■ What are the most effective policies for increasing the number of older workers in the workforce?

If you are thinking of employing more older workers, you will also be trying to find ways to attract them to your company. But before you start offering free zimmer frames, you may want to know what the Institute of Manpower Studies survey found to be the most effective incentives for older workers.

- The survey found that respondents considered 'more flexible working time' to be the most effective policy for increasing their older worker employment.

- Next most effective was said to be 'encouraging line managers to recruit older workers'.

- This was followed by 'Promoting more older workers'.

Source: Last in the Queue? Institute of Manpower Studies, 1991

Disabled employees

■ *What proportion of employers meet the legal quota of disabled employees?*

By law, every organisation with more than 20 employees should have 3% of their staff made up of disabled people. If you are concerned about where you stand in relation to this law, then these figures may be of interest to you.

- One survey found that only just over 50% of the organisations surveyed employed any disabled people at all.
- Of these, only just over 10% (5% of all companies) met the legal requirement of 3% of the workforce registered disabled.
- When non-registered disabled people were included, however, this number rose to 44%.
- Even using this figure, it still seems that less than 25% of companies met the 3% requirement.
- Employment of people with disabilities was found to be much more common in larger companies.

Source: Employers' Attitudes towards People with Disabilities, Institute of Employment Studies, 1993

■ *Why are people with disabilities not employed?*

It seems, then, that many companies do not meet the requirement of 3% disabled workers. Why are these companies not employing disabled people?

- It is often because they don't apply. A total of 75% of the companies surveyed who had no disabled employees cited this as the reason.
- Only 4.2% said that they had ever rejected a disabled applicant because their disability was seen as a barrier to the job.
- However, over 65% of the organisations with no disabled employees said that there were particular problems associated with employing disabled people.

Source: Employers' Attitudes towards People with Disabilities, Institute of Employment Studies, 1993

■ *What are the advantages and disadvantages of employing disabled workers?*

If you are considering reviewing your position on disabled workers, then you will no doubt want to know what advantages and disadvantages you can expect from employing the disabled. The following figures relate to all the companies surveyed, of whom just over half actually employed disabled people.

- Only 29% of companies said that they could see clear benefits to employing disabled people.

- These advantages fell into two broad categories – the motivation and dedication of the disabled employee, and enhanced company image.

- The most common reservation about employing disabled people was their reduced ability to do the job and their productivity level, which was cited as a disadvantage by 56% of respondents.

- However, 75% of the organisations who were employing disabled employees said that they had experienced no problems or difficulties at all in doing so.

Source: Employers' Attitudes towards People with Disabilities, Institute of Employment Studies, 1993

■ *To what extent do extra provisions need to be made for disabled employees?*

Another thing you will have to consider if you are going to take on more disabled personnel is what extra facilities you will have to provide.

- Approximately 50% of the organisations employing disabled people said that they had not had to make any special arrangements for them.

- However, 43% of all companies said that they thought there would, in practice, be extra costs associated with recruiting or employing disabled people.

Source: Employers' Attitudes towards People with Disabilities, Institute of Employment Studies, 1993

■ How many companies have special facilities for disabled people?

There is, of course, a legal requirement for the number of disabled employees in companies of a certain size. If you are going to meet this requirement, you may need to provide special facilities for your disabled employees. If you don't have such facilities, then are you behind the times, or are there many other companies in your position? As it turns out, you are not alone – only 31% of companies have special facilities for people with disabilities.

Source: Skill Needs in Britain 1994, IFF research for Employment Department

■ What proportion of companies have an explicit policy with regard to recruiting disabled people?

Recruitment can be very political territory, particularly when it involves issues such as the recruitment of disabled people. One way to clear up any ambiguities in this area is to have a formal policy with regard to recruitment. But if you do not have a specific policy regarding the recruitment of disabled people, then are you really missing out on something, or are there many other companies who are also lacking in this respect?

- One survey found that fewer than 50% of organisations had an explicit policy on recruitment of disabled workers.
- Only 25% had such a policy actually written down.
- Unsurprisingly, the incidence of such policies was much higher in larger companies.

Source: Employers' Attitudes towards People with Disabilities, Institute of Employment Studies, 1993

■ What proportion of organisations actively seek to employ disabled people?

Many minority groups are overlooked in the labour market. You could be missing out on finding the staff you need simply because they are disabled. So if you are not actually trying to employ disabled people, are you missing the boat? Or are you in line with common practice?

- Only 20% of organisations have an active recruitment policy for disabled workers.

- This is, again, much more common in larger companies.

- Of companies who already employed disabled people, 33% said that they had such a policy.

- Only 5% of companies with no disabled employees had one.

Source: Employers' Attitudes towards People with Disabilities, Institute of Employment Studies, 1993

■ How do companies go about recruiting disabled people?

If you are thinking of trying to recruit disabled workers, then you will want to know what options are open to you.

- The IES survey found that two methods were used very commonly – by over 50% of the companies operating such a recruitment policy.

- The first of these was welcoming disabled applicants in job advertisements.

- The other was notifying the Employment Service disability specialists of any vacancies.

Source: Employers' Attitudes towards People with Disabilities, Institute of Employment Studies, 1993

SALARIES, BONUSES AND BENEFITS

■ What is the average management salary?

If you have to set salaries for the employees in your organisation, then you will want to know what the average national salary is for an employee of their grade. So the table below gives the average salaries for 1997 for 8 levels of directors and managers. The lowest grade included – Senior staff – is taken to be the level directly above line management. Of course, your company may well not have this many levels in its hierarchy. However, you will undoubtedly be able to recognise certain posts as relating to one of the levels given.

Grade	Basic annual salary
Chief executive	£117,670
Other directors	£74,504
Senior function head	£59,260
Function head	£44,207
Department manager	£37,742
Section manager	£34,109
Section leader	£30,594
Senior staff	£24,783

Source: *National Management Salary Survey 1997*, Remuneration Economics

■ *What proportion of employees are satisfied with their salaries?*

Are you reviewing your payment levels to staff? Have you conducted an employee survey with respect to employee satisfaction with pay? Then you may well want some objective standard by which to judge the normal level of staff satisfaction on this issue. One survey reported the following findings:

Completely satisfied with pay	6%
Very satisfied with pay	18%
Fairly satisfied with pay	42%
Ambivalent about/unsatisfied with current pay levels	33%

Skilled manual workers were generally less satisfied with their pay than others, but satisfaction was fairly uniform among all other job classes.

Source: *Employee Commitment and the Skills Revolution*, Policy Studies Institute, 1993

■ How many companies link human resources and payroll responsibilities?

There is a strong link between pay and aspects of human resources management, especially in cases such as pay rises and bonuses, let alone performance-related or profit-related pay. Given this, it might make sense to put the two functions together in some way. But how many companies actually acknowledge this link?

● In only 20% of organisations are both payroll and human resources systems controlled by the same person.

● In 33% of companies, there is no link at all between the human resources and payroll systems.

Source: People and Technology, Benchmark Research Ltd for Coopers & Lybrand and Oracle, 1994

■ How many companies have a formal remuneration policy?

Remunerations have to be considered by every company. This does not mean that every company will go so far as to have a formal policy covering this area. If you do not have one, though, it seems that you are in the minority according to one survey, which found that 60% of companies do have a formal remuneration policy.

Source: Counting Costs to Keep Competitive, Confederation of British Industry, 1994

■ What proportion of employees receive incentive payments?

There are many forms of incentive payments. The question posed by this survey was intended to cover all of them, including bonuses and commissions. If you do not currently run any incentive systems, you might like to know how many employees across the country do benefit from such a pay policy.

● 27% of employees received some sort of incentive payment.

● Often these employees received more than one such payment.

● Employees who received individual incentives were almost four times more likely to receive workplace or organisational incentives than those who did not.

Source: Employee Commitment and the Skills Revolution, Policy Studies Institute, 1993

■ *What proportion of earnings do incentive payments represent?*

The most difficult decision about incentives is at what level any payment should be given. One way to measure this is to calculate what proportion of annual earnings come from incentive payments. And one way to judge at what level you should set payments is to find out what the average level is.

- 31% of employees on incentives (9% of all employees) received more than 10% of their annual pay from incentive schemes.

- Another 31% received between 10% and 5% of their annual earnings from such schemes.

- Over a third (38%) received less than 5% of their annual pay from this source.

Source: Employee Commitment and the Skills Revolution, Policy Studies Institute, 1993

■ *How common, and how sizeable, are premium payments?*

Many workers receive some form of extra payment for variability in hours worked, or for working in adverse conditions. But if you are concerned, for instance, about how much overtime you are paying out, then you might like to know what the usual levels for such premium payments are.

- Over half of the individuals surveyed (53%) received at least one form of premium payment.

- Payments for adverse working conditions were found to be rare.

- However, about 40% of workers received overtime payments.

- Night working was by far the most common shift-work for which workers received premium payments.

- Premium payments accounted for over 10% of annual salary for nearly 20% of all employees.

- For 10% of employees, they accounted for 25% or more of the annual salary.

Source: Employee Commitment and the Skills Revolution, Policy Studies Institute, 1993

■ *What proportion of employees are paid in cash?*

Cash-in-hand payment has certainly been decreasing over the past few decades. If you are still paying some of your employees in this way, you may want to know just how common, or uncommon, the practice is.

- 35% of the manual workers covered by the survey were paid in cash.

- Only 12% of non-manual workers, however, received their pay in this form.

Source: The New Industrial Relations? Policy Studies Institute, 1994 (data from *Workplace Industrial Relations Survey,* 1990)

Benefits

■ *What effects do fringe benefits have on recruitment and retention?*

Is it really worthwhile to introduce fringe benefits? Do they work? Are they likely to attract recruits, and are they likely to encourage employees to stay? The following table provides some answers.

Benefit	Reason took job	Reason stayed in job
Fringe benefits	17%	22%
Occupational pensions	10%	15%
Sick pay	7%	8%
Time off for domestic responsibilities	5%	8%

- No other benefits rated above 3% on either scale.

Source: Employee Commitment and the Skills Revolution, Policy Studies Institute, 1993

■ What benefits are most commonly available?

If you are reviewing your policies towards fringe benefits for your employees, then you might want to know what benefits are most commonly available. The list below shows what proportion of employees are eligible for each of the benefits given (* indicates benefits which go beyond the basic state scheme).

Occupational pension scheme*	61%
Sick pay*	57%
Time off for domestic problems	
with full or part pay	51%
unpaid	34%
Subsidised or free meals	31%
Maternity pay*	27%
Goods or services at discount	25%
Recreation or sports facilities	25%
Use of company car or van	20%
Private health scheme	20%
Free transport / help with travel costs	18%
Accommodation or housing	18%
Life assurance	17%
Finance or loans (e.g. house purchase)	15%
Career break schemes	11%
Child care assistance	4%

Source: *Employee Commitment and the Skills Revolution*, Policy Studies Institute, 1993

■ What percentage of managers and company directors receive company cars?

The company car is one of the best-established status symbols of western culture, but what status do you have to have to earn it? Is it reasonable for most managers to consider themselves entitled to a company car, or is this accolade reserved for only a select few company directors?

- 94% of directors have a company car.

- Managers, however, are not so lucky, with only 58% receiving this perk.

Source: *National Management Salary Survey 1995*, Remuneration Economics

Pay settlements

■ *What is the average level of pay awards?*

Pay awards can be a very controversial area. It is easy to become stuck between the need to keep costs down and the need to pay a decent wage. So what sort of pay increases are most companies making in their attempts to tread this fine line? The following figures are estimates from the Confederation of British Industry databank for the financial year August 1993–July 1994.

- The average pay award attributable to a pay settlement in the manufacturing industry was 2.5% of salary.

- In the service sector, the corresponding figure was 3.0%.

- The percentage of companies giving different sizes of awards breaks down like this:

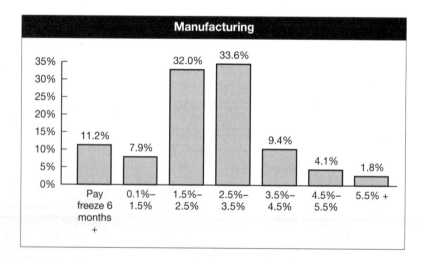

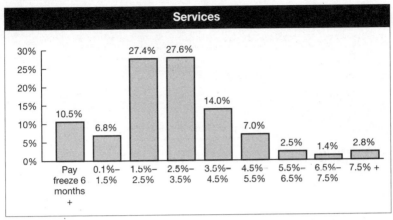

Source: Counting Costs to Keep Competitive, Confederation of British Industry, 1994

■ *What are the main pressures on pay settlements?*

How do you sort out the real issues from the minor considerations when agreeing a pay settlement? The Confederation of British Industry survey asked employers which upward and downward pressures on pay settlements they considered 'very important'. The results are broken down for the service and manufacturing sectors.

Service sector: upward pressures

Costs of living	29%
Need to recruit/retain employees	24%
Good labour productivity	23%
High profits	22%

Service sector: downward pressures

Inability to raise prices	36%
Low profits	25%
Redundancy risks	18%
Low cost of living	17%
Low orders	14%

69

Manufacturing sector: upward pressures

High cost of living	27%
Good labour productivity	16%
High profits	15%
High order levels	12%

Manufacturing sector: downward pressures

Inability to increase prices	48%
Low/deteriorating profits	33%
Low cost of living increases	22%
Risk of redundancy	18%
Low order levels	18%

Source: Counting Costs to Keep Competitive, Confederation of British Industry, 1994

■ *What are the main determinants of wage levels for new employees?*

Are wages decided by what the firm can afford, by what your competitors are paying, or by what other people in your firm are paid? It seems that overall the most common determinant is the level of pay received by other comparable employees within the firm (37%).

Main determinants of wage levels for new employees

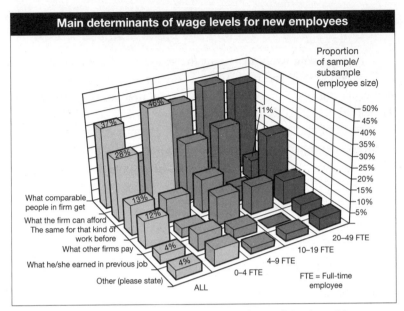

Source: Recruitment, Lloyds Bank/SBRT Quarterly Small Business Management Report Vol. 5 No. 2, July 1997

Bonuses

■ *What proportion of pay are individual bonuses usually worth?*

Bonuses can be an important part of the earnings of many of your staff. Or they can be at a level which makes them less significant as an addition to base salary. What is a reasonable level for bonuses? One survey asked companies what the bonuses they awarded were worth as a percentage of base salary.

- For top management, bonuses added up to, on average, 15% of salary.

- Semi-skilled and unskilled workers received, on average, an extra 13% of their salary in bonuses.

- Bonuses for clerical and supervisory staff came to an average of only 5% of base pay.

Source: Counting Costs to Keep Competitive, Confederation of British Industry, 1994

71

■ *What proportion of directors and managers receive bonuses, and how much are these bonuses worth?*

If you are making decisions about the salaries and bonuses awarded to your employees, and particularly more senior employees, then you will no doubt want to know what common practice over bonuses is. The table below gives figures for the percentage of staff receiving bonuses and the average proportion of their earnings that these bonuses represent for 8 grades of directors and managers. Senior staff – the lowest grade – is taken to be the level directly above line management.

Grade	Percentage receiving bonus	Bonus as percentage of earnings
Chief executive	69.4%	20.9%
Other directors	70.4%	20.0%
Senior function head	63.4%	16.4%
Function head	67.8%	11.6%
Department manager	62.7%	9.8%
Section manager	53.4%	10.5%
Section leader	59.9%	11.8%
Senior staff	56.1%	10.8%

Source: National Management Salary Survey 1997, Remuneration Economics

■ *How much are management and directors' bonuses worth in cash terms?*

It is all very well talking about bonus payments as a percentage of total earnings, but sometimes it is more helpful to see the straight cash figures. The table below shows the average bonus for the same 8 grades of directors and managers – with bonus as a percentage of salary, for comparison.

Average bonus in cash terms		
Grade	Average bonus	Bonus as percentage of salary
Chief executive	£23,383	20.9%
Other directors	£14,525	20.0%
Senior function head	£10,176	16.4%
Function head	£5,192	11.6%
Department manager	£3,755	9.8%
Section manager	£3,720	10.5%
Section leader	£3,782	11.8%
Senior staff	£2,655	10.8%

Source: National Management Salary Survey 1997, Remuneration Economics

CHECKLIST

■ *How can you make sure that your recruitment procedures succeed?*

John Fenton, a well-known sales and marketing training expert, has recently devised a course to help managers pick winners when recruiting staff. He provides the following checklist:

John Fenton's checklist for picking winners

1. **Job specification:** Do we really need to recruit? If so, how do we wish the person to operate?
2. **Person profile:** Bearing in mind the task we last performed, what qualities should we advertise to attract the right type of applicant?
3. **The search:** Who do we know and how should we advertise to attract the right type of applicant?

73

4. **Letters, application forms and photographs**: What can we really discover from a letter? Do we need a (quality) application form? Would a photograph help?

5. **Initial interview**: How well prepared are we to interview and to sell to the applicants? Do we do the initial interview over the telephone or face to face? If face to face, do we have the numbers, words and psychometric tests ready to use?

6. **Second interview**: Which areas need further investigation? How are we going to test the shortlisted applicants on these areas? Is the draft contract of employment up to date? And the company rules? And the company car rules?

7. **References**: Are we sure, in each case, that we have the person's line managers to telephone. Which questions have we prepared to use?

8. **Being sure**: Do we need to meet the candidate's spouse? If so, can we do it over dinner, and check out their home too?

9. **Hiring and turning down letters**: Will our hiring letter overcome competition and our turndown letter leave a good image?

10. **The welcome**: How can we construct the first day to give the recruit total reassurance that he/she has made the right decision?

Source: John Fenton International Training, 1997

STAFF RELATIONS

GOVERNMENT REQUIREMENTS

Government requirements have quite an impact on staff relations. There are many regulations covering staff relations – from unfair dismissal claims to the nitty gritty of PAYE and National Insurance. Employers are increasingly concerned about compliance costs, as the burden of government requirements grows. New legislation is also about to change the nature of staff relations.

Compliance costs

■ Which businesses find government regulations a financial burden?

Are you one of those businesses which feels overwhelmed by the costs of complying with tax, VAT, health and safety and environmental regulations, and government forms?
The chances are, then, that your firm is small.

● Total compliance costs are generally more important (as share of turnover) for smaller firms.

Source: Compliance Costs, NatWest SBRT Quarterly Survey of Small Businesses in Britain, Vol. 12, no. 1, 1996

■ Are compliance costs very high?

The average cost of time taken to comply with all government regulations is 6.2% of turnover. A more detailed breakdown is given in the following table.

	Income/ corporation tax, PAYE, NIC	VAT	Government statistical forms	Health/ safety/ environment regulations	Other	Total compliance costs	Sample
Cost of time spent complying with government requirements as a percentage of turnover, by turnover size band							
Less than £20,000	3.06	1.77	0.33	0.61	1.37	7.14	27
£20,000–£49,999	2.95	2.47	0.56	2.09	0.42	8.50	61
£50,000–£149,999	2.55	2.81	0.37	0.68	0.55	6.96	89
£150,000–£349,999	2.28	1.83	0.40	0.90	0.45	5.85	80
£350,000–£749,999	1.72	1.37	0.21	0.45	0.69	4.45	51
£750,000–£1,499,999	1.89	1.01	0.34	1.25	0.39	4.78	38
£1,500,000 and over	1.78	1.17	0.29	0.83	0.05	4.12	39
All	2.33	1.96	0.38	1.02	0.51	6.20	396

Source: Compliance Costs, NatWest SBRT Quarterly Survey of Small Businesses in Britain, Vol. 12, No. 1, 1996.

■ Does the average cost of compliance vary between categories?

The table above shows how smaller firms suffer relatively more overall. This is even more pronounced when certain individual categories of compliance costs are considered:

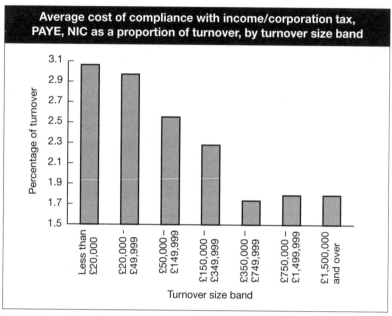

Source: Compliance Costs, NatWest SBRT Quarterly Survey of Small Businesses in Britain, Vol. 12, No. 1, 1996.

■ *What are the largest components in compliance costs?*

The same survey gave a breakdown of compliance costs, both in terms of percentage of turnover and as a percentage of total compliance costs. The largest components in compliance costs were as shown in the following table.

Component	Percentage of turnover	Percentage of total compliance costs
Income/corporation tax, PAYE and NIC	2.33%	40.0%
VAT	1.97%	29.0%
HSE/environment regulations	1.0%	17.1%
Government statistical forms	0.38%	4.5%
Other (fire, import/export, pensions, etc.)	0.5%	3.42%

Source: Compliance Costs, NatWest SBRT Quarterly Survey of Small Businesses in Britain, Vol. 12, No. 1, 1996

Changes

■ *Have government requirements changed recently?*

With a change of government, employment policy has also changed. The government is now committed to:

- The introduction of a national minimum wage.
- A reduction in the two-year qualifying service for unfair dismissal claims protection for those engaged in lawful industrial action.
- Compulsory trade union recognition.
- The implementation of outstanding European Union Directives.
- Signing up to the European Social Chapter.

Source: New Agenda, IRPC Group Ltd, 1997

■ *What does the European Social Chapter include?*

While the UK government had opted out of the European Social Chapter, it retained a right of veto on social and employment policies to be implemented. Adopting the European Social Chapter means that certain European Directives must now be implemented. These are:

1. The Parental Leave Directive – granting the right to a minimum of three months' unpaid leave to each parent until the child is eight years of age.

2. The European Works Council Directive – requiring companies with over 1,000 employees and a minimum of 150 employees in two member states to set up a European Works Council to provide information to and consult with employees on significant measures affecting employees' interests.

Source: New Agenda, IRPC Group Ltd, 1997

UNIONS AND STAFF CONSULTATION

Consultation with staff

■ *To what extent do managers consult with their staff?*

Managers often have to make decisions which affect their staff. How often do staff actually have a say on these issues? If you would rather make decisions based on your judgement with no input from your employees, are you running a particularly dictatorial workplace?

- If you do not consult with staff on any issues at all, then you are certainly in a minority – less than 10% of managers adopt this approach.

- As for how many issues are open to such consultation, the median number of issues on which managers consult with staff is 6.

- Consultation' in this survey was defined as any situation in which 'management asks about things and listens before making decisions'.

Source: *Consultation and Communication*, ACAS, 1990

■ *On what issues does management consult with staff?*

If you want to open up a communication channel with your staff, you will have to decide what issues to deal with in this way. The following chart shows what issues are most commonly opened for staff consultation, together with the percentage of establishments in which managers consult on these issues.

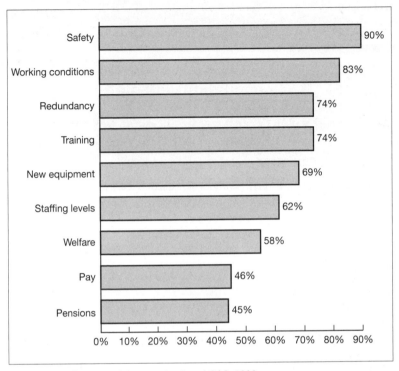

Source: *Consultation and Communication*, ACAS, 1990

■ *What factors affect the level of consultation in a company?*

Naturally there are many factors that can affect how much consultation occurs between managers and staff. The ACAS survey concentrated on union recognition and on whether the company is British-owned or not. The figures below indicate what percentage of companies in each class consult on more than 6 issues (this being the overall median average number). So if you are in a foreign-owned company that recognises unions, you should not be surprised if your consultation procedures are more comprehensive than average.

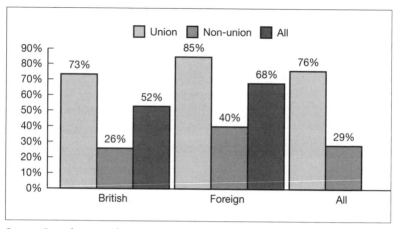

Source: Consultation and Communication, ACAS, 1990

■ *What methods of communication or consultation are most often used?*

If you are considering your position with respect to internal communications, then you may want to know what the most common methods are, and how frequently they are used. The following chart shows what proportion of trading sector companies used each of the methods listed at the time of the survey, and also the proportion of employees who were covered by such a scheme. Multiple answers were permitted.

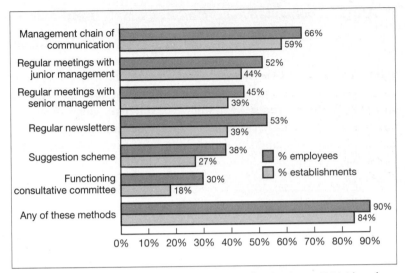

STAFF RELATIONS

Source: *The New Industrial Relations?* Policy Studies Institute, 1994 (data from *Workplace Industrial Relations Survey*, 1990)

■ *How many employees take part in some sort of employee involvement activity?*

Knowing what methods of consultation and communication are used gives no idea of how widespread their use is. The Institute of Personnel and Development wanted to know how many employees were part of an employee involvement activity.

● Nearly half the workforce – 45% – report that they take part directly in some form of employee involvement activity.

● These activities range from making suggestions to quality circles.

Source: *Employee Motivation and the Psychological Contract*, IPD Employee Attitude Survey, 1997

■ *Are joint consultative committees widely used?*

Perhaps you are already committed to consulting with staff on various management issues, but cannot decide what format this negotiation should take. One obvious choice is a committee, but how favoured is this option in practice? The table below shows what proportion of organisations use joint consultative committees of management and staff. Organisations are divided into manufacturing and services sectors, and small (less than 300 employees) and large (more than 300 employees) companies.

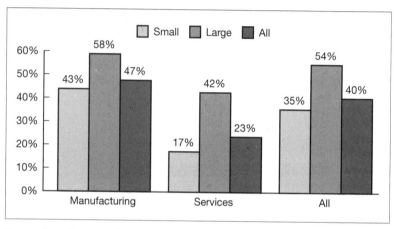

Source: Consultation and Communication, ACAS, 1990

■ *What issues are most commonly discussed by joint consultative committees?*

If you do decide to set up a committee to give your staff a chance to air their views, then what views will you be wanting them to air? Naturally there are some subjects which work well in a committee situation. Others may be better dealt with in other ways. But what subjects fall into each category? The following chart gives a list of subjects discussed on joint consultative committees, together with the percentage of respondents who said the issue was one of the three most time-consuming, and the percentage who said it was discussed at least to some extent.

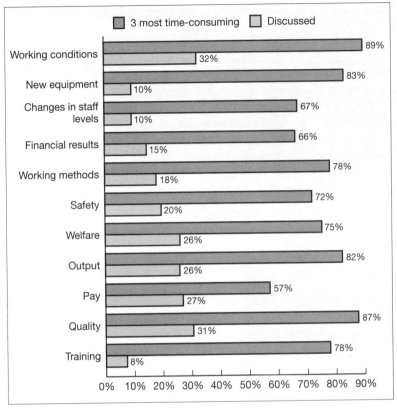

Source: *Consultation and Communication*, ACAS, 1990

STAFF RELATIONS

■ *How would a management–employee committee with decision-making power affect your relations with employees?*

Any committee of this type could affect more than just the decisions you make. Such action obviously makes staff feel more involved in the working of the company, and could actually improve staff relations. But before you jump to conclusions, are such committees generally considered to improve staff relations, or is this just wishful thinking? The chart below shows what percentage of managers think that such a committee makes a significant improvement in staff relations, no major difference, or even makes them worse.

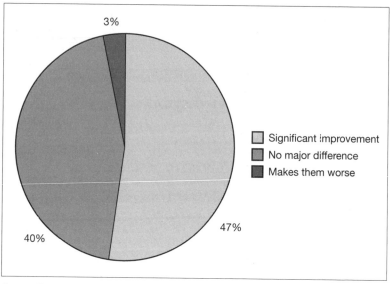

Source: *IPD Survey*, June 1995

■ *To what extent are quality circles used for staff feedback?*

'Quality circles' for this survey were defined as 'groups of workers, from the same work area, who voluntarily meet on a regular basis to identify and analyse their own work-related problems' and which 'present recommendations to management'. This is a viable alternative to holding joint committees, but how well accepted is this form of staff feedback?

- 27% of companies surveyed said that they currently operate this system, or a close approximation.

- This was more common among foreign-owned companies, 40% of which operate one or more quality circles.

- Only 23% of British-owned companies operate this system.

Source: *Consultation and Communication*, ACAS, 1990

■ What proportion of employees belong to a quality circle?

Another way to measure the prevalence of quality circles is to find out what proportion of individuals belong to one.

- 20% of employees belong to a quality circle.
- This proportion is slightly higher among men (22%) than among women (18%).

Source: Employee Commitment and the Skills Revolution, Policy Studies Institute, 1993

■ To what extent do quality circles actually influence work organisation?

Quality circles may be a good idea for providing staff feedback, but do they actually work in practice? In one survey, employees involved in quality circles were asked what level of influence they thought such groups had on the way that work was organised.

- 30% of men and 25% of women thought that quality circles had a great deal of influence.
- A further 48% of men and 52% of women thought that they had a fair amount of influence.

The survey also asked respondents what degree of influence they felt they had over decisions that changed the way they did their work.

- 47% of employees in a quality circle thought that they had a great deal or a fair amount of influence.
- Only 23% of employees not in such a group felt this way.

Source: Employee Commitment and the Skills Revolution, Policy Studies Institute, 1993

■ What issues are discussed in quality circles?

As with committees, there are some issues which are well suited to discussion in quality circles and some which are not so appropriate. The list overleaf gives some gauge of this, showing what percentage of companies with quality circles use them for discussion of each subject.

Product quality	95%
Cost reduction	72%
Output levels	66%
Communication between workers and management	60%
Communication between work-groups	55%
Safety	47%

Source: Consultation and Communication, ACAS, 1990

■ To what extent are joint working parties used?

Joint working parties are essentially joint committees convened to produce an agreed solution to a specific problem. They can be a very useful tool in cases where there is a particular issue that needs attention, but are they actually used, or are they just a good idea that is rarely put into practice? The answer to this question depends on several factors, such as the ownership of the company (British or foreign), union recognition, and company size. The following table gives the percentage of companies using joint working parties in all of these groups.

	British		Foreign		All	
	non-union	union	non-union	union	non-union	union
Small	21%	38%	43%	56%	29%	40%
Large	40%	67%	22%	75%	39%	69%
All	23%	49%	37%	65%	30%	52%

Source: Consultation and Communication, ACAS, 1990

■ What issues are most commonly dealt with by joint working parties?

Of course, some issues are more appropriate to joint working parties than others. If you have a particular problem, how can you judge whether it is wise to deal with it in this way? One answer is to see how they have been used by other companies. The following chart shows what percentage of joint working parties are convened to deal with each of the given issues or subject areas.

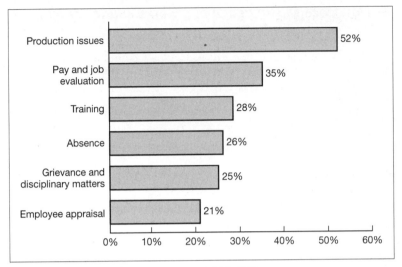

Source: *Consultation and Communication*, ACAS, 1990

■ *How common are works councils, and for what grade of employees are they most often used?*

Another method for allowing staff feedback is to have an elected works council. But is this method a widely accepted one, or is it generally restricted to only a few establishments?

- Overall, 20% of employees reported that there was a works council or similar consultative committee at their place of work.

- 70% of those surveyed, however, said that there was no such committee, and another 9% were unsure.

- Such councils were most commonly mentioned by technicians and supervisors (in 30% of cases) and by professionals and managers (29%).

- They were only mentioned by 14% of semi- and non-skilled manual workers.

- Size also seems to be a factor here – only 10% of people in companies with less than 25 employees said that they had a works council.

- 38% of people in companies with over 500 employees mentioned such a committee.

Source: *Employee Commitment and the Skills Revolution*, Policy Studies Institute, 1993

■ How does the influence of a works council differ from that of a union?

There are many similarities between works councils and unions in their provision of feedback from employees. There are also, of course, some differences. These may be particularly important if you are trying to decide between these two systems of staff consultation.

- Works councils were found to have significantly more influence over work organisation and equipment decisions than unions.

- They also had more influence over work practices, which was seen to be the biggest area of influence – 48% of respondents with such a council said it had a 'great deal' or a 'fair amount' of influence.

- They were seen to have less influence than unions over issues concerning hours and pay.

For information on union influence see What areas of work do unions have the most influence over? p.94.

Source: Employee Commitment and the Skills Revolution, Policy Studies Institute, 1993

■ Do works councils affect perceptions of employee–management relationships?

If you are considering introducing a works council, or if you are reviewing one that you currently have, then you will want to know about any effect that it will have on the climate of staff–management relations in your company. One survey found that management relations were perceived as very good by 15% fewer employees in establishments with work councils than in those without.

Source: Employee Commitment and the Skills Revolution, Policy Studies Institute, 1993

■ How will future European legislation affect the development of works councils?

New Social Chapter plans will impose tough sanctions on companies failing to consult employees on corporate policy and may force them to reinstate workers. The European Commission is currently planning national works councils for all but the smallest companies.

Plans for national works councils are especially aimed at the UK and Ireland, the only member countries without consultation arrangements. The other 13 member states already have arrangements for domestic consultation. The Commission is calling for a new directive to aim 'to develop arrangements for anticipating and forestalling the social consequences that may arise from changes in the life, organisation and running of a company'.

Source: Employers Face up to EU Consultation Fight, People Management, September 1997

Unions

■ On what issues do managers most commonly negotiate with staff?

The figures in the previous section show that organisations which recognise unions have much higher levels of staff consultation than others. But what about actual negotiation? For these purposes, negotiation was defined as 'joint decision making involving bargaining between representatives of management and representatives of employees'. The figures overleaf are for union-recognising establishments only, and indicate the most common subjects for negotiation together with the percentage of establishments in which negotiation takes place.

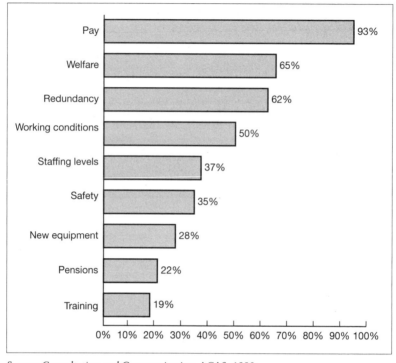

Source: Consultation and Communication, ACAS, 1990

■ *How prevalent are trade unions?*

Not all workplaces recognise trade unions, but if you are reviewing your trade union situation, then you might like to know just what sort of level of trade union recognition there is in British business.

- Overall, 59% of employees said that trade unions were represented at their workplace.

- Of these employees with trade unions present, 91% said that there were unions who represented the type of work that they did.

- In total, 43% of employees were found to be trade union members. Membership was slightly more likely for men (46% of male employees) than for women (39%).

Source: Employee Commitment and the Skills Revolution, Policy Studies Institute, 1993

An earlier survey gives more detailed figures for union recognition, this time measured by the proportion of workplaces with union recognition, rather than by the proportion of employees.

- This survey found that 40% of all trading sector workplaces recognised one or more unions.

- Union recognition was more common in the manufacturing sector, where 45% of establishments recognised at least one union.

- In contrast, only 38% of service sector establishments recognised unions.

- The figures are also broken down by the size of the establishment:

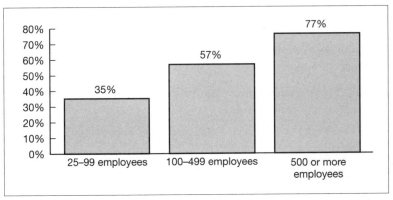

Source: *The New Industrial Relations?* Policy Studies Institute, 1994 (data from *Workplace Industrial Relations Survey*, 1990)

■ What proportion of establishments recognise only one union?

One significant development in the recognition of unions through the end of the 1980s was the tendency for workplaces to recognise only one union, rather than several. But what proportion of unionised establishments have dealt with unionisation in this way? If you are reconsidering your position on union recognition, then some figures on this may be useful:

- 54% of all workplaces with union members recognised only one union.

- This was most common in workplaces established since 1984, 64% of which recognised a single union.

- Only 52% of older workplaces had this form of union arrangement.

Source: *The New Industrial Relations?* Policy Studies Institute, 1994 (data from *Workplace Industrial Relations Survey*, 1990)

■ *Are trade unions usually encouraged or discouraged?*

Even if trade unions are represented at your workplace, it does not mean that you will encourage people to join them. On the other hand, you may feel that unionisation of your workplace is very desirable. But what is the most common attitude towards unions in the business community?

- Only 9% of employees felt that their employers discouraged them from joining trade unions.

- 14% felt that they were encouraged by their employer to join a union.

- Most commonly, however, employees did not see trade unions as an issue in their workplace – 45% of those surveyed felt this way.

- A further 33% said that their employers simply accepted the fact that some workers join unions.

Source: *Employee Commitment and the Skills Revolution*, Policy Studies Institute, 1993

■ *What areas of work do unions have the most influence over?*

If you are beginning to allow unions into your workplace, or if unions are represented and you are concerned about their level of influence, then you might like to know what influence you can expect them to have over your organisation. The following figures show the proportion of employees in unionised establishments who felt that unions had a 'great deal' or a 'fair amount' of influence over:

Pay	63%
Work hours	54%
Working practices	43%
The way that work was organised	25%
Introduction of new equipment	24%

Source: Employee Commitment and the Skills Revolution, Policy Studies Institute, 1993

■ Does the presence of a trade union affect perceptions of employee–management relations?

If you already have a union in your workplace, or are thinking of introducing one, then you will be interested to know about any effect on company culture. One survey found that management relations were perceived as very good by 15% fewer employees in unionised establishments than in non-unionised ones.

Source: Employee Commitment and the Skills Revolution, Policy Studies Institute, 1993

STAFF RELATIONS

INDUSTRIAL TRIBUNALS

Currently, around 70,000 industrial tribunal applications are made every year. *The 1992 Survey of Industrial Tribunal Applications* by Social and Community Planning Research for the Employment Department gives a detailed breakdown of a sample of industrial tribunal applications covering the five major jurisdictions under which cases are brought. Interviews were conducted with 1,990 employers and 537 applicants in the summer of 1992. The applications covered by the report were all made between April 1990 and March 1991.

Unfair dismissal

■ Are union members more likely to apply to an industrial tribunal for unfair dismissal?

Industrial tribunals can be a very harrowing and costly experience for everyone involved. If you are concerned about the possibility of such a case being brought against your company, then you will want to do everything you can to avoid this happening. But does unionisation have any impact on this?

- Although several applicants said that they had been moved to apply for a tribunal because of their union, this was far from being the most common reason.

- The proportion of industrial tribunal applicants for unfair dismissal who were union members was found to be 32%.

- The proportion who were non-union members was 60%.

Source: The 1992 Survey of Industrial Tribunal Applications, Nigel Tremlett and Nitya Banerji, Employment Department Research Series No. 22

■ Do industrial tribunals normally involve companies who already have a record of applications against them?

Some companies have a bad record for industrial tribunal applications against them. Does this mean that those with clean records can consider themselves safer? According to the SCPR survey, the proportion of industrial tribunal applications for unfair dismissal which constituted the first such case at that workplace was 64%, and the proportion for which it was not the first case was only 27%.

Source: The 1992 Survey of Industrial Tribunal Applications, Nigel Tremlett and Nitya Banerji, Employment Department Research Series No. 22

■ What are the main reasons for dismissals which are appealed against?

Staff are dismissed for all kinds of reasons, but which of these carry the greatest risk of ending in a tribunal court? The SCPR survey asked both employers and employees involved in industrial tribunal applications why the dismissal had taken place. These were the main reasons given by employers for dismissal in cases of unfair dismissal:

Economic squeeze/need for redundancies	24%
Dishonesty/theft	15%
Disobedience/breaking rules	13%
Poor attendance record	11%
Insufficient quality of work	10%

These were the main reasons given by employees for dismissal in cases of unfair dismissal:

Economic squeeze/need for redundancies	27%
Disobedience/breaking rules	11%
Poor attendance record	10%
Ill health	10%
Change in job specification	8%

Source: The 1992 Survey of Industrial Tribunal Applications, Nigel Tremlett and Nitya Banerji, Employment Department Research Series No. 22

■ How many industrial tribunal applicants have applied before?

Are tribunal applications usually made by 'troublemakers'? Or is it just as likely that they will be made by people who have never taken advantage of this system before? If some of your employees have previously lodged such cases, will you have to be extra careful? As it turns out, only 2% of applicants covered by the survey had ever applied for an industrial tribunal before.

Source: The 1992 Survey of Industrial Tribunal Applications, Nigel Tremlett and Nitya Banerji, Employment Department Research Series No. 22

■ How far do industrial tribunal applications usually go?

Obviously going to a tribunal is a time-consuming and unpleasant process. For this reason, all applications have a conciliation or a pre-hearing assessment.

● 27% of applications are resolved after this hearing or assessment.

● 33% go on to a full tribunal hearing.

● The other 40% are resolved before the tribunal by some other means.

Source: The 1992 Survey of Industrial Tribunal Applications, Nigel Tremlett and Nitya Banerji, Employment Department Research Series No. 22

■ How many tribunals find in favour of the applicant, and what is the actual cost?

If you are concerned about the possibilities of being involved in an industrial tribunal case, or if you are already involved and want to know more about your situation, then the first things on your mind will probably be what your chances of losing are, and how much you are likely to have to pay.

- 41% of unfair dismissal tribunals rule in favour of the applicant.
- The median amount of compensation awarded is £1,923.

Source: The 1992 Survey of Industrial Tribunal Applications, Nigel Tremlett and Nitya Banerji, Employment Department Research Series No. 22

■ What other costs are associated with industrial tribunals?

Compensation is not the only cost to the employer of industrial tribunal applications. Simply responding and getting involved takes up time and, of course, money. But if you do end up in this situation, what sort of amount can you expect to be shelling out?

- The median cost to companies of responding to an industrial tribunal application against them was found to be £1,486.

The cost varied depending on the type of case:

Unfair dismissal	£1,845
Redundancy payment	£781
Wages act	£293
Sex discrimination	£1,500
Race discrimination	£2,300

Source: The 1992 Survey of Industrial Tribunal Applications, Nigel Tremlett and Nitya Banerji, Employment Department Research Series No. 22

REDUNDANCIES

Union agreements

■ How many organisations have union agreements on redundancy?

Not all companies recognise any trade unions within their organisation. Those that do can have very different levels of collaboration with them. If your company recognises a union, should you therefore have an agreement with them about redundancy? Obviously this is your choice, but according to one survey:

- 78% of companies who recognise a union have a redundancy consultancy agreement with the union.
- 50% of these companies have agreed redundancy procedures with the union.

Source: Managing Redundancy, IRS Employment Trends, March 1995

■ What factors influence decisions when selecting for redundancy?

In the past, many companies used to select redundancies on the 'last in first out' principle. This is still used in some cases. But more often there are other considerations which take higher priority. What factors need to be taken into account? One survey asked this question, and the most commonly cited factors (in order of importance) were:

- The jobs that staff perform (cited by 96% of companies surveyed)
- The availability of volunteers
- Skills assessment (cited by 74% of companies)
- Performance appraisal (cited by 60% of companies)
- Attendance
- Length of service
- The ability to perform alternative jobs.

Approximately 25% of companies questioned said that they take all of the factors above into account when selecting for redundancy.

Source: Managing Redundancy, IRS Employment Trends, March 1995

STAFF RELATIONS

■ How are skills assessed for redundancy selection?

A skills assessment seems a sensible and popular way of selecting which staff to make redundant. How would you actually perform such an assessment in practice? The IRS survey asked this question, and found that:

- Over half the organisations that use skills assessment as a criterion for selecting for redundancy used some form of appraisal system.

- The majority of these appraisal systems were competency-based.

- Approximately 25% of those using skills assessment used a skills matrix which assessed staff against specific skills and knowledge required for the job.

- Some companies used training records as part of the skills assessment.

- NVQs were also mentioned as a way of assessing skills.

Source: Managing Redundancy, IRS Employment Trends, March 1995

■ How is performance assessed for redundancy selection?

Performance appraisal is another popular criterion for selecting for redundancy. Again, such an appraisal can be carried out in different ways. So if you want to use this method, what are your options, and which are most popular?

- 78% of companies surveyed have a formal performance appraisal scheme which assesses an individual's work record against the achievement of certain objectives or standards.

- Just under 20% of companies assessing performance use other personnel records such as those relating to competencies, sales, quality standards and operational time.

- A few companies have less formal procedures which rely on assessments from managers or supervisors.

Source: Managing Redundancy, IRS Employment Trends, March 1995

■ *How can you assess the ability to perform alternative jobs?*

It may make sense to judge whom you should make redundant by looking at their ability to perform other jobs. This may be easier said than done. If you were in this situation, what methods could you use to make such an assessment?

- Around 50% of organisations which consider this factor use formal appraisal schemes to determine adaptability.

- Other aspects which are often taken into consideration are
  - past employment record;
  - transferability of skills and experience to other work;
  - performance in previous job changes;
  - performance in previous training situations;
  - management assessment.

- Some companies use aptitude tests, assessment centres or even psychometric tests.

Source: Managing Redundancy, IRS Employment Trends, March 1995

■ *By what means are redundancies achieved?*

Redundancy is no longer a case of simply giving people the sack. In these days of redeployment, early retirement and the like, there are many other ways of reducing your numbers of staff. But how realistic is it to expect to reduce staff numbers simply by means of redeployment, for example? If you have to make some redundancy decisions, then the figures below might help you to assess your options.

- Only 14% of organisations cut staff numbers using only compulsory redundancy.

- Another 14% of companies said that they use a combination of the techniques offered as options (redeployment, natural wastage, early retirement, voluntary redundancy and compulsory redundancy).

- A mixture of voluntary and compulsory redundancy was used by 10% of companies.

- None of the companies covered by this survey used only redeployment or only natural wastage.

Source: Employment Policies in the Recession, IRS Employment Trends, February 1993

■ To what extent is voluntary redundancy used?

You can, of course, ask for volunteers. If you are thinking of doing this to help with your redundancy selection, then you are not alone – 88% of companies say that they seek to avoid compulsory redundancy with voluntary redundancy measures. Only 76% of companies, however, said that they had actually used this procedure to make staff redundant.

Source: Managing Redundancy, IRS Employment Trends, March 1995

■ To what extent is the principle of 'last in first out' used?

The LIFO principle, as it is known, is popular with ACAS and also with many unions, but is it wise to make redundancy decisions on this basis? The consensus seems to be that it is not, with only 24% of companies covered by the IRS survey using LIFO in cases of compulsory redundancy. However, union influence is very significant here, since LIFO is used by 50% of organisations with union agreements.

Source: Managing Redundancy, IRS Employment Trends, March 1995

■ What are the arguments in favour of 'last in first out'?

The LIFO system does appear to be somewhat controversial – popular with some and unpopular with others – which indicates that there are good reasons to use it. But if you are deciding whether or not to use it, it will help to know what the main reasons are for its use.

● LIFO is most often used as a last resort, where other criteria have failed to differentiate sufficiently between individuals.

● The other reasons cited for using LIFO were that it is seen as being fair, and that it is part of a union agreement.

Source: Managing Redundancy, IRS Employment Trends, March 1995

■ What are the arguments against using 'last in first out'?

Having heard the pro-LIFO side of the argument, you will now also want to know why so many organisations choose not to use it as a selection criterion.

- By far the most common reason for avoiding LIFO – cited by 50% of companies who do not use it – is that it disregards the future needs of the business and the retention of the best and most skilled staff.

- Other companies said that they did not use LIFO because they were able to avoid compulsory redundancy measures.

- A few companies (6%) said that they rejected LIFO because it had the potential to be discriminatory.

Source: Managing Redundancy, IRS Employment Trends, March 1995

■ Do most companies stick to the statutory minimum severance payments?

There is a statutory minimum provision for severance pay, but this does not mean that you cannot be more generous. But if you do stick to the minimum, and fulfil your legal obligation, are you meaner than most? I am afraid you are – the IRS survey found that a heart-warming 90% of companies provide severance payments exceeding the statutory minimum. Such overpayment can be arranged in various ways, including:

- Improving on the formula determining the number of weeks' pay to which an employee is entitled.

- Using a broader definition of 'a week's pay' than the legislation.

- Reducing or removing length-of-service qualifications.

Source: Managing Redundancy, IRS Employment Trends, March 1995

■ What is a reasonable service qualification for severance pay?

Many companies only grant severance pay to employees who have been employed for a certain length of time, but is this one month or ten years? If you want to put a minimum service restriction on your provision of severance pay, it might help to know what sort of time-frame is usually given. The following percentage of organisations gave time-frames of:

Under one year	6%
Two years	33%
Five years	4%
No minimum service or minimum hours qualification	26%
No minimum hours qualification	68%

Source: *Managing Redundancy*, IRS Employment Trends, March 1995

■ What qualifies as 'length of service' in such calculations?

An employee's length of service is not always totally straightforward to calculate. Sometimes it is calculated differently for part-time employees, and different treatment may be given to periods of leave. But what is the standard practice for calculating length of service with regard to severance pay entitlement?

- 90% of respondents treated part-time service the same way as full-time service for this purpose.

- 90% also included periods of long-term sickness and maternity leave in these calculations.

Source: *Managing Redundancy*, IRS Employment Trends, March 1995

■ How many companies provide counselling for employees who are made redundant?

Counselling services are used by many companies to offer support and guidance to their employees. Redundancy can naturally be a very upsetting experience, but to what extent should employees who are made redundant expect counselling to be provided for them by their employer? Apparently this is quite a widespread practice, with 75% of companies providing such counselling services.

Source: *Employment Policies in the Recession*, IRS Employment Trends, February 1993

Outplacement

■ How many companies provide outplacement services?

Outplacement services are widely available in the current business marketplace, but to what extent are they actually used? If you do not use such a service, are you one of many or do you have some catching up to do? According to the IRS survey, 68% of organisations provide outplacement services for employees who are made redundant.

Source: Managing Redundancy, IRS Employment Trends, March 1995

■ For what grades of staff are outplacement services usually provided?

If you are thinking of providing outplacement services for staff who are made redundant, you will have to decide whether these services should be available across the board, or only to certain grades of staff. So it might help to know what grades of staff are normally covered by outplacement services.

- In over 60% of companies which provided outplacement services, these were available to all levels of staff.
- In about 33% of cases, however, outplacement services were only provided at more senior management grades.

Source: Managing Redundancy, IRS Employment Trends, March 1995

■ Are outplacement services usually provided in-house or by external companies?

Another decision you will have to make if you are considering providing outplacement services is whether to make this provision with your own company or to bring in an external agency. This is a difficult decision, and it seems that most companies, one way or another, do involve an external agency in the process.

- 91% of companies providing outplacement services use a specialist agency.
- 35% use in-house services.
- This gives an overlap of 26% who use a combination of both.
- Only 9% rely entirely on in-house services.

Source: Managing Redundancy, IRS Employment Trends, March 1995

RELOCATION

■ *What retraining do staff need when they relocate?*

When staff move from one site to another, they are often given extra training on how to perform their (possibly new) job in a definitely new environment. This may simply cover how to use the new computer system, or it may be much wider-ranging. But are the standard levels of retraining actually sufficient? One survey sent questionnaires to relocatees in two companies. Respondents were asked to rate the training and induction procedures they went through on relocation.

- 40% of staff in the first company gave these procedures a negative rating.

- A similar 38% in the second company also gave negative ratings.

The sample used is very limited, so these figures cannot reliably be taken as representative of all relocation programmes. More usefully, though, the survey also tried to ascertain where this dissatisfaction stemmed from. Again, this is still very specific to the companies concerned, but the three main points that were raised are worth considering before you plan such a retraining programme.

- Many staff felt that technical training was good, but that there was a lack of training in interpersonal and people management skills.

- Specialist workers who were trying to move into more general management roles often did not feel that adequate opportunities had been provided for retraining in the necessary skills.

- Many staff said that the training covered skills necessary for the company to function, but did not take into account the needs of the staff.

Source: 'Employee Job Mobility and Relocation', Personnel Review, Vol. 19, No. 6

■ *How stressful is relocation?*

Moving house is no one's idea of a great way to spend a holiday. Does the assistance given during relocation help to reduce the stress of this upheaval? The figures below come from the same survey of two companies, and again are not representative of the country as a whole. However, they are quite revealing of some general factors influencing stress.

- Over 50% of staff in both companies described the experience of relocation as stressful.

- Stress was most often reported by married couples (in 75% of cases in one company, and 70% in the other).

- Just over 50% of couples with children in both companies said that the experience was stressful for their children.

Source: 'Employee Job Mobility and Relocation', Personnel Review, Vol. 19, No. 6

PENSIONS

■ *Why should you provide pension plans for employees?*

Pensions are provided for at least some staff by many companies, but why exactly is this? If you are thinking of introducing a pension scheme, or discontinuing one that you are currently running, then it might help to understand what reasons companies have for providing this incentive for employees. One survey gave five potential reasons for having a pension scheme, and asked respondents to rank them in order of importance from 1 (most important) to 5 (least important). The table overleaf shows the average ranking for each suggestion, and the percentage of respondents who considered it most important.

Motivation	Average rank	Marked as most important
Ensures company is competitive in the labour market	2.2	33%
Part of company's paternalistic approach to benefit provision and contributes to image as a good employer	2.2	28%
Acts as an aid to employee motivation	2.8	21%
Provides the ability to retire employees on reasonable pensions at company's convenience	3.7	9%
Has been in existence many years and could not easily be discontinued	4.0	9%

Source: A View from the Top, Confederation of British Industry, 1994

■ What are the most important issues with regard to planning pension schemes?

Of course, you may well have a pension scheme which you wish to continue, but there could still be issues surrounding this which may be cause for concern. But which of these should take priority in your plans for the scheme? The table below gives six potential concerns for the next five years which were ranked in importance by senior executives from 1 (most important) to 5 (least important). The figures show the average rank for each concern, and the percentage of executives who marked it as most important.

Concern	Average rank	Marked as most important
Contain pension costs at current level	1.9	53%
Reduce pension costs	3.5	15%
Reduce administrative burden	3.5	7%
Restructure scheme to meet recent or prospective UK or EC legislation	3.6	11%
Improve pension benefits	3.8	11%
Place more responsibility on employees to meet the cost of their pensions	4.6	3%

Source: A View from the Top, Confederation of British Industry, 1994

STAFF RELATIONS

■ *How appreciative of pension schemes are employees?*

When you have a pension scheme as part of your benefits package, you will obviously want to feel that you are getting some advantage from offering it. But do staff really appreciate the pension provision that you provide for them? The Confederation of British Industry asked senior executives whether they thought their employees appreciated their pension schemes. The possible answers were 'Yes', 'Yes, but not as much as we would like', 'No', and 'Don't know'. The responses are shown below.

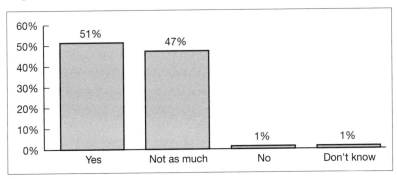

Source: A View from the Top, Confederation of British Industry, 1994

■ How can employee appreciation of pension schemes be improved?

The figures above show that almost half of companies providing pension plans feel that they are not fully appreciated. If you fall into this category, what can you do to improve the situation? The Confederation of British Industry survey asked what steps companies were taking to improve employee appreciation. The table below shows what proportion of companies were adopting each measure.

Improve communication arrangements	61%
Provide individual benefit counselling	18%
Introduce new pension arrangements	12%
Make pensions part of employee bargaining	4%
Other	5%

Source: A View from the Top, Confederation of British Industry, 1994

■ What changes in the labour force have most impact on pension provision?

The profile of the labour force is constantly changing, and this naturally has repercussions for pension provisions. But what expected changes are most relevant to the planning of pension schemes? Senior executives were asked to rank several expected changes from 1 (most important) to 5 (least important). The average rank for each is shown below, along with the percentage who considered it most important.

Expected change	Average rank	Marked as most important
Shortening length of service/ end of lifetime employment with one employer	2.0	48%
Average age of workers rising	2.6	34%
More part-time employees	3.3	7%
More female employees	3.4	6%
More temporary employees	3.8	5%

Source: A View from the Top, Confederation of British Industry, 1994

■ *How long should you take to recover pension surpluses?*

When a pension scheme produces surpluses, these can be recovered in various ways. But as well as deciding how to recover them, it is also important to decide what time-span you would expect this to take. One survey asked employers how long they would expect to take over recovering any surplus. The percentage indicating each time-span is shown below. It is worth noting that there is no option between 5 years and 10–15 years, and it cannot be determined how many respondents would have indicated a 5–10 years option had there been one (or what option they indicated instead).

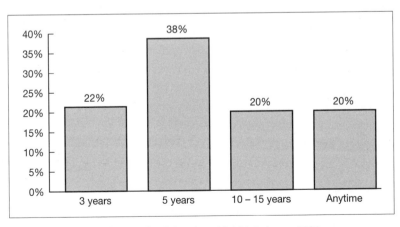

Source: A View from the Top, Confederation of British Industry, 1994

■ *What is the best type of pension provision to make?*

Naturally this varies from company to company. Some general perceptions of pension schemes might be useful if you have to make decisions in this area. The Confederation of British Industry asked senior executives what pension scheme they would use if they had a chance to start from scratch, with the benefit of hindsight. A total of 83% said that they would still introduce a pension scheme. The breakdown of responses is shown below.

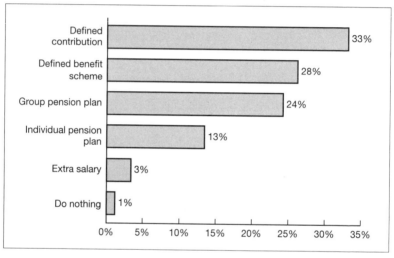

Source: A View from the Top, Confederation of British Industry, 1994

STAFF ATTITUDES

Employees

■ *What aspects of their job are most employees satisfied, or dissatisfied, with?*

If you want to improve staff morale, motivation, or your workforce's behaviour, then you may well want to increase their overall job satisfaction. Before doing this, you may want to run a survey to see what aspects of their jobs they are least and most satisfied with. In this case, it helps to know what the average responses across the country are. Alternatively, you may want to make your decisions simply on the basis of national figures. Either way, the figures below could be of use to you, showing what percentage of people surveyed reported that they were either completely or very satisfied with each area of their job:

Friendliness of colleagues	71%
Chances to use their own initiative	57%
Opportunities to use their abilities	54%
Work they had to do	53%
Sufficient variety in their work	49%
Relationship with their supervisor or boss	52%
Hours that they worked	44%
Amount of work	39%
Training provided by their organisation	33%
Ability and efficiency of management at their place of work	32%
Promotion prospects	32%
Pay received	25%

- Overall job satisfaction varied very little between different job levels.

Source: Employee Commitment and the Skills Revolution, Policy Studies Institute, 1993

■ *What are the possible reasons for middle management resistance to employee involvement?*

Opinions on employee involvement can be mixed, and sometimes there is a specific resistance to it at the middle management level. But what are the causes of this particular resistance? One report puts it down to three main categories of reason:

1 Protection of self-interest
2 Lack of competence to facilitate employee involvement
3 Mixed signals from top management and the organisation

Source: Middle Managers – Their Contribution to Employee Involvement, London Business School 1994, for the Department of Employment

■ *How can you increase employee involvement?*

You may want more employee involvement in your organisation, but how is this actually going to be achieved? The London Business School report gives five main factors that actually encourage employee involvement.

Five factors encouraging employee involvement
1 High performance expectations combined with frequently expressed confidence in staff
2 Autonomy from bureaucratic constraint
3 Meaningful goals
4 Celebration of successful achievement
5 Removal of sources of 'adverse emotional arousal', e.g. job insecurity or high levels of uncertainty

Source: Middle Managers – Their Contribution to Employee Involvement, London Business School 1994, for the Department of Employment

■ To what extent do staff have a say in the way that their company operates?

A lot is said about employee involvement, but in a cross-section of the working community, how involved do staff really feel? One survey asked workers how much influence they felt they would have over a decision that changed the way they do their job.

- Overall, 32% felt that they would have either a great deal or quite a lot of say.
- Another 18% said that they would have a little say.
- 50% said that they would have no say or were unsure.
- Managers and professionals seemed to feel much more involved here, with 45% saying that they would have a great deal or quite a lot of influence.
- This claim was made by 32% of technical and supervisory staff, 28% of lower non-manual employees, and 26% of skilled manual workers.
- Only 20% of semi- or non-skilled manual workers felt that they would have this level of say in such decisions.

Source: Employee Commitment and the Skills Revolution, Policy Studies Institute, 1993

■ Are employees happy with the level of input they have into organisational decisions?

Employee involvement may have increased significantly over the last few decades, but has it come far enough? Does current company culture give employees as much say as they would like, or are there still improvements to be made?

- 49% of employees thought that they should have more say in organisational decisions.
- This feeling was strongest among technicians and supervisors, 55% of whom were dissatisfied with their level of input, and skilled manual workers, 53% of whom felt the same.
- However, dissatisfaction spread across all job levels, with even 47% of professional and managerial employees wanting to participate more in such decisions.

Source: Employee Commitment and the Skills Revolution, Policy Studies Institute, 1993

■ *Does employee involvement affect employee perceptions of changes at work?*

Employees may want to participate in decisions for a variety of reasons, and involving them may satisfy these desires. But does allowing them to participate actually change their perceptions of decisions that are made?

- Overall, 50% of employees who had experienced recent organisational change, and who claimed to have no influence over work decisions, said that this change had had little or no benefit.

- However, only 22% of those who had experienced changes but who claimed to have a high level of involvement in work decisions said that the change had had little or no benefit.

Source: Employee Commitment and the Skills Revolution, Policy Studies Institute, 1993

■ *Does employee involvement affect perceptions of employee–management relations?*

As with attitudes to change, increased employee involvement may improve staff perceptions of other things. If you are wondering whether it is worth increasing the level of employee involvement in your organisation, then these figures may interest you.

- Where employees felt that their level of participation in work decisions was negligible, 17% felt that staff–management relations were very good.

- Where participation was high, however, 47% felt that this was the case.

Source: Employee Commitment and the Skills Revolution, Policy Studies Institute, 1993

Leadership

■ *Is there a change in leadership style?*

What style will future business leadership take? Old style command and control leadership is perhaps becoming less appropriate, but how prevalent is it?

Korn Ferry International and the Economist Intelligence Unit undertook a survey of leadership styles. The survey reports that:

- Leadership is in transition. Today it is still paternalistic, entrepreneurial and involved in command and control.

- In the future it is expected to be entrepreneurial; driven by ideas, products, marketing and sharing – power, ideas and accountability.

Source: 'Developing Tomorrow's Leaders', Ken Brotherton's speech at the IPD's National Conference, 23 October 1997

■ *Is there a change in leadership language?*

Ken Brotherton, partner at Korn Ferry International, argues that organisations will need a 'new language of leadership'. He says:

> *Management used to speak of organisations being designed, planned and managed, with feedback loops, control systems, compliance and measurement devices. Today's companies like to describe themselves using words such as 'empowered', 'process-oriented', 'networks', 'alliances', 'shared values and cultures', 'consensus' and 'involvement'. The leitmotif of this vocabulary shift is that co-ordinating, facilitating and enabling seem to be in the process of ousting directing and commanding.*

Source: 'Developing Tomorrow's Leaders', Ken Brotherton's speech at the IPD's National Conference, 23 October 1997

■ *How will leadership be benchmarked in the future?*

If the style of leadership is changing, then methods of evaluating it will have to change too. So how will a CEO's effectiveness be measured in the future?

- Chief executives are measured today firstly by profitability, then satisfaction, then sustained growth.

- In the future, they will probably be assessed firstly by customer satisfaction, then by long-term return to investors, then profitability.

Source: 'Developing Tomorrow's Leaders', Ken Brotherton's speech at the IPD's National Conference, 23 October 1997

Company culture

■ What effect does 'flattening' your organisation have on company culture?

There are many reasons for restructuring a company to create a 'flatter' hierarchy. But changes like this are bound to have an effect on the people who work there, in terms of how they are treated and how they feel towards the company. What effects do a flatter structure create? Well, many managers have a very positive impression of their restructured company. The most common words used to describe it were:

● Open

● Honest

● Informal

● Consultative

● Progressive.

Unfortunately, however, there were also some disadvantages. The two most significant ones were:

● Flatter organisations are seen as less 'caring'. This was found to be truer of managers further down the organisation than of their senior counterparts.

● Over 50% of managers felt that, since restructuring, managers were held accountable but lacked the authority actually to take decisions.

Source: Are Managers Getting the Message? Institute of Management, 1992

■ Do staff like flatter structures?

Roffey Park Management Institute surveyed 200 organisations and 800 staff. They found that staff perceptions of delayering are 'generally negative'. Why are staff suspicious? Linda Holbeche, Roffey's research director, says:

> *During the first phase of the survey in 1994, we found that flatter structures were having a very damaging effect on employees. People felt that they had no guarantee of a job, and no prospects of promotion. They were uncertain about the future, confused about their roles, and complained of heavier workloads.*

There would also appear to be growing contradictions as high-flyer schemes return. Employees who have compromised their own ambitions in future organisations now see newer employees on fast tracks which were not available to them.

Source: 'Managing Careers in a Flatter Organisation', Linda Holbeche's speech at the IPD National Conference, 23 October 1997

■ How can you guarantee the success of a flatter organisation?

Linda Holbeche advocates a coherent human resources strategy, to counteract this negative response to flatter organisations. Organisational support such as mentoring and peer coaching is vital; good leadership is critical.

- Participative management styles, feedback and clear business vision can contribute to higher employee morale.

- Organisations need to think carefully about the range of career development options they offer – and the fact that they might be giving conflicting messages to their employees.

Source: 'Managing Careers in a Flatter Organisation', Linda Holbeche's speech at the IPD National Conference, 23 October 1997

■ Do leaner organisations have better staff relations?

According to a book published recently, the opposite may apply. Many companies have, in the name of leaner organisation, introduced policies which have shattered staff loyalty and reversed the efficiency they were intended to create.

The book documents cases of how, in the City of London – 'the UK's best example of cost-based leanness' – some firms have resorted to spying on staff in an effort to spot disloyalty.

Source: From Leanness to Fitness – Developing Corporate Muscle, Michel Syrett and Jean Lammiman, IPD, October 1997

■ How do lean organisations make sure that they are efficient?

Syrett and Lammiman recommend that the 'slimming' of a company be approached in much the same way as a healthy diet. Companies should:

Avoid being overweight, but once the optimum weight has been achieved they should work hard to turn their fat into muscle where it is needed.

This can be achieved by using personnel professionals in much the same way as sports stars use physiotherapists – to train, counsel and support their staff.

- Leanness should never mean slashing whole layers of employees and then hoping for the best.

- Well-thought out leanness can create the fitness needed to innovate, capture fresh markets and ensure long-term success.

Source: 'Developing Tomorrow's Leaders', Ken Brotherton's speech at the IPD's National Conference, 23 October 1997

■ How many organisations treat manual workers the same as non-manual workers?

Traditionally there has been a significant distinction between manual and non-manual workers, often highlighted by such terminology as 'workers' and 'staff'. But is this distinction still applicable in business today, or are many companies opting for a 'single status' organisation? If you still use different procedures for manual and non-manual workers, then you may like to know whether this is a common practice, or whether it is outdated.

- Just over half of the organisations surveyed (51%) pay both types of staff at the same intervals – be it weekly, fortnightly, or monthly.

- Similarly, 52% of companies used the same methods of recording attendance (clocking in, etc.) for manual and non-manual workers.

- 73% of organisations use the same method of payment (e.g. cheque, cash, direct transfer) for all their workers.

Source: The New Industrial Relations? Policy Studies Institute, 1994 (data from *Workplace Industrial Relations Survey*, 1990)

Promotions

■ *What proportion of employees are aiming for a promotion?*

There are only ever a limited number of promotions to go round. If everyone is clamouring to move up the echelons of your company, then some are bound to be disappointed. This can be a difficult situation to manage. But what proportion of workers really are concerned about getting a better job?

- In one survey, 51% of respondents said that they were 'aiming to get a better job or to be promoted'.
- Unfortunately, this still seems to outnumber the opportunities, with only 39% considering that their chances of promotion were better than 50/50.

Source: Employee Commitment and the Skills Revolution, Policy Studies Institute, 1993

■ *Do employees feel that there are enough opportunities for promotion in their company?*

If you want to make sure of keeping skilled staff, then you may need to satisfy their desire for promotion. This means, at the very least, making them feel that they have better career opportunities if they stay with the company than if they leave. So what proportion of employees are satisfied with their employers in this respect?

- 49% of employees thought that changing employers was the best route to getting a promotion.
- Only 41% said that their best chance for being promoted was to stay with their current employer.

Source: Employee Commitment and the Skills Revolution, Policy Studies Institute, 1993

STAFF BEHAVIOUR

Violence

■ How common is physical or verbal workplace violence?

Sometimes staff can get out of hand, but how often does this situation really break down into one that would be described as 'violent'? According to one survey, 11% of UK workers have observed violence in their workplace in the last year, and in 33% of these cases, this involved actual physical violence. These are, of course, only the figures for observed instances, certainly not for all that occurred.

But it seems that this is not just one-off cases of someone blowing their top. Over 40% of workers who had experienced violence had been involved in more than 5 violent incidents in the last year.

Source: Is your Workmate your Worst Enemy? IPD survey, June 1995

■ How does this violence break down?

Men seem to be considerably more at risk of violent treatment in the workplace than do women. The IPD survey found that 7.2% of male workers had experienced threats, abuse or assaults in the last year, as against 2% of female workers.

Although it is more common for a boss to act violently to one of their staff than the other way round, there is often no such hierarchical division between the people involved. The survey found that in 63% of cases the people involved were at the same level of the staff hierarchy. As for the other instances, in 23% of cases the aggressor was a superior, and in the remaining 14% they were a subordinate.

Source: Is your Workmate your Worst Enemy? IPD survey, June 1995

Sexual harassment

■ How many companies have a written policy on sexual harassment?

If a case of sexual harassment does occur at your workplace, then you will want to be prepared for it. One way to make such preparation is to have a formal policy on this issue. But is this really necessary?

- For many it seems that it is – 43% of workers are aware that their employer has a written policy on sexual harassment.

- Also, 45% of workers say that their employer provides support or guidance for employees alleging sexual harassment.

Source: The Institute of Personnel and Development Survey on Sexual Harassment in the Workplace, IPD survey, February 1995

■ How can sexual harassment be dealt with?

Sexual harassment in the workplace is the subject of much discussion. It is certainly an issue which may confront you. But if allegations are made, what is the best way to deal with the situation?

- 83% of workers say that sexual harassment cases should be resolved by the employer.

- 46% say that this should be an informal, rather than a formal, solution.

- Only 10% say that such cases should always go to court.

- 42% of female workers say that they would always take a case of sexual harassment to court.

- 25% of male workers feel the same.

- It is worth noting that 7% of workers are aware of men being sexually harassed by women in the workplace – quite a few considering that most cases of sexual harassment have no witness.

Source: The Institute of Personnel and Development Survey on Sexual Harassment in the Workplace, IPD survey, February 1995

■ Who do employees turn to when they have suffered sexual harassment?

If someone is subjected to sexual harassment at work, then there will have to be someone that they go to first to take action on the incident. If you are concerned about such happenings at your workplace, then you might want to get an idea of who the potential victims are likely to turn to first.

- 67% of workers say that they would turn to their boss for help and advice if they were being sexually harassed.
- Nearly 50% of those with personnel professionals would go to them.
- 33% said that they would go to their union representative.

Source: The Institute of Personnel and Development Survey on Sexual Harassment in the Workplace, IPD survey, February 1995

STAFF TURNOVER

■ What is the average level of staff turnover?

Naturally this can vary a lot according to industry, level of staff, and even regional considerations. For the purposes of this survey, 'staff turnover' was defined as:

$$\text{Percentage employee turnover} = \frac{100 \times (\text{no. new recruits} + \text{no. leavers})}{2 \times \text{no. employees 12 months ago}}$$

According to this survey, then, and this calculation of turnover, the overall national average level of staff turnover was 11.5%.

Source: Skill Needs in Britain 1994, IFF research for Employment Department

■ What is the average level of turnover for management and directors?

Of course, turnover naturally varies between different grades of staff. If it is management turnover that you are concerned about, then you may want to see some figures that are more specific to your problem.

- In 1997, some 8.9% of company directors left their jobs.
- 2.6% of directors resigned from their posts.
- In the same period, 11.1% of managers (above line manager level) left their jobs for one reason or another.
- For some 3.4% of managers, resignation was the reason.

Source: National Management Salary Survey 1997, Remuneration Economics

■ What are the basic facts of staff turnover?

If you have a problem with staff turnover in your organisation, then there are many possible causes, as well as many possible treatments. But the first thing that you will probably want to do is to get a broader understanding of staff turnover, to see if your problem fits into any recognised pattern. One report managed to identify these eight 'irrefutable facts' of staff turnover:

Eight irrefutable facts of staff turnover
1 Young, single employees with short service are the highest risk
2 Dissatisfied and uncommitted employees are most likely to leave
3 Employees who are neither satisfied nor committed in the first month of employment are most likely to leave within a year
4 The majority of turnover is within the control of the employer
5 Recruits with unrealistic expectations are most likely to leave within six months
6 Turnover is self-perpetuating
7 Job redesign and realistic recruitment are the best ways to reduce turnover
8 Dissatisfaction with pay is very rarely the main cause of high turnover

Source: Staff Retention: A Manager's Guide, Institute of Manpower Studies 1990, HMSO Copyright

STAFF RELATIONS

■ How does turnover of management level staff vary with age?

Age obviously does play a part in considerations of staff turnover, but what is the profile of this relationship? If you are concerned about turnover among your managers or directors, then the chart below is likely to interest you. It shows what percentage of managers and directors in each age group left their posts in 1996. It also shows what percentage left through resignation and what percentage were made redundant in each group (small percentages left for other reasons such as death or retirement).

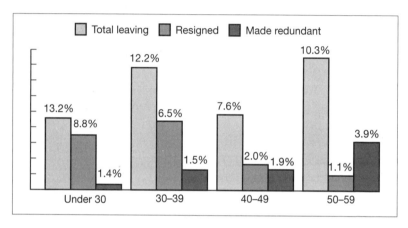

- 35.6% of managers and directors over 59 years old left their jobs during this time.
- Over half of these (21.7% of the total sample) retired.
- Of the total sample of over 59s, 1.3% resigned and 9.9% were made redundant.

Source: National Management Salary Survey 1997, Remuneration Economics

■ What is the role of pay in staff turnover?

You may want to solve your turnover problems with pay rises, but will this actually work? One report identifies these relationships between turnover and pay:

1	Few people leave for jobs with less pay
2	Leavers typically express similar dissatisfaction with pay as stayers
3	An offer of a pay rise will keep less than 10% of leavers
4	Leavers only seek to maximise pay after they have decided to leave
5	Dissatisfaction with some aspect of the job other than pay is the most common cause of resignation.

Source: Staff Retention: A Manager's Guide, Institute of Manpower Studies 1990, HMSO Copyright

STAFF RELATIONS

■ *What are the costs of turnover?*

Turnover is costly, but what is the real price of losing staff? It varies from organisation to organisation, of course, but to calculate it you will need a checklist. Turnover cost can be broadly categorised in four categories:

- **Separation costs.** Administrative costs (e.g. pensions, exit interviews, etc.).

- **Temporary replacement costs.** The costs of getting the work done while the post is vacant (e.g. overtime, temps, etc.).

- **Recruitment and selection costs.** The direct costs and the cost in manager's time.

- **Induction and training costs.** Direct costs and pay during unproductive early stages.

Source: Staff Retention: A Manager's Guide, Institute of Manpower Studies 1990, HMSO Copyright

■ *What are the most common reasons for leaving?*

Another way to look at staff turnover is from the employees' point of view – why are these people leaving your company? To this end, the Institute of Manpower Studies report identifies seven main causes of resignation:

The seven main causes of resignation

1 Insufficient job satisfaction
2 Insufficient career opportunities
3 Not feeling valued
4 Poor relationship with boss
5 Job does not meet expectations
6 Work is dull and repetitive
7 Promotion system seen as unfair

Source: Staff Retention: A Manager's Guide, Institute of Manpower Studies 1990, HMSO Copyright

■ *What constitutes job satisfaction?*

If you are concerned about morale and job satisfaction, and suspect that addressing this problem might help with your turnover situation, then you will also need a deeper understanding of what this satisfaction is. The tasks that your staff perform are not the totality of what they perceive as their job. Dissatisfaction may come from this, but it may arise from a number of other factors. The most commonly accepted components of job satisfaction are:

1 The work itself
2 The immediate boss
3 Colleagues
4 Pay
5 Working conditions/environment.

Source: Staff Retention: A Manager's Guide, Institute of Manpower Studies 1990, HMSO Copyright

COMMUNICATION

Negotiation

■ *How is negotiation defined?*

Negotiation applies equally to purchasing and to industrial relations. Two typical definitions are:

1 The process whereby two or more parties decide what each will give and take in an exchange between them.
2 The process of communicating, discussing and bargaining with the object of reaching an agreement.

Source: Negotiation, Ken Burnett, The Chartered Institute of Purchasing and Supply, 1997

■ *What determines a successful outcome?*

The key determinant of a successful outcome is an understanding and appreciation of the position of the other side in the negotiations. This approach is known as partnership, or win/win negotiation – as opposed to the traditional adversarial approach which has marked the more acrimonious industrial disputes.

Source: Negotiation, Ken Burnett, The Chartered Institute of Purchasing and Supply, 1997

■ *Do differences in bargaining strength affect outcome?*

Advocates of the traditional adversarial style maintain that partnership negotiations can only take place when the two parties have equal bargaining strength. It would appear that differences in bargaining strength are less important than how thoroughly each side has researched the topic under discussion.

Source: Negotiation, Ken Burnett, The Chartered Institute of Purchasing and Supply, 1997

STAFF RELATIONS

■ *What are the characteristics of a successful negotiator?*

The National Association of Purchasing Management – the US counterpart of the CIPS – has identified the following 8 vital characteristics:

Eight vital characteristics of a successful negotiator
1 Ability to think and plan ahead
2 Competitiveness
3 Personal integrity
4 Analytical ability
5 Decisiveness
6 Ability to gain respect
7 Tact
8 Ability to listen

Source: Negotiation, Ken Burnett, The Chartered Institute of Purchasing and Supply, 1997

■ *How do you avoid making mistakes in negotiations?*

The easiest way to avoid mistakes is to take advice – and Ken Burnett provides a list of the most commonly encountered mistakes:

1 Failure to make adequate preparations before negotiations start.

2 Failure to interpret correctly the signs and signals from the other side; body language and facial expression often convey as much as, if not more than, speech.

3 Too much haste – time pressures can result in premature, and often unsatisfactory, agreements.

4 Having unrealistic expectations from the discussions. Often these expectations can be too high – but they can also be too low.

5 Inability to distinguish between counter-attacking and negotiating.

6 Adopting the win–lose mentality.

7 A successful negotiation ends as a meaningful and constructive relationship begins. So don't sour this relationship by trying to squeeze last minute concessions.

8 Never show triumph – or the other party will resolve to win next time.

Source: Negotiation, Ken Burnett, The Chartered Institute of Purchasing and Supply, 1997

■ *How do you increase your chances of success?*

Ken Burnett offers five tips, taken from *It's a Deal*, by Steele, Murphy and Russill – an excellent practical handbook on negotiation:

1. **Trade or bargain on the straw issues** – if you have to make concessions, try to do so on the relatively unimportant issues.
2. **Aim high** – the more you ask for, the more you get. However, the figure must be credible.
3. **Learn to listen** – often so much more profitable than talking.
4. **Elicit offers – don't make them** – get the other side to reveal what their targets or figures are.
5. **Learn to say thank you** – always thank the other side for the concessions they make. This is not a sign of weakness, but is simple courtesy and will smooth the negotiation process.

Source: Negotiation, Ken Burnett, The Chartered Institute of Purchasing and Supply, 1997

Counselling

■ *What do Employee Assistance Programme providers actually provide?*

Many companies supply some form of counselling service for their staff, and one way to do this is through an EAP provider. But before you make any arrangements for these services, you will need to know what exactly these organisations provide for your company. One survey asked EAP providers what they considered the core activities of an EAP.

- The provision of face-to-face counselling was the most commonly agreed element of EAPs, cited by over 90% of respondents.

- Initial and ongoing advertisement of the EAP was seen by 80% of providers as one of their core activities.

- At least 80% also mentioned orientation sessions for managers and employees.

- Approximately 70% said that providing statistical and detailed feedback to the client organisation was a core activity.

- Giving advice to managers was cited by nearly 70% of EAP providers.

Source: An Assessment of UK EAPs and Workplace Counselling Programmes, Highley and Cooper 1995 (Manchester School of Management, UMIST)

■ What form of counselling do EAP providers usually supply?

While it may be very useful to provide counselling services for those among your staff who feel they need them, you may not want to pay for half your staff to embark upon years of intensive Freudian psychoanalysis. Fortunately, however, this is not the usual EAP approach, and 90% of providers offer services consisting of approximately 6 sessions with the aim of resolving a particular problem.

Source: An Assessment of UK EAPs and Workplace Counselling Programmes, Highley and Cooper 1995 (Manchester School of Management, UMIST)

■ Should workplace counselling services extend to the families of employees?

It is often hard to be detached from the family, and it may be that the distress a member of your staff is experiencing is closely tied in with that of a member of their family. But if this is the case, will, or should, your workplace counselling arrangements cover this person? If you want an arrangement that does extend to family members, then these facts might interest you.

- In 87% of cases, Employee Assistance Programmes do extend to family members.

- Only 28% of internal counselling arrangements, however, provide this service.

Source: An Assessment of UK EAPs and Workplace Counselling Programmes, Highley and Cooper 1995 (Manchester School of Management, UMIST)

■ Should you perform a 'stress audit' before deciding whether to introduce counselling?

Any new business initiative is normally preceded by a needs analysis or audit to determine whether it is actually necessary. But if you are thinking of introducing a counselling initiative, how important, or indeed practical, would such an exercise be? If you do decide to by-pass this procedure, then you will certainly not be the first to have done so – only 30% of companies perform any kind of stress audit before introducing counselling services.

Source: An Assessment of UK EAPs and Workplace Counselling Programmes, Highley and Cooper 1995 (Manchester School of Management, UMIST)

■ How reliable are the counselling services of EAP providers?

When you employ an external organisation to perform a function within your organisation, you expect the personnel who will be assigned to your organisation to be fully qualified and experienced. But is this something that you can rely upon when you go to an EAP provider? Whilst some companies are entirely reputable and reliable, the results of the Highley and Cooper survey suggest that it may well be worth checking on these points before you sign any cheques.

- 11% of counsellors surveyed were found to have no formal qualifications in counselling.

- A further 11% were found to have only a basic Certificate in Counselling.

- Also, 18% of counsellors were found to have had no experience of short-term counselling work.

Source: An Assessment of UK EAPs and Workplace Counselling Programmes, Highley and Cooper 1995 (Manchester School of Management, UMIST)

Internal communication

■ Are internal communications improving?

Internal communication can be a major issue in many companies. How often do revisions of this procedure actually take place, and how effective are these changes? One survey asked managers if their internal communication systems had changed over the last two years.

- 60% of them said yes, it had.

- Unfortunately, only 40% said that their internal communications strategy was now clearer than it had been.

Source: Are Managers Getting the Message? Institute of Management, 1992

■ *What forms of internal communication are being used?*

Some ways of passing information around an organisation can be much clearer and more effective than others. If you are reviewing your internal communication structure, then you may want to take recent developments into consideration. So, which of these channels is growing the fastest?

- 40% of managers said that face-to-face communications (meetings, briefings, etc.) had increased since restructuring of internal communications.

- 65% of managers said that they were now spending more time engaged in meetings.

Source: Are Managers Getting the Message? Institute of Management, 1992

■ *What is the most effective channel for communication?*

If you make decisions about the internal communication procedures in your company, then it is up to you to minimise misunderstandings and failed communication. So if you really want to get the message across clearly, and make sure it is understood, what is the best way to communicate it? Not by letter or fax or e-mail, it seems.

- Over 67% of managers said that they found face-to-face communication to be more effective than any method based on paper or technology.

- Under 50% of managers said that they found paper-based communication to be effective.

Source: Are Managers Getting the Message? Institute of Management, 1992

■ *Is paper a dead medium?*

With ever-improving technological communication, and a preference for face-to-face meetings, you might expect communication on paper to be a thing of the past. But if you find that this does not tally with your own experience, and suspect that your company has overlooked these other methods of communication, you may be surprised to find that this is not the case.

- Over 40% of managers reported a rise in the number of memos and circulars used in their organisation.

- 33% said that paper-based communication in general was still increasing.

Source: Are Managers Getting the Message? Institute of Management, 1992

■ *How many companies have internal magazines or newsletters?*

One obvious way to improve communication within an organisation, and to instill a feeling of community among employees, is to have a magazine or newsletter that deals with internal company issues and news. If you do not make use of this approach to internal communication, are you overlooking a valuable and widely used resource, or are you treating it with the usual level of scepticism? The chart below shows what proportion of establishments have newsletters or magazines, broken down by size (more or less than 300 employees) and ownership (British or foreign).

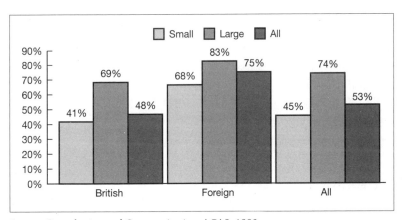

Source: Consultation and Communication, ACAS, 1990

■ How many companies use team briefings as a vehicle for internal communication?

You may want to disseminate information downwards through your organisation all the way to the shop floor, and be sure that the message gets across. One way to do this is to hold team meetings between supervisors and their staff. If you are thinking of doing this, then you may want to know how commonly used this system is. The following chart shows what percentage of organisations used team briefings, divided according to whether the company is British- or foreign-owned, and whether it has more or less than 300 employees.

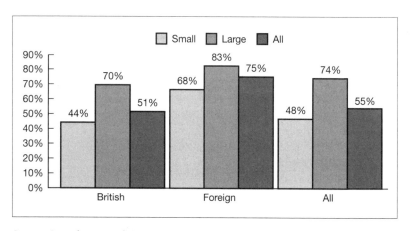

Source: Consultation and Communication, ACAS, 1990

■ To what extent are noticeboards used?

Noticeboards are a simple, convenient and effective way to spread information, but how widely used are they? If you think that you can get along fine without a noticeboard, are there many others who think like you? Apparently not – according to one survey a resounding 98% of companies do have noticeboards.

Source: Consultation and Communication, ACAS, 1990

■ *How are employees informed about what goes on at their place of work, and are they able to give feedback?*

There are various ways of letting your employees know what is happening in your organisation, some of which provide more opportunity for feedback than others. If you are only using noticeboards and newsletters to spread news, then are you giving your employees a fair chance to have their say?

- 75% of employees in this survey reported that they received information through notices or news sheets. (If this seems to contradict the ACAS information above, bear in mind that such facilities are not necessarily available to everyone in a company.)

- Information meetings were held to keep 70% of employees up to date.

- 63% of people surveyed were in organisations which held meetings in which they could express their views.

Source: Employee Commitment and the Skills Revolution, Policy Studies Institute, 1993

■ *Are employees satisfied with the level of communication they receive?*

If you are in line with current practice over internal communications, is this good enough, or is it likely that your employees would want you to go still further?

- Overall, 30% of employees said they were 'completely' or 'very' satisfied with the level of internal communication in their company.

- Another 42% were 'fairly' satisfied with the communication level.

- Only 29% of those surveyed were ambivalent or dissatisfied with internal communications.

- The level of dissatisfaction was generally much higher in larger companies: 46% of those in companies with less than 10 employees were 'completely' or 'very' satisfied, as against 19% in companies with 100–499 employees and 21% in those with over 500 employees.

Source: Employee Commitment and the Skills Revolution, Policy Studies Institute, 1993

STAFF RELATIONS

■ *What forms of internal communication increase employee satisfaction with communication levels?*

If you are worried about whether your employees are happy with the standard of communication in your organisation, you will want to know what measures have the greatest effect on increasing this satisfaction.

● The provision of written information does not seem to have a great effect on satisfaction levels.

● Employees who are involved in information-giving meetings are generally more satisfied, with 4% more saying that they are 'completely' or 'very' satisfied and 20% less being dissatisfied to any degree.

● Setting up meetings where employees can air their views seems by far the most effective method, with 12% more of these employees being 'completely' or 'very' satisfied, and the proportion of dissatisfied staff plummeting from 44% to 20%.

Source: Employee Commitment and the Skills Revolution, Policy Studies Institute, 1993

STAFF EFFECTIVENESS

ABSENCE FROM WORK

Sickness absence

■ *What is the average level of sickness absence?*

Sickness absence is a fact of life for all organisations, but for some it can be a real problem. But how can you tell if the amount of working time you lose every year to sickness absence is par for the course or a matter for genuine concern? The national average amount of time lost through sickness absence in 1994 was 3.4% of working time, averaging just under 8 days in the year per worker.

This figure can be broken down by sector and type of staff to give you a better idea of where you stand:

Manufacturing sector:

- The average length of time lost to sickness absence in 1994 was 9 days for full-time manual employees.
- The corresponding figure for full-time non-manual employees was 5.1 days.

Service sector:

- The 1994 figure for time lost was 11 days for full-time manual workers.
- For full-time non-manual workers, however, it was only 7.6 days.

Source: Confederation of British Industry Employment Affairs Report No. 65, August 1995

■ *Is company size an important factor for levels of sickness absence?*

If you are in a large company and find that your sickness levels are above the national average, does this need serious attention or does it just go with the territory of employing so many people? In this instance, the latter does seem to be the case:

- Employers of more than 5,000 staff experienced sickness absence totalling, on average, 4.3% of working time.

- Those employing under 100 staff lost an average of only 2.3% of time to sickness absence.

- The correlation between company size and absence levels is also strong between these extremes.

Source: *Counting Costs to Keep Competitive*, Confederation of British Industry, 1994

■ What is the average direct cost of sickness absence?

Naturally, the cost of losing an employee for a few days varies greatly depending on who the employee is. It is very hard to measure the loss in work not done or delayed and other indirect costs. The average cost of simply replacing that staff member, however, came to £466 per employee in 1994. This makes the total direct cost of sickness absence in Britain about £10 billion over the year.

Source: *Confederation of British Industry Employment Affairs Report* No. 65, August 1995

■ What are the main causes of sickness absence?

Being ill is, unsurprisingly, top of the list here. However, there are other factors that can play a part in an employee's decision to call in sick rather than just take another handkerchief with them. But what other issues are involved, and how significant are they considered to be? One survey asked employers what factors they thought influenced levels of staff absence.

Cause	Percentage employers citing as factor for manual staff	Percentage employers citing as factor for non-manual staff
Genuine sickness	90%	95%
Lack of commitment	77%	67%
Family responsibilities	65%	72%

Source: *Confederation of British Industry Employment Affairs Report* No. 65, August 1995

■ *Does giving absence statistics to line managers reduce absence levels?*

If absence levels are high, it can be very hard for middle or senior management to monitor them effectively. One way around this problem is to give line managers access to the statistics to aid their contribution to solving the problem. But does this really work? The consensus of opinion seems to be that it does, with 83% of employers believing that providing absence statistics to line managers has a measurable impact on absence levels.

Source: Confederation of British Industry Employment Affairs Report No. 65, August 1995

■ *What guidance do line managers and supervisors receive on handling absence?*

Even if your managers have some responsibility for absence level, you may still be considering giving them a bit more guidance over how to control absence among their staff. But is this a radical departure from conventional policy or is it a universal policy? The fact of the matter is somewhere between the two.

- 55% of companies provide line managers or supervisors with written guidance on handling employee sickness.

- A very significant proportion of organisations provide some form of training on this subject.

Source: Sickness Absence Monitoring and Control – A Survey of Practice, IRS Employment Trends, September 1994

■ *What are the benefits of monitoring absence?*

If you are introducing or reviewing absence monitoring procedures, then the first thing on your mind will probably be to reduce absence levels to an acceptable minimum. However, there can be many other consequences of the procedure that could be beneficial to your organisation, and which might be worth bearing in mind. The main ones cited by respondents to one survey were:

- Reducing absence levels, naturally.

- Raising awareness of the issue of absence control.

- Increasing line managers' responsibility for management of sickness absence.

- Ensuring consistency in the assessment of absence, and fairness in the treatment of those concerned, especially the genuinely ill.

Source: Sickness Absence Monitoring and Control – A Survey of Practice, IRS Employment Trends, September 1994

■ *What people and departments are absence records normally made available to?*

In the vast majority of organisations, absence records are held by the personnel department, but often other groups also have access to these data. If you are reviewing this situation in your organisation, then you may want to know what is 'common practice' with regard to disseminating this information.

- In 95% of organisations, absence statistics are made available to senior management.

- Also, line managers have access to this information in 93% of companies.

- 36% of companies make these records available to trade union representatives, although sometimes only on request.

Source: Sickness Absence Monitoring and Control – A Survey of Practice, IRS Employment Trends, September 1994

■ *How should absence records be broken down?*

As with any raw data, absence records can be processed in a variety of ways. If you would like guidance on whether to analyse your data simply using the division between manual and non-manual, or whether to include some other classification system, then here are the most common ways of breaking down the information.

- Breakdown by department is the most common method, used by 84% of organisations.

- 36% of companies use a breakdown by manual/non-manual groups.

- 36% of companies also break absence down by type of absence (including long or short term).

- 32% divide the information according to work group (e.g. production, craft, office etc.).

- In the great majority of cases, more than one breakdown is undertaken.

Source: Sickness Absence Monitoring and Control – A Survey of Practice, IRS Employment Trends, September 1994

■ *Is it useful to have separate policies towards long- and short-term absence, and is this a common procedure?*

Is the difference between long- and short-term absence only one of degree? Or should each warrant different procedures in your organisation? A total of 59% of employers believe that separate policies towards short- and long-term absence would benefit their organisation. Unfortunately, however, the practice is not as widespread as it is popular – only 24% of companies actually have such policies.

Source: Confederation of British Industry Employment Affairs Report No. 65, August 1995

■ *How effective is computer monitoring of absence levels?*

One way to keep tabs on staff absence is with a computer system. Such systems, however, are quite an investment. So you would not want to make this kind of outlay on a gamble that it might work.

- Computer monitoring of absence is quite well regarded, with 69% of employers believing that it is effective in reducing absence.

- Moreover, 51% of companies covered by the Confederation of British Industry survey did operate such systems, and these companies were found to have lower absence levels than others.

Source: Confederation of British Industry Employment Affairs Report No. 65, August 1995

■ *Do disciplinary procedures help to reduce absence?*

When absence levels are high, you may feel that some action has to be taken. Taking disciplinary action is a possibility, but will it actually help? Most employers seem to think so, with 82% saying they believe that disciplinary procedures have a high to medium impact on absence levels.

Source: Counting Costs to Keep Competitive, Confederation of British Industry, 1994

■ *Do return-to-work interviews help reduce absence levels?*

Of course, disciplinary action may seem a bit harsh in some cases, and a quiet word might do just as well. But are interviews for staff returning from absence really effective in reducing the phenomenon? According to 52% of employers, this is an effective system.

Source: Counting Costs to Keep Competitive, Confederation of British Industry, 1994

■ *How many companies give return-to-work interviews?*

The majority of employers seem to think that return-to-work interviews are an effective way of controlling absence, but how many companies actually run such interviews? Is it a standard policy or one that is only used rarely?

- According to one survey, 76% of organisations use a return-to-work interview after some or all periods of absence.

- In over 90% of cases, this is conducted by the line manager or supervisor.

Source: Sickness Absence Monitoring and Control – A Survey of Practice, IRS Employment Trends, September 1994

■ *Do return-to-work interviews cut down on absences in future?*

A recent Institute of Personnel and Development book underlines the importance of return-to-work interviews. They enable managers to stamp out 'malingering', to understand the nature of a domestic problem if there is one, and to show that they care. However, the book also finds that ill health is still the major course of absences – so the return-to-work interview will not solve the absence problem by itself.

Source: From Absence to Attendance, Alistair Evans and Steven Palmer, IPD, 1997

STAFF EFFECTIVENESS

145

■ How many companies reward good attendance?

Rather than punishing bad attendance, another way to try to reduce absence is to encourage good attendance with an incentive. This seems like a logical approach to the problem, but is it a generally accepted strategy?

- It seems not – only 5% of companies actually offer a cash incentive for good attendance.

- In addition to this, however, some companies do take attendance into account when calculating other bonuses.

Source: Sickness Absence Monitoring and Control – A Survey of Practice, IRS Employment Trends, September 1994

■ Can you minimise absence by avoiding the recruitment of poor attenders?

Another way to reduce absence is not to recruit it in the first place. To what extent is this a viable option? According to one survey, 74% of employers think that this is an effective way to reduce absence levels.

Source: Counting Costs to Keep Competitive, Confederation of British Industry, 1994

■ How frequently should sickness absence records be monitored?

If you keep sickness absence records, you will have to decide what to do with this information. How often do you monitor the level of absence? What is a reasonable frequency with which to do this? One survey asked companies how often they monitor their sickness absence levels.

- 83% of companies surveyed monitor their absence records frequently.
- Of these, 81% do so on a monthly basis.
- Weekly monitoring is used by 29%.
- 25% monitor only on a quarterly basis.
- A rigorous 11% do so on every day.

Source: Sickness Absence Monitoring and Control – A Survey of Practice, IRS Employment Trends, September 1994

■ Who should be responsible for monitoring absence levels?

If you are reviewing your policies on monitoring sickness absence, then you will also have to decide who is responsible for such monitoring. So what are the most common solutions to this problem?

- The personnel or human resources department is responsible for absence monitoring in 90% of organisations.

- 79% give the responsibility directly to line managers.

- The responsibility often rests on both of these groups, as is the case with 72% of companies.

- In only 29% of cases is the wages department given the responsibility of monitoring absence.

- Also used, but only very occasionally, were occupational health departments, team leaders, and outside consultancies.

Source: Sickness Absence Monitoring and Control – A Survey of Practice, IRS Employment Trends, September 1994

■ To what extent are 'triggers' used in employee absence procedures?

Having data on employee absence can be very helpful. There are times when you will want to act upon this information. But how can you decide what these times are? Some companies use 'triggers' for this purpose – arrangements whereby certain absence patterns in an employee or group of employees will lead to some action being taken. Such triggers may be informal, or may consist of an arithmetic formula applied to the absence figures. One survey found that this 'trigger' mechanism was used, in one form or another, by 73% of companies.

Source: Sickness Absence Monitoring and Control – A Survey of Practice, IRS Employment Trends, September 1994

■ What actions can be taken for employees with unsatisfactory attendance records?

If a situation does occur in which you want to take action on the absence of a particular member of staff, you will then be confronted with the decision of what action to take. Different circumstances may require different measures. However, you may be more comfortable

STAFF EFFECTIVENESS

with this decision if you have a clear idea of your options. Here is a list of the most common methods of dealing with staff absence:

- Counselling – to determine whether there is an underlying problem and to offer assistance if appropriate.

- Setting attendance targets – and/or setting a review period.

- Using the normal disciplinary procedures – such as would be used for unacceptable behaviour, for example.

- Involvement of company doctor or occupational health department – to make further medical assessments or advise on ill-health retirement or dismissal.

- Exclusion from sick pay scheme – provided contractual circumstances permit.

- Dismissal – in extreme circumstances.

Source: Sickness Absence Monitoring and Control – A Survey of Practice, IRS Employment Trends, September 1994

Maternity leave and career breaks

■ *What kind of career break schemes do companies operate?*

If you are considering operating a career break scheme within your company, then all sorts of issues have to be faced. What re-entry provisions should you make? What kind of keep-in-touch scheme should you operate? How often are these various possibilities actually used? The following list gives the percentage of companies which offered career breaks which offered each provision.

Re-entry provisions, either during break or on return	65%
Arrangements for periods of work during leave period	44%
Training during break	33%
Other keep-in-touch schemes	33%
Training for the employee on restart	33%
Option of returning to previous job after break	54%
Provision for employee to return to job of similar grade	42%
Option of full- or part-time work on re-entry	65%

Source: Retaining Women Employees: Measures to Counteract Labour Shortages,
Institute of Manpower Studies, 1990

■ *Why do companies introduce career break schemes?*

Before deciding whether to introduce a career break scheme, you will
need to decide whether this measure fits the needs of your company.
Below is a list of possible reasons for introducing such a scheme,
together with the proportion of companies which said, for each
reason, that it was one of the factors that prompted them to introduce such a scheme.

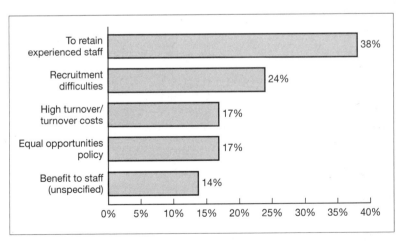

Source: Retaining Women Employees: Measures to Counteract Labour Shortages,
Institute of Manpower Studies, 1990

■ *How long a break do most women take for maternity leave?*

Some women take as little time off work to have children as they can, whereas others may take a much longer 'career break'. Naturally, in any particular situation, the way to find out how long the break will be is to ask the person involved. If you are developing a policy towards maternity leave, you will also want to take into consideration the overall pattern of career breaks. The charts below show this pattern for part-time workers, women who have always been full-time workers, and an overall figure (including also women who are full-time but have previously been part-time).

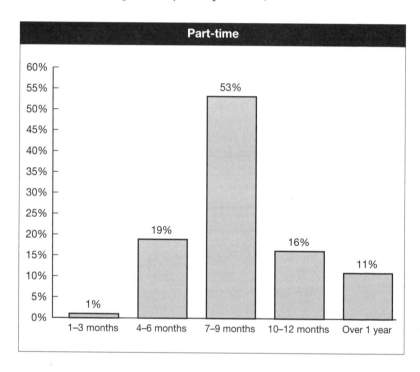

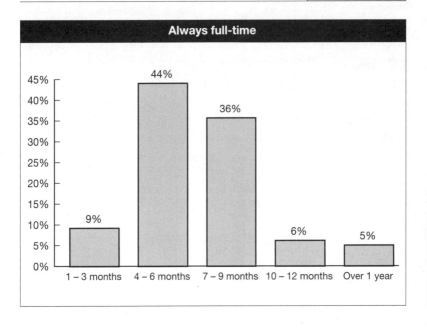

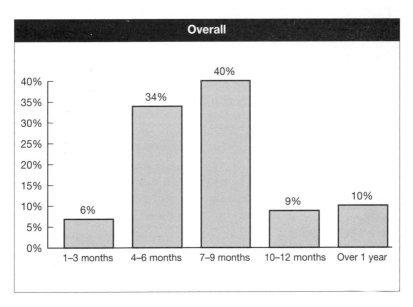

Another factor than can affect the length of the break taken is the level of the job that the employee is in at the time of the break. The following chart shows the average length of career breaks for junior and senior professionals and junior, middle and senior management.

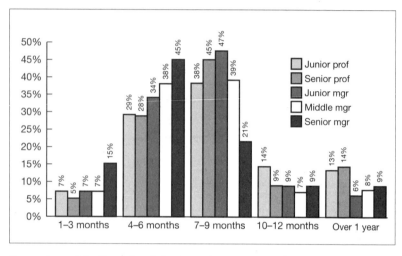

Source: Beyond the Career Break, Institute of Manpower Studies, 1992

■ *Are women who have already had a career break for children less likely to return to work after another break?*

One factor that will affect the likelihood of a woman returning to work after having a child is whether she has had the experience before. But if you employ someone who has already had a career break, what are the chances that they will not return after having another child? The Institute of Manpower Studies survey asked women who had and who had not previously taken career breaks how they felt about returning to work – 'very unsure', 'thought I would', or 'very sure'. The figures show that women who have already taken a break are more sure of their return to work after subsequent breaks.

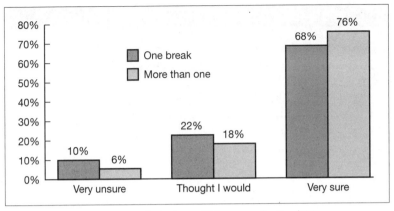

Source: *Beyond the Career Break*, Institute of Manpower Studies, 1992

STAFF EFFECTIVENESS

■ What factors influence the decision to return to work?

Some very valuable staff may decide to take career breaks while in your organisation. If this happens, then you will probably want to ensure that they return to work for you afterwards. But in what ways can you encourage this, and what issues are of only minor importance? The survey asked women who had taken career breaks to rank various factors by their importance in the decision to return to work. The responses were sorted by the average ranking.

Most important factors affecting decision to return to work

1 The ability to organise satisfactory childcare
2 Having a healthy baby
3 Having the support of my partner
4 My desire to work for my own satisfaction
5 My ability to fit my job with domestic responsibilities
6 Financial need

Least important factors affecting decision to return to work
1 Knowing other women who had successfully returned
2 The effective administration of the career break by my employer
3 The support of my colleagues at work
4 Having the support of other family members
5 The need for my baby to be weaned or part-weaned
6 The general attitude of my employer

Source: Beyond the Career Break, Institute of Manpower Studies, 1992

■ When employees take career breaks, what jobs do they come back to?

Of course, there are many options available for women taking career breaks other than having their jobs held for them. For some it may mean a promotion, and for an unfortunate few it may mean a return to work at a lower level than the original job. But does this happen often, or are women justified in expecting to come back to the same job, or at least the same level of job as they left? (It is worth noting that all the women surveyed had returned to their original employer after their career break, so these figures do not necessarily apply to women who change employers on their return to work.)

- All in all, 54% of women surveyed returned to the same job that they left.

- A further 40% came back to a job at the same level as the one that they left.

- An unfortunate 9% returned to a job that was at a lower level than the job they had previously held.

- Only 7% of those surveyed experienced a promotion after their career break.

Source: Beyond the Career Break, Institute of Manpower Studies, 1992

■ *How many companies will hold an employee's job for her while she takes a career break?*

If a member of staff wants to take a break from work to have children, she may want to be sure that she will have a job to come back to after the experience. But is this a reasonable expectation, and what proportion of companies actually provide this option? The Institute of Manpower Studies survey covered women who returned to their original place of work after a career break, and found that 58% of these women had their jobs held for them (either left vacant or filled on a temporary basis) when they took their career break.

Source: Beyond the Career Break, Institute of Manpower Studies, 1992

■ *How many companies allow childcare leave, and for how long?*

There may well be circumstances in which a working mother needs to take time off work for special circumstances relating to childcare (e.g. illness of the child or the regular carer). If you are reviewing your policies towards working mothers, then this may be one arrangement that you wish to consider introducing. But how much of a precedent is there for childcare leave, and what form does it usually take?

- Childcare leave was found to be operated by 23% of companies.

- In over 90% of these companies, it was given on an informal basis.

- The length of leave ranged from less than a week to over a year. The chart below shows what percentage of companies allow childcare leave for each length of time (given in weeks).

- 81% of organisations allowing leave gave paid leave for some length of time (ranging from less than a week to one year).

- Of companies allowing leave, 79% granted leave on full pay for some length of time.

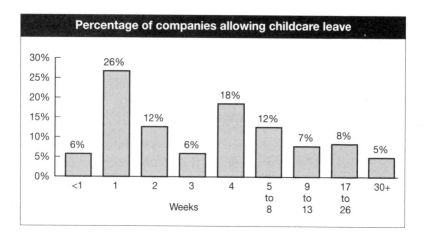

- The chart below shows what proportion of companies with childcare leave provide it on full pay for each specified period (again, the figures relate to weeks).

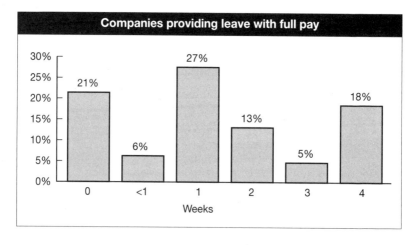

- In addition, 2% of companies provided full pay for 8 weeks, 5% provided it for 13 weeks, and a generous 2% provided it for 26 weeks.

Source: Retaining Women Employees: Measures to Counteract Labour Shortages, Institute of Manpower Studies, 1990

■ What length of service qualifications are usually placed on childcare leave?

As with many perks and benefits, some companies restrict childcare leave allowances to employees who have served with the company for a certain length of time. But if you are thinking of using such a qualifying period, what length of time seems reasonable?

- 19% of companies allowing childcare leave have no qualifying period for full-time staff, and 23% have none for part-timers.

- Including these companies, 47% have restrictions of 6 months or less for full-timers, and 46% have similar restrictions for part-timers.

- After 1 year, full-time employees in 84% of companies with childcare leave schemes will be eligible, as will 86% of part time workers.

Source: Retaining Women Employees: Measures to Counteract Labour Shortages, Institute of Manpower Studies, 1990

■ How many companies offer term-time working arrangements?

Some working mothers need special working arrangements to be able to cope with their domestic responsibilities. One arrangement that can be used for such employees is that they only work during term-time. But if you are considering this option, you might like to know how much of a precedent there is for such an arrangement.

- In fact, it is a fairly limited practice, being operated by only 6% of companies.

- It is more often operated for manual, clerical, sales and administrative staff than for managers and professionals.

Source: Retaining Women Employees: Measures to Counteract Labour Shortages, Institute of Manpower Studies, 1990

STAFF EFFECTIVENESS

■ Why do companies introduce term-time working schemes?

Precedent may well not be the only factor in your decision to adopt term-time working schemes for some employees. How much weight should you give to other factors? It may be helpful to know what reasons have led other companies to introduce such schemes. The graph below shows what percentage of companies currently running schemes consider each of the factors below to be a reason that they introduced the scheme.

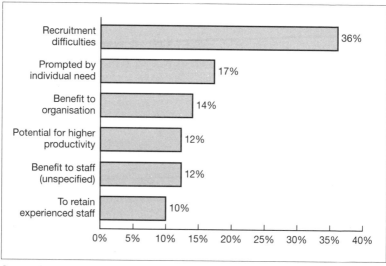

Source: *Retaining Women Employees: Measures to Counteract Labour Shortages,* Institute of Manpower Studies, 1990

■ Do career breaks affect an employee's career commitment?

Many women do come back to their career after having children. Are they always as committed to their work as they were before? Naturally this varies from person to person, but if you are developing a policy, then it might help to have a more general impression of the situation. The charts below show what percentage of women returners described their job commitment after their career break as 'more ambitious', 'just as committed', 'career will wait', 'aspirations lower', or 'not so committed' for each of three groups – part-timers, those who had always worked full-time, and an overall figure (including women who had at some stage worked part-time).

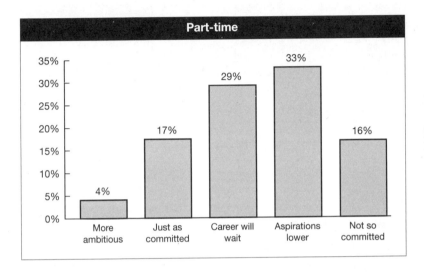

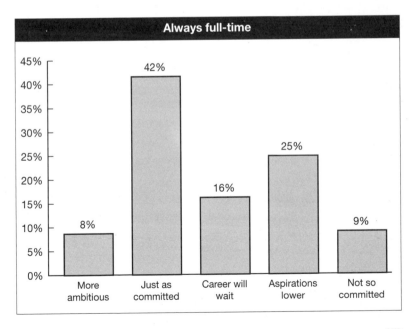

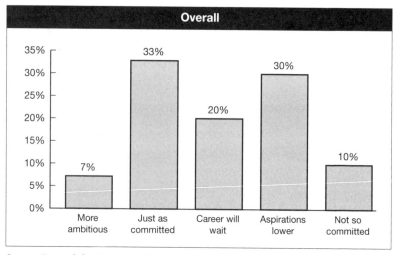

Source: *Beyond the Career Break*, Institute of Manpower Studies, 1992

■ *What advice would women returners give to other women thinking of taking a career break?*

Taking a career break to have children can be a big decision, and if you or someone in your organisation is thinking of doing this, then some support and advice could be very useful. The Institute of Manpower Studies survey asked women returners what advice they would give to women who were thinking of taking a career break. The most common specific advice, in descending order of frequency, is shown below.

Most common advice to women about career breaks

1 Organise good childcare
2 Enlist your partner's co-operation
3 Seek flexible arrangements at work
4 Delegate more tasks to others
5 Get properly organised
6 Develop a balanced attitude to home and work demands
7 Set realistic standards for what you can achieve
8 Don't feel guilty about working
9 Establish priorities

Source: *Beyond the Career Break*, Institute of Manpower Studies, 1992

■ *What advice would women returners give to the companies seeking to employ them?*

Women returners can be very valuable employees, but as such they do have special needs. If you are seeking to make the most of this section of the workforce, then you will want to know what they need from an employer. The Institute of Manpower Studies survey asked women returners what advice they would give to companies employing them, or others like them. In descending order, the most common comments were:

Most common advice to companies about career breaks

1 Be more flexible and understanding
2 Offer more opportunities for part-time work/job-sharing
3 Provide workplace nurseries/crèches
4 Judge people by their performance/don't stereotype mothers
5 Treat returners as equal with colleagues (e.g. for promotion)
6 Offer financial help with childcare

Source: Beyond the Career Break, Institute of Manpower Studies, 1992

HOURS AND HOLIDAYS

Hours

■ *What is the most common number of hours worked per week?*

Are you slave driving your staff, or are you being a softie? With the Working Hours Directive in the news, limiting employees to a 48 hour week, current working hours are of particular interest:

Manual workers

- Just under half of manual groups (41%) have basic working hours which are below 39 a week. The 39 hour week remains the most typical arrangement for manual employees.

- More than a quarter of agreements for manual workers contain working weeks of 37 or 37.5 working hours.

- A third are for less than 37 hours.

Non-manual workers

- 26% are contracted to work 35 hours and 24% are contracted to work 37 hours a week.

- 17% have contracts for 37.5 hours per week.

Single-status workplaces

These are workplaces that do not differentiate between manual and non-manual employees. 38% of employees here have weekly hours of 37; 27% have 37.5%, and only 17% work 39 hours or more.

Source: Hours and Holidays 1996, IDS Study 614

■ *What alternatives to weekly hours are there?*

Rather than specify working hours in weekly terms, some companies define working hours over several weeks:

- Volvo Trucks, for example, specifies 148 hours over 4 weeks.

- The BBC specifies 160 hours over the same time period.

- Blue Circle Cement averages the working hours of its drivers over a three month period, making a 'quarterly' working time of 767 hours.

Source: Hours and Holidays 1996, IDS Study 614

■ Do many companies use annual hours?

Under annual hours, working time is calculated over the complete year rather than a week, often taking annual and public holidays into account. This can be particularly appropriate for continuous manufacturing processes, or situations which would otherwise require a significant degree of overtime working. Incomes Data Services currently has 20 organisations on its records which have annual hours systems. However, several other employers are planning to introduce this system in the near future.

Source: Hours and Holidays 1996, IDS Study 614

There are obviously two categories of workers who are not encompassed by a survey into full-time working patterns. One is part-time workers, who generally work a proportion of a full-timer's hours. The question then is whether they receive the same benefits pro rata. The other category is the self-employed, who define their own hours.

STAFF EFFECTIVENESS

■ How hard do the self-employed work?

The benefits of being self-employed are obvious – being your own boss; the challenge, and the possible rewards. So do the benefits really outweigh the costs? Increased freedom is not worth much if hours are too long.

● A self-employed business person works an average of 9.5 hours each day, six days a week.

Source: Starting up in Business, Barclays Research on Small Business Characteristics, Barclays Bank plc, 1995

■ Does the number of hours worked by the self-employed vary substantially?

Interestingly enough, there is substantial variation in working hours across ethnic groupings. Asian small businesses put in the longest day of all – an average of 11.5 hours, as shown in the following table.

Hours/day	White business owner/manager	Black business owner/manager	Asian business owner/manager
4 hours or less	5%	1%	0%
4–8 hours	9%	6%	8%
8–10 hours	34%	27%	25%
10–12 hours	29%	34%	31%
12–14 hours	17%	19%	23%
14–16 hours	3%	12%	7%
16 hours or more	3%	2%	5%
Average number of hours	10.25	11.10	11.27

Asians work the longest week – averaging 5.96 days compared with 5.69 days for black businesses and 5.58 days for white businesses.

Source: Cultural Change and the Small Firm, Barclays Review, 1997

■ *Do part-timers receive the same benefits as full-time workers?*

Should all benefits be applied equally to part-time and full-time workers? If you are reviewing your contracts for part-time employees, you may be interested to know what the current state of play is regarding the various benefits. Overall, it was found that the majority of organisations treat part-timers on an equal or pro rata basis for every benefit for which there were significant figures. For more detail, though, the list below shows which benefits, according to the IRS survey, are provided at an equal or pro rata rate for part-time employees by different proportions of employers (100%, 90%, etc.).

100% of companies treat as equal:

- Bereavement leave

Over 90% of companies treat as equal:

- Redundancy pay
- Selection for redundancy
- Performance appraisal
- Staff discounts

- Basic and service holiday entitlement and pay
- Unsocial hours premia
- Sick pay
- Location allowances
- Call-out or stand-by payments

Over 80% of companies treat as equal:

- Shift premia
- Performance pay
- Sales commissions or bonuses
- Maternity and paternity leave
- Subsistence/lodgings allowances
- Private health insurance
- Output bonuses

Under 75% of companies treat as equal:

- Company loans/mortgages
- Pensions
- Profit sharing

Source: Part-time Working 2: Changing Terms and Conditions of Employment, IRS Employment Trends, April 1993

■ *Do part-timers receive standard bank holidays?*

If you are employing part-time workers, you may have to decide whether, or to what degree, to grant them paid bank holidays. If you are in this position, then you may well want to know what arrangements are most usually made by other companies.

- 66% of companies only granted paid bank holidays to part-time staff on bank holidays when they would normally be working.
- In 18% of companies, part-timers were granted paid bank holidays regardless of whether they would normally be working on that day.
- Only 3% of organisations did not grant paid bank holidays to part-timers at all.

Source: Part-time Working 2: Changing Terms and Conditions of Employment, IRS Employment Trends, April 1993

STAFF EFFECTIVENESS

■ Does working part-time damage career opportunities?

Some companies rely on part-time workers to function fully. Does this mean that these staff have the same career opportunities as the full-time staff that work alongside them? If your part-time workers feel that they are losing out in this area, then they are probably not the only ones. The following information comes from a survey of women who have returned to work after having children. It is not, therefore, a representative sample of all part-time workers, but the results are still revealing. Respondents were given various statements, including the two below. They were asked to rate their agreement on a scale of 1 to 5, with 1 being strong agreement and 5 strong disagreement. The data given below combine the figures for ratings of 4 and 5 (disagreement, weak and strong), and show the percentage of respondents giving each response.

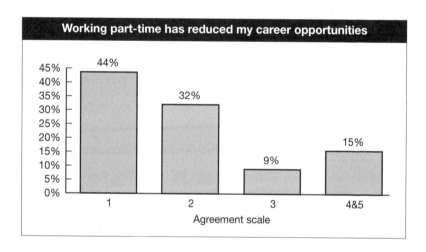

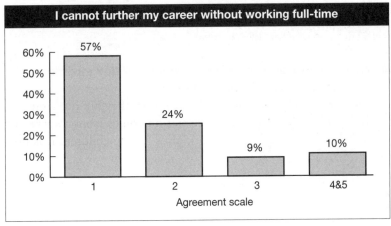

Source: Beyond the Career Break, Institute of Manpower Studies, 1992

STAFF EFFECTIVENESS

Holidays

■ *What is the average level of holiday entitlement?*

Very few people will take a job that offers no holiday time, but every day that an employee takes as a holiday is one day's less work. All staff must have some holiday entitlement, but how much is reasonable for them and reasonable for you? One way to assess this is to look at the figures for holiday entitlement. The following chart shows what percentage of companies offer a basic holiday entitlement of each length.

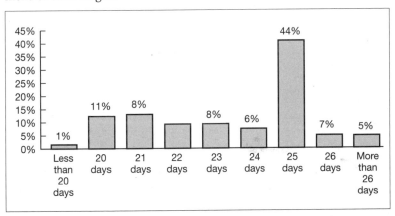

- The mean average basic holiday entitlement is 22.4 days a year.

Source: Hours and Holidays 1996, IDS Study 614

■ How many companies offer extra holiday entitlement to long-standing employees?

Many companies offer extra holiday time over and above this basic rate. This bonus may be based on the grade of the employee or, more commonly, on the length of the employee's service. If you are reviewing your holiday provisions, then you may want to know how common this practice is. It seems that such service-related entitlements were available to around half of the employees covered by this survey, but the results vary for manual and non-manual employees.

- 41% of manual workers receive some service-related holiday entitlement.
- 64% of non-manual workers receive such a bonus.

Source: Hours and Holidays 1996, IDS Study 614

■ How are service-related holiday entitlements incremented?

If you are running or intending to run a service-related programme for holiday entitlement, you will not want to be insultingly stingy with your bonuses, but neither will you want to be over-generous. So how do such schemes usually operate? How much extra holiday is given? At what lengths of service? What is the maximum holiday time?

- Most commonly, there is one extra entitlement offered at a certain length of service.
- Two, three and four step entitlements (offered at different lengths of service) are also common.
- The most common qualifying periods are at 5, 10, 15, 20 and 25 years.
- On average, maximum holiday entitlement is 4 days more than the basic entitlement.
- Some companies offer a cash alternative to additional holiday entitlement.

Source: Hours and Holidays 1996, IDS Study 614

■ How many companies have customary days off?

Some schools have days off for 'Founder's day' or other dates in the school calendar. Similarly, some companies also have certain holidays in addition to public holidays and their personal holiday allowance. If this idea appeals to you, then you may want to know if other companies do it. This practice, although making a strong statement about company identity, is still quite rare, being used by only 15% of organisations.

Source: Hours and Holidays 1996, IDS Study 614

■ Do managers take all the holiday that they are entitled to?

Holidays are not compulsory. If you find that you or your staff often cannot afford to take holiday time off, then are you enormously overworked, or is this a situation that crops up quite often?

● 42% of senior managers and 33% of middle management do not take their full holiday entitlement, due to work pressures.

● Nearly 50% of those surveyed said that their companies contact them when they are on holiday or off sick.

● It is worth noting that the survey sample (407) was split equally between senior managers, middle managers, junior managers, supervisors and others, and is hence more representative of management staff than others.

Source: IPD survey, released June 1995

■ How important is holiday relative to pay?

If you have the unenviable job of trying to balance your staff's pay packet against any bonus package that you could provide them with, then you may want to know which is most likely to be higher on your employees' priority lists. In fact, about 30% of workers (but only 22% of senior managers) would accept less pay for more holiday time.

Source: IPD survey, released June 1995

STAFF EFFECTIVENESS

169

Christmas

■ *How many companies expect their staff to work over Christmas?*

Many people like to forget all about work at Christmas and immerse themselves in Christmas spirit (or spirits). But some companies cannot afford to give time off to all their staff over the period. Naturally staff working over Christmas are usually given premium payments, but if you ask some of your employees to come in over Christmas, are you being a humbug? Well, maybe, but you are not alone, because 45% of companies, according to one survey, say that their staff work, or could be called to work, over Christmas.

Source: Christmas in the Office – Party Time or Double Time? IRS Employment Trends, December 1992

■ *How many companies hold Christmas parties?*

It is, after all, a time for celebration, and how better to celebrate than an office party? In fact, it seems that not all companies feel this way, but before you cancel your plans for a Christmas bash, bear in mind that 60% of companies do hold an office party over Christmas.

Source: Christmas in the Office – Party Time or Double Time? IRS Employment Trends, December 1992

■ *How many companies give staff Christmas bonuses?*

Another quaint yuletide custom is the Christmas bonus, but has this stood the test of time, or is it an outdated Christmas ritual? If you give Christmas bonuses, or are thinking of starting, then you may want to know what other companies' policies are.

- Less than 10% of companies provide a cash bonus for their staff at Christmas.
- 36% of companies, however, provide a non-pay gift or a benefit-in-kind to show their goodwill.

Source: Christmas in the Office – Party Time or Double Time? IRS Employment Trends, December 1992

TIME MANAGEMENT

■ *What is the average working week?*

Well, everyone knows that 9am–5pm for 5 days a week is 35 hours (with an hour a day for lunch). But not everyone works exactly these hours. So if your staff are working a 38 hour week, does that make you a slave driver, or is this par for the course? The following figures should help to shed some light on this question.

- Manual workers work an average of 38.3 hours a week.

- Their non-manual counterparts, on the other hand, get away with an average of only 36.7 hours.

- And in workplaces with no distinction between these groups, the average working week is 37.6 hours.

- The 'finance and insurance' sector was found to have the lowest average working week – only the standard 35 hours.

Source: Hours and Holidays 1996, IDS Study 614

■ *Is there enough time in the day?*

So most people do end up working more than the standard 35 hour week. And if you find that the work you have to do simply does not fit into the 9 to 5 schedule, then you are not alone. Some 60% of workers say that they cannot meet deadlines within normal working hours. (The sample for this survey was split equally between senior managers, middle managers, junior managers, supervisors and others, and is hence more representative of management staff than others.)

Source: IPD survey, released June 1995

■ *How much time pressure do people consider themselves to be under, and how much free time do they actually have?*

There is no doubt that we live in a pressured society. But there will always be some groups of people who feel the pressure more than others. So if you find that women working part-time in your organisation feel more hassled than men working full-time, don't worry that you are being too hard on them – the chart below, showing what proportion of people in each group agreed with the statement 'I never have enough time to get things done', proves that this goes with the territory.

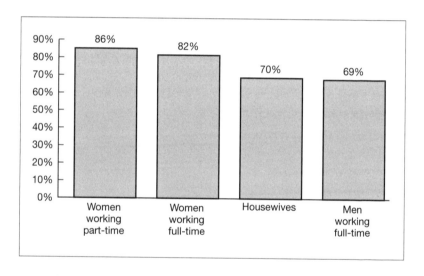

It is interesting to compare these figures with the actual amount of time that each of these groups is committed for. The chart below shows the total essential, non-discretionary time use for each group, in hours per week (including work, travelling time, essential domestic activities, etc.).

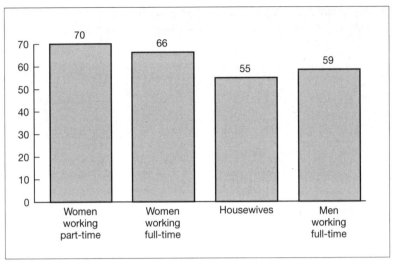

Source: *Time Use Survey*, The Henley Centre, 1994

■ *So how can you make sure that your time is effectively managed?*

'To say that time is money is to devalue time.' That is how John Fenton, the well-known trainer, begins his training session on time management. He suggests that the first job of the day, every day, is to fill in a sheet something like this:

Priorities	Codes:	Notes:
	I Important	
	U Urgent	
	A Active	
	R Reactive	
	T Trivial	
Musts		
Shoulds		
Coulds		

Source: John Fenton International Training, 1997

■ *How do you avoid running out of time?*

John Fenton has two tips – other than to prioritise:

1. Think in chunks of time. So if each month has 20 working days, then split it according to the demands on your time. As an example, a sales manager might decide to spend 5 days selling with his salespeople, 5 days on key personal accounts, 5 days on administration and planning and 5 days on recruiting, training and strategic meetings with other departments.

2. The second tip is – whenever you add a new task, take at least one away. Look at your least productive tasks. Either scrap them, or delegate them.

Source: John Fenton International Training, 1997

MOTIVATION

■ *Why do people go to work?*

If you want to motivate your staff, then a good place to start is by understanding why they go to work in the first place. Simply paying the rent is not the only reason for taking a job.

- Earning money for paying essentials was, not surprisingly, the most common reason for working, cited by 76% of men and 53% of women.

- However, 51% of men and 56% of women say that they go to work because they enjoy working.

- 46% of women and 23% of men say that they go to work at least in part because they enjoy the company to be found there.

- Following a career was given as a reason for working by 28% of women and 33% of men.

Source: Employee Commitment and the Skills Revolution, Policy Studies Institute, 1993

■ *Why do people start their own businesses?*

There are a variety of reasons for starting a small business. Freedom seems to be the overriding motivation, as suggested by the following table.

Factors influencing decision	White business owner/manager	Black business owner/manager	Asian business owner/manager
Freedom of being your own boss	65%	71%	62%
Challenge of running a business	49%	48%	49%
Potential to earn more money	51%	50%	45%
Lack of employment opportunities	22%	30%	23%
Family tradition	17%	8%	34%
Establishing a business for the family to inherit	9%	11%	20%
None of these	6%	1%	1%

Sir Herman Ouseley, Chairman of The Commission for Racial Equality, makes the following comment about members of ethnic minorities' motivations for starting up in business:

> *Driven by the frustrations caused by racial discrimination and the need to succeed against the odds, it's not surprising that ethnic minority small businesses and new business start-ups represent a growth area in the economy. Ethnic minorities are increasingly aware that they cannot rely on others for employment, and they are utilising their skills and qualities for their economic development and that of the localities in which they live and work.*

Source: *Cultural Change and the Small Firm*, Barclays Review, 1997

■ *What do people look for in a job?*

If you want to keep your employees satisfied with their job, you will have to do more than simply make sure that they are being paid enough. But what factors do people look for in a job?

Enjoying the work	84%
Job security	83%
A good relationship with the supervisor	80%
Potential to use their abilities	78%
Able to use their initiative	75%
Friendly people to work with	74%
Good training provision	72%
Good pay	71%
Good physical working conditions	70%

Source: Employee Commitment and the Skills Revolution, Policy Studies Institute, 1993

■ *Does the average employee want to go to work?*

Most British workers can't wait to get to work, according to a recent IPD survey. They are also hard workers, who put in extra hours out of choice:

- 57% of employees said that they wake up in the morning and really look forward to going to work.

- Over half – 53% – also said that they had a lot of choice about how hard they worked, compared with 26% who said they had little or no choice.

- Many people do more than they are required to – for example, 62% help new workers; 50% stay late to help out when necessary.

Source: Employee Motivation and the Psychological Contract, IPD Employee Attitude Survey, 1997

■ *Do people feel that they are fairly treated at work?*

Encouragingly, the same survey shows that most people feel that they are fairly treated:

- A resounding 90% believe that they are generally treated fairly.
- 79% trust their organisation to keep its promises to employees.
- 71% trust that managers will look after the best interests of employees.
- 70% feel that managers have always or to a large extent kept promises about job security.

Source: Employee Motivation and the Psychological Contract, IPD Employee Attitude Survey, 1997

■ *Is a structured motivation programme a necessary part of corporate strategy?*

It would obviously be nice always to have well motivated staff, but is it really necessary to have an official, structured programme for motivating your employees? If you do not have such a programme, then are you being lazy about motivation? One survey conducted by *Marketing Week* delved into this issue. It is worth noting that the questionnaire was distributed not only in the magazine but also at an exhibition on incentives, which may suggest that many individuals responding were particularly interested in motivation. The results, however, are still well worth considering.

- A full 100% of respondents saw structured motivation programmes as a necessary part of corporate strategy.
- In stark contrast, however, only 64% said that their company had endeavoured to motivate personnel 'in any way'.

Source: 'Garnishing the Corporate Carrot', *Marketing Week*, November 1990

■ *Which occupational groups are most in need of motivation?*

Motivation is one of the many issues in business that are relevant to all parts of the company. As with so many of these issues, it is not always possible to deal with all the company at once. But if you had to decide which of your staff were top priority for a motivation initiative, where would you start? One survey asked this question, and the responses may help you with this decision if you have to make it.

- The sales force was the most common response to 'Who in the UK is most in need of motivation?' This answer was given by 27% of respondents. Despite this, 95% of those surveyed said that other staff are also in need of motivation.

- Administrative and support staff were cited by 24% of those surveyed.

- 18% said that dealer networks were top of the motivation priority list.

- Manual workers were considered the most in need of motivation by 16% of respondents.

- Middle management were seen as the next most likely group to need motivation, mentioned by 8% of those surveyed.

- The group least likely to need motivation, cited by only 7%, was senior management.

Source: 'Garnishing the Corporate Carrot', *Marketing Week*, November 1990

■ *What is the purpose of motivation programmes?*

If you are in charge of motivation within your organisation, then you could treat motivation as a way to improve sales, or alternatively as a way of improving communication with customers. But which of the options available is most commonly considered to be the main goal of a motivation programme? These are the main objectives of improving motivation according to the *Marketing Week* survey:

Improving sales	38%
Generating a more positive attitude among employees	27%
Customer care	23%
Improving the communication of product information to customers	12%

Source: 'Garnishing the Corporate Carrot', *Marketing Week*, November 1990

■ *Who has responsibility for motivation?*

Motivation is a serious issue, but it is one which may not have a clear responsibility attached. If you do want to become more involved in staff motivation issues, then you will have to give someone the job of dealing with this area of the business. But who should this responsibility rest with? The answers are given in the following chart.

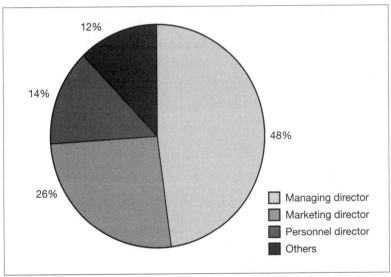

12%	
14%	
48%	
26%	

- Managing director
- Marketing director
- Personnel director
- Others

Source: 'Garnishing the Corporate Carrot', *Marketing Week*, November 1990

■ *How does your company motivate its employees?*

Motivation could be described as 'having sufficient reason' for doing something. To motivate is therefore 'to furnish with a reason or motive'. Tasks, meanwhile, are either pleasant or unpleasant. If the task is pleasant, then there will be little need for motivation. If the task is unpleasant, then management will either have to offer a reward for doing it – or a penalty for not doing it. The traditional carrot and stick. John Fenton, who made his name as a sales guru, has devised tips for positive motivation. He says:

> *Motivation is achieved by the promise of satisfaction of individual needs. Each individual has different needs and wants, and these change ... motivation must relate to the promise of something in the future ... there is a level beyond which each individual cannot be motivated.*

A modern researcher into needs, Abraham Maslow, devised a hierarchy of needs. He divided needs into 5 categories:

1. Self-actualisation needs – self-fulfilment
2. Esteem needs – status, recognition, self-respect
3. Affiliation needs – acceptance by equals, friends, belonging
4. Safety needs – physical and financial security
5. Physiological needs – air, water, shelter, rest, food.

Working from the bottom of the list up, each individual must be satisfied at each level of need before feeling free to seek satisfaction at the next level above. If a lower level is threatened, then attention will revert to that level to 'repair the foundations'.

John Fenton maintains that positive motivation can only be achieved by concentrating on the positive factors:

ACHIEVEMENT   RECOGNITION   RESPONSIBILITY
        ADVANCEMENT   PERSONAL GROWTH

Source: John Fenton Training International, 1997

■ What rewards are the most motivating?

A reward-based scheme is an obvious choice for increasing employee motivation, but what rewards should be offered? You will want to offer whatever motivates your staff the most, but what exactly is this? The *Marketing Week* survey asked respondents what rewards they thought had the greatest effect on motivation.

Money	28%
Travel rewards	24%
Merchandise	15%
Vouchers	12%
Activity experiences such as go-karting or canoeing	11%
Attendance at a major sporting event	10%

Source: 'Garnishing the Corporate Carrot', *Marketing Week*, November 1990

■ What factors most affect how much effort staff put into their job?

If you want to motivate your staff, then you will need to know what measures have a significant effect on the effort your staff put in to their work, and which may turn out to be just token gestures. One survey asked respondents which of the factors below were 'things important in determining how hard you work in your job'. The list is given in order of factors most commonly cited down to those which were cited least.

The eight most important factors for working hard

- Personal discretion
- Targets
- Clients/customers
- Supervisor/boss
- Fellow workers/colleagues
- Reports/appraisals
- Pay incentives
- Machine/assembly line

Source: Employee Commitment and the Skills Revolution, Policy Studies Institute, 1993

STAFF EFFECTIVENESS

■ *If an incentive scheme offers travel to employees, should partners be included?*

You may wish to reward some employees for good work by giving them a travel award, but does this mean that you will have to let their spouse or partner come along for the ride?

- According to 63% of those surveyed, it is essential that partners be included in staff travel awards.

- A further 28% said that the inclusion of partners is important.

- Only 9% of respondents said that including a ticket for the nearest and dearest was not very important.

Source: 'Garnishing the Corporate Carrot', *Marketing Week*, November 1990

■ *How committed are people to their work?*

Not everyone wants to have a job, but many people are motivated to work simply for its own sake. But how many people work for the sake of working, and does this depend on what work they perform?

- 67% of people would prefer to have a job even if there were no financial necessity.

- This proportion decreases as the work descends from managerial or professional level to lower non-manual work, to technical and supervisory posts and skilled manual work, being lowest with semi- or non-skilled manual workers.

- Although 73% of managers and professionals would prefer to continue working, 61% of semi- or non-skilled manual workers would still want a job even if there were no necessity.

Source: Employee Commitment and the Skills Revolution, Policy Studies Institute, 1993

■ *How does commitment vary with educational qualifications?*

Commitment, for the purposes of this survey, was considered to be an employee's desire to continue working even if there were no financial need. So, if you are looking for this kind of commitment in your workforce, are you most likely to find it among unqualified staff or those with a strong educational background?

- 77% of people with degree level qualifications said that they would stay in work even if they did not need the money.

- This figure dropped to 69% among employees with only CSE level qualifications.

- Only 58% of employees with no educational qualifications said that they would stay in work under these circumstances.

Source: Employee Commitment and the Skills Revolution, Policy Studies Institute, 1993

■ *What are the major influences on organisational commitment?*

You may well be concerned about your employees' commitment to work in general, but the chances are that you will be even more concerned about their specific commitment to working for your company. If you are trying to develop such organisation-oriented commitment within your workforce, you will be interested to know which factors have a strong effect on this.

- Unlike work commitment, organisation commitment was not found to be related to the level of academic qualifications.

- A high level of correlation was found between skill utilisation, personal development and careers and levels of organisational attachment.

- The belief that training provision had increased, and would be available in the future, was strongly related to organisational commitment – more so than actually receiving training.

- Employees who felt that their supervisor helped them to learn their job were significantly more committed to their organisation than others.

- High organisational attachment was also observed among employees who thought that their job prospects were better with their current employer than they would be if they changed employers.

- Aspects of participation and involvement, such as 'having a say' and 'taking part in decisions' correlated strongly with high organisational commitment.

- Egalitarianism also seemed popular, with commitment generally being higher in organisations where there was no difference in fringe benefits or privileges between different grades of staff, in organisations where supervisors did the same work as their subordinates, and for employees who considered their supervisor to be 'fair'.

- Organisation commitment was also substantially influenced by all aspects of job satisfaction.

Source: Employee Commitment and the Skills Revolution, Policy Studies Institute, 1993

STAFF EFFECTIVENESS

TEAMS

■ To what extent is team working used?

How many organisations actually use this new management style? Team working, it seems, is fairly widely used, being operated to some extent by 40% of companies.

Source: Team Working and Pay, IES, 1995

■ How often is team-based pay used?

It is one thing to have employees working together in teams. It is something else actually to pay them on this basis. It turns out that team bonuses and skill-based pay are still quite uncommon, being used by only 10% of the companies who use team working.

Source: Team Working and Pay, IES, 1995

■ For what occupations is team working most often used?

If you want to introduce a team working initiative, who are the most likely candidates? Some organisational structures are much more appropriate for managers and others are better suited to manual workers, but it seems that this is not the case with team working. Team working initiatives are used fairly evenly across a range of occupational groups. The percentage of companies operating team work systems with each occupational group is shown below:

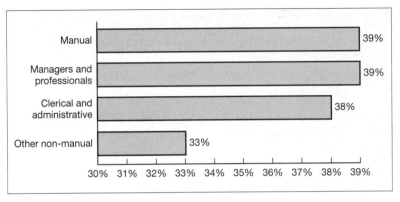

Source: Team Working and Pay, IES, 1995

STAFF EFFECTIVENESS

■ What are the advantages of team-based pay?

Obviously different payment systems affect staff, and therefore your organisation as a whole, in different ways. The most common alternative to team pay is individual merit pay. The IES has identified several advantages of team pay over this and other payment systems.

- Team pay rewards team work and co-operation.
- It encourages groups to improve work systems.
- It increases flexibility and the ability to respond to changing needs.
- It encourages information sharing and communication between individuals.
- It makes individual staff focus more on the wider organisation.
- It is not incorporated into base pay.

Source: Team Working and Pay, IES, 1995

■ How much are team-based pay systems used within the companies that use them?

It would be possible to nominate only one team in your organisation as eligible for team pay, but often there are many teams who could be paid on this basis. On the other hand, you may not want to go overboard and pay every member of staff as a team member. So how many teams receiving this pay are there in most companies? In fact, companies that operate team pay have an average of 3.5 schemes of this type.

Source: Counting Costs to Keep Competitive, Confederation of British Industry, 1994

■ What proportion of pay does team pay constitute?

As with all bonus systems, it is often hard to know how large such bonuses should be. Should they constitute the majority of the pay cheque, or simply be a little pocket money?

- For semi/unskilled workers, team incentives are equivalent to an average of 20% of base salary.
- For top management, team pay adds up to, on average, only 7% of base salary.

Source: Counting Costs to Keep Competitive, Confederation of British Industry, 1994

■ Does team working work?

Team working is often employed as a central strategy for ensuring adaptability and effectiveness in today's organisations. Business psychologist Alison Hardingham, of Interactive Skills, argues that many organisations hamper the best efforts of the teams they create:

> *The problem is not working in teams – teamwork is the most natural thing in the world. The problem is often the organisational context which throws up barriers to effective teamworking.*

Organisations set up competitive tensions between team members, or change the goalposts, or appoint individuals to competing teams.

Research also indicates that, for many tasks, team performance is often much less effective than the same individuals working alone.

Source: 'Effective Teamworking', Alison Hardingham's speech to the IPD National Conference, 23 October 1997

■ How can teams resolve the problems they face?

Alison Hardingham advocates two solutions:

1. Realise the team's humanity. By getting members to share their values, experiences and motivations with each other, a sense of belonging is reawakened.
2. Disciplines and structures to govern the conduct of the team. These will control natural rivalries, antagonistic dynamics and tendencies not to listen.

Source: 'Effective Teamworking', Alison Hardingham's speech to the IPD National Conference, 23 October 1997

PERSONAL DEVELOPMENT

Appraisal

■ How common are formal appraisals, and how often are they used to plan training?

Most staff are evaluated in some way, but this does not have to be by means of a formal appraisal. Even if it is, there is still a question of whether training plans should then take account of the findings of such an appraisal. If you are thinking of introducing an appraisal system, and possibly linking it to training plans, you might want to know the extent to which this practice is currently used. The figures below apply only to staff who have supervisors (90% of the sample – excluding some senior managers and others).

- 55% of employees with supervisors were found to have formal appraisals.
- This varied according to job level, with over 60% of supervisors, technicians and non-manual workers having appraisals, as against 43% of manual workers.
- Of all employees having appraisals, 66% reported that they were used for planning training and development.
- This, however, was also dependent upon job level, with 80% of managers and professionals having appraisals linked to training plans, but only 40% of semi- and non-skilled manual workers.

Source: Employee Commitment and The Skills Revolution, Policy Studies Institute, 1993

■ How often are appraisals linked to pay?

Another area that you may want to consider if you are reviewing your appraisal system (or lack of it) is the linking of appraisals to pay. It is possible to give bonuses and pay rises on the basis of appraisals, but how common is this practice, and who most commonly receives such benefits? These figures come from the same survey as the previous question, but apply to all employees, with or without supervisors.

- 53% of employees said that they received formal appraisals.
- 33% of these (18% of all employees) felt that these affected their earnings to some extent.
- Lower non-manual staff were the group most likely to have pay linked to appraisals.
- However, 60% of those having appraisals (33% of all employees) felt that the outcome of these could influence their job prospects, and hence affect their earnings in the long run.

Source: Employee Commitment and the Skills Revolution, Policy Studies Institute, 1993

■ *Do appraisals increase motivation?*

Appraisal systems can be useful for monitoring and evaluating employee performance. They can also have additional benefits within your company. If you are considering whether to introduce, abolish or update an appraisal system, these figures may influence your decision.

- About 40% of employees who received formal appraisals said that 'reports and appraisals' influenced how hard they worked.
- Furthermore, nearly 70% of employees having appraisals said that their effort was affected by 'targets', which were also cited as a motivator by nearly 40% of employees who were not formally appraised.

Source: Employee Commitment and the Skills Revolution, Policy Studies Institute, 1993

Personal development plans

■ *How many companies have introduced personal development plans for their staff?*

Personal development plans are intended to help employees develop the skills needed for future careers as well as their present jobs. A total of 69% of companies surveyed had introduced personal development plans, and more companies are emphasising staff development than performance-related pay:

- 74% of participants state that their performance management processes focus mainly on staff development.

- Only 38% believe that performance-related pay is an essential part of performance management.

Source: IPD Survey of Performance Management Policies and Practices in the UK, IPD, 1997

■ How enthusiastic are staff about objective setting?

Companies support the process of objective setting – 70% rated it very or mostly effective – but how do staff feel?

- Only 45% of staff believe it is very or mostly effective.

- 37% of respondents said that performance management is time-consuming and bureaucratic.

Source: IPD Survey of Performance Management Policies and Practices in the UK, IPD, 1997

■ How do companies set up an effective performance management system?

Michael Armstrong, an IPD course director, says that companies trying to create a successful performance management process need to be clear what they mean by performance:

> *Performance can mean different things to different people. Employees cannot have faith in a system unless they understand where the organisation sees itself going and how they can help it achieve those objectives.*

He also stresses the importance of showing individuals how the process will benefit them:

- There was considerable interest amongst survey respondents in 360 degree feedback, and 11 companies surveyed had introduced formal schemes.

Source: IPD Survey of Performance Management Policies and Practices in the UK, IPD, 1997

STAFF EFFECTIVENESS

METHODS OF PAY

Variable pay systems

■ What are the main reasons for operating variable pay systems?

Before you start trying to choose a variable pay system, you will naturally want to know what the arguments are for introducing one at all. According to one survey, the most common reasons for introducing variable pay, in order of priority, were:

• Motivating employees

• Communication of business objectives

• Retaining employees.

Source: Counting Costs to Keep Competitive, Confederation of British Industry, 1994

■ What are the most commonly used variable pay systems?

If you do decide that you want to introduce a variable pay system, you will then be faced with the daunting prospect of choosing between the many schemes that you could potentially be running. One thread that may help guide you through this maze is to know which are the most popular systems currently being used.

• Individual bonuses are most common, being used by 75% of companies.

• SAYE share option schemes are the next most popular, in use in 38% of companies.

• Discretionary share options come close behind, being used in 35% of companies.

Source: Counting Costs to Keep Competitive, Confederation of British Industry, 1994

One less recent survey has more comprehensive data on this subject, as is shown in the chart below. This gives figures for the proportion of trading sector establishments running each of the five types of scheme mentioned, and also breaks this information down by the size of the enterprise.

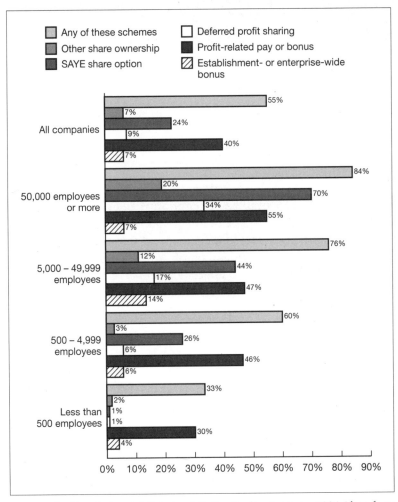

STAFF EFFECTIVENESS

Source: The New Industrial Relations? Policy Studies Institute, 1994 (data from *Workplace Industrial Relations Survey*, 1990)

191

■ *What are the most effective variable payment systems?*

Which systems are considered to be most efficient in changing company culture? One survey asked companies who ran variable pay systems which ones they considered to be most effective overall. Ironically, the highest scorers were not the systems most commonly in use. The most effective systems were considered to be:

● Spot awards

● Skill/competency pay

● Restricted shares.

Source: Counting Costs to Keep Competitive, Confederation of British Industry, 1994

■ *What payment systems are most effective for different goals?*

An overall effectiveness rating might be helpful, but sometimes there will be one particular goal that takes priority, and the effectiveness of a system in other areas will be of minor concern. Of course, there are various potential goals that you may have in introducing a new payment system, and the Confederation of British Industry survey asked respondents to rate schemes' effectiveness on a range of objectives. The most effective schemes for each desired outcome are listed below.

More closely link pay to performance:

● Individual bonus

● Spot awards

● Team incentives.

Encourage participation/empowerment:

● Spot awards

● Team incentives

● Profit sharing share schemes.

Communicate business objectives:

● Individual bonuses

● Skill/competency pay

● Discretionary options.

Aid staff retention:

- Cash profit share/profit-related pay
- Discretionary options
- Restricted shares.

Source: Counting Costs to Keep Competitive, Confederation of British Industry, 1994

Performance-related pay

■ *Why are performance-related pay schemes used?*

A lot is said about performance-related pay, and it is often used, to some degree or another. But what are the main reasons behind the introduction of such schemes? A mini-survey by the Institute of Manpower Studies asked this question. Respondents were allowed to give more than one answer – the proportion giving each reason is shown below.

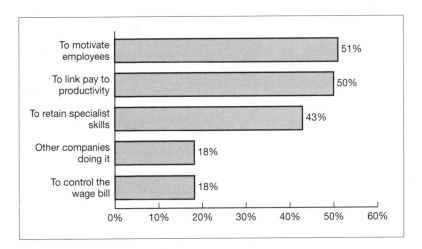

This was a mini-survey of only 90 companies, so while results are revealing, they cannot necessarily be considered entirely representative of performance-related pay users in general.

Source: Pay and Performance – The Employer Experience, Institute of Manpower Studies (now Institute of Employment Studies) 1992

■ *By what standards is performance usually measured?*

One issue that is raised by the introduction of any performance-related system of pay is how performance is to be judged. Naturally this will vary from company to company, but if you are designing or reviewing such a system, it may help to know what the most common measures are.

- For senior and middle management, the most common measures are profitability and revenue or income generation.

- For supervisory and clerical staff, performance is most often judged on the basis of work quality and timeliness.

- For manual workers, the most common measures are production volume and quality.

Source: Counting Costs to Keep Competitive, Confederation of British Industry, 1994

■ *How much of annual pay is performance-related?*

If you are setting up or reviewing a performance-related pay system, then you will want to know how much pay to give out on a performance-related basis, and how to distribute it.

- The Institute of Manpower Studies mini-survey found that approximately 10% of the salary bill was usually set aside for performance-related pay schemes.

- This was most usually paid on an annual basis, with under 5% of the sample distributing them on a quarterly or six-monthly basis.

Source: Pay and Performance – The Employer Experience, Institute of Manpower Studies (now Institute of Employment Studies) 1992

■ *How can you monitor the effectiveness of performance-related pay?*

If you are setting up a performance-related pay system, for whatever reason, then you may well want to know whether it is achieving your desired aims. In order to find this out, you will have to monitor the scheme in some way, but what monitoring method should you use?

Many methods can be used, but some are more popular than others. The Institute of Manpower Studies survey asked employers which of the following methods they used (they were allowed to give more than one answer), and the percentage using each method is shown below.

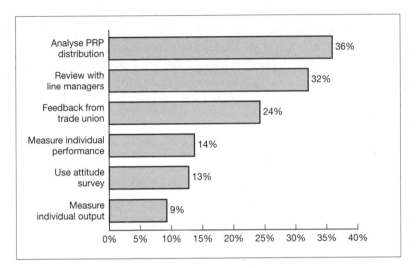

STAFF EFFECTIVENESS

Source: Pay and Performance – The Employer Experience, Institute of Manpower Studies (now Institute of Employment Studies) 1992

■ *What are the main costs of performance-related pay schemes?*

If you are thinking about setting up such a scheme, you'll need to know what sort of costs will be incurred if you do so. The Institute of Manpower Studies mini-survey revealed five main areas of expense:

The five main areas of expense

1 External consultancy
2 Training of line managers
3 Preparation of documentation for managers and staff
4 Communication strategy
5 Management time

Source: Pay and Performance – The Employer Experience, Institute of Manpower Studies (now Institute of Employment Studies) 1992

■ *How effective is performance-related pay?*

Very few studies have actually covered the overall effectiveness of performance-related pay. Possibly the largest of these – *Performance Related Pay: The Employee Experience* – was conducted by the Institute of Manpower Studies, examining the attitudes of almost 1,000 employees. The survey itself, however, covered only three organisations, and hence the results can in no way be considered universally applicable. It is interesting, though, to see what the results were, since it is the most comprehensive study available.

Results from the investigation were clear on three points about performance-related pay:

---

1 It does not serve to motivate employees, and may even act as a demotivator.

---

2 There was little evidence to suggest that performance-related pay helps retain high performers, and no evidence that it encourages poor performers to leave.

---

3 Employees are negative or neutral about its impact on organisational culture.

This is all very discouraging for performance-related pay. However, the study did produce three factors which seemed to contribute significantly to the apparent failure of the schemes. These were:

---

1 Employees who have been involved in the design and implementation of the scheme are more likely to be motivated by it.

---

2 Employee reaction to performance-related pay seems strongly dependent on the relationship with their line manager – when this is good, employees are much more likely to react positively.

---

3 Fairness, or perceived fairness, is crucial to the success of a scheme. The line manager can also play a major role in this aspect of performance-related pay.

Source: Performance Related Pay: The Employee Experience, Institute of Manpower Studies (now Institute of Employment Studies), 1992

■ *How widely used is performance-related pay?*

It is often hard to tell, when something is heavily advertised and talked about, how much of the story is about real change and how much is just hype. In the case of performance-related pay, that means finding out what proportion of organisations actually use it. The IPM and Nedo asked this question in a survey in 1991.

- 47% of private sector companies operated performance-related pay schemes for all non-manual grades (management and others).

- In the public sector, 37% of companies were operating performance-related pay for some non-manual grades. Most of these, however, were confined to management level.

Source: 'What's Changed about Incentive Pay?' *Personnel Management*, October 1991, from an IPM/Nedo survey

■ *For what grades is performance-related pay used?*

Performance-related pay schemes can cover only a few management staff, or most of the employees in the company. One factor in your decision may be what precedent there is in this area. So how far do most companies go with their performance-related pay schemes? It seems that this varies considerably between the private and public sectors.

- Only 10% of public sector companies had secretarial, clerical, or administrative staff who were on a performance-related pay scheme.

- In the private sector, however, 56% of companies had performance-related pay schemes for at least some of their non-management, non-manual staff.

Source: 'What's Changed about Incentive Pay?' *Personnel Management*, October 1991, from an IPM/Nedo survey

STAFF EFFECTIVENESS

197

Other payment schemes

■ *How widely used is merit pay?*

Many companies use performance-related pay schemes, but what of less publicised payment systems such as merit pay? Is this alternative option often taken? By some it is – 21% of companies surveyed used it for some of their non-manual employees.

Source: 'What's Changed about Incentive Pay?' *Personnel Management*, October 1991, from an IPM/Nedo survey

■ *To what extent are piece-rate and measured daily work schemes still used?*

Many new pay schemes are being introduced, but what of the older schemes that they are often thought to replace? If you are thinking of introducing a performance-related payment system then you will want to take all your options into consideration. But are these other payment systems dying out, or are they still in use? The answer to this question seems to vary considerably between different sectors.

• Piece-rate payment is used by 23% of manufacturing companies.

• However, it is used by 39% of public sector organisations.

• Measured daily work schemes are used by only 7% of manufacturing companies.

• But they are still in place in 41% of public sector organisations.

Source: 'What's Changed about Incentive Pay?' *Personnel Management*, October 1991, from an IPM/Nedo survey

■ *For what grades of staff are share option schemes used?*

Share option schemes are quite a popular method of providing variable pay, but, as with many systems, they do not always cover the entire company. If you are thinking of introducing this kind of scheme, it might help to know what grades such schemes usually cover.

- Discretionary share options and restricted shares tend to be limited to senior and top management.

- SAYE share options and profit sharing share schemes more often cover all grades of staff.

Source: *Counting Costs to Keep Competitive*, Confederation of British Industry, 1994

■ What proportion of employees are in a profit sharing or share scheme?

Profit sharing and share option schemes are popular types of incentive scheme, but how popular are they? One survey asked employees whether they took part in 'a profit sharing scheme, employee share scheme or share option scheme'.

- 15% of employees said that they did take part in a scheme fitting this description.

- 83% of these also stated that they took part in a workplace or organisational incentive scheme.

Source: *Employee Commitment and the Skills Revolution*, Policy Studies Institute, 1993

Profit-related pay

The Inland Revenue offers a tax incentive on profit-related pay (PRP) schemes that conform to certain guidelines that it has set out. The most detailed figures concerning PRP schemes, therefore, are those concerning the schemes that are registered with the Inland Revenue. The figures below all refer to this data set.

■ How many registered PRP schemes exist?

The first thing you will want to know if you are considering the option of starting up a PRP scheme is how many other companies have taken advantage of this method of pay. The number of PRP schemes registered with the Inland Revenue at the end of June 1994 was 7,486. A total of 1,856,600 employees were covered by these schemes.

Source: (See p. 200).

■ How large are PRP schemes?

Naturally, running a PRP scheme for only a handful of your staff is very different from running it for thousands of employees. So, where in this range do most PRP schemes lie? The chart below shows what proportion of PRP schemes cover different numbers of employees (0 to 10, 11 to 50, etc.).

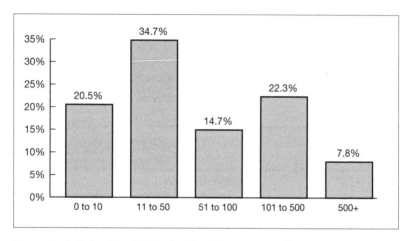

Source: Profit-Related Pay, IDS Study 564. All figures from Inland Revenue

■ *What proportion of pay does PRP represent?*

Again, there is a great difference between a scheme that offers only a small amount of PRP, almost as a bonus, and one in which a substantial amount of pay is linked to company performance. So which of these is the most popular option?

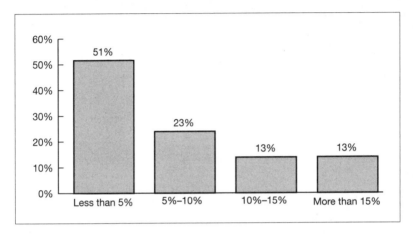

Source: Profit-Related Pay, IDS Study 564. All figures from Inland Revenue

- The mean average percentage of pay that PRP constituted was 10.4%.

- 74% of employers used PRP to pay out bonuses or incentives to their staff.

Source: Profit Related Pay, An Employer Survey, Inland Revenue, 1994

The figures below all come from the 1994 Inland Revenue survey *Profit-Related Pay, An Employer Survey.* The reference is given on page 204.

STAFF EFFECTIVENESS

■ What are the main reasons for introducing PRP?

If you are considering introducing a PRP scheme in your company, then one way to gauge whether this is appropriate for your needs is to find out what the usual reasons are for starting up such a scheme.

- The main motivations for introducing PRP schemes (among those registered with the Inland Revenue) are tax efficiency and employee involvement.

- Less important, but significant, factors are making employees work harder or more efficiently, and making employees more aware of the need for cost control.

- 36% of all PRP schemes operators said that the scheme would not have been introduced were it not for the tax relief incentives.

■ What are the actual effects of PRP schemes?

Before you embark upon introducing a scheme, you will want to know what sort of effects you can expect it to have on your company.

- The most significant effects of PRP were said to be tax efficiency and employee involvement.

- Less significant were increased productivity, improved staff retention/recruitment, better cost control (by the employees), and 'the stamp of a good employer'.

- Unfortunately, only a quarter of the respondents of the survey responded to this question.

- Also, over 80% of employers who introduced a PRP scheme after 1992 were unable to judge its effectiveness on any measure.

■ How long does it take to draw up a PRP scheme?

One of the things that you will have to plan for, if you do decide to adopt a profit-related pay system, is the length of time that it will take to draw up the scheme. So what sort of time is it reasonable to expect? Respondents to the questionnaire were asked how long it had taken them to draw up the scheme they were currently running. The overall figures were as follows:

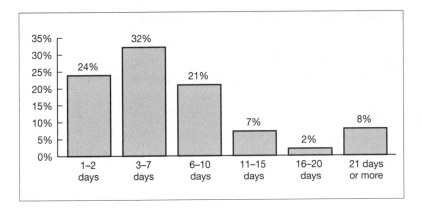

- The figures were naturally larger for larger companies – the most common responses for companies of 500+ employees were 6–10 days (32%) and 21+ days (26%).

■ *How frequently are PRP payments made?*

If you set up a scheme, you will also have to tackle how often to make the relevant payments. Naturally this is up to you, but if you would like some guidance, then the figures below show what percentage of respondents made their payments at each interval.

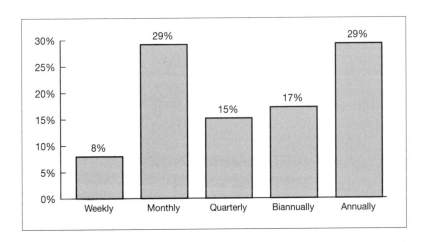

■ *What are the disadvantages of PRP?*

Of course, every system has some drawbacks. Before you commit yourself to a PRP system, you might want to know what the down side could be. According to the Inland Revenue survey, the most strongly felt concern about PRP was that it builds up expectations that may be difficult to satisfy when profits dip.

Source: Profit Related Pay, An Employer Survey, Inland Revenue, 1994

DISCIPLINE

■ *What degree of lateness or poor performance leads to dismissal?*

If an employee is persistently late in arriving at work or persistently not working as hard as they should, then you would naturally want to take some form of disciplinary action. But if they continued in their behaviour no matter what you did, how long would you leave it before giving them the sack? One survey asked employees how long they thought it would take someone doing their sort of job to be dismissed if they were persistently late, or if they persistently did not work hard.

Reason for dismissal	1 month	1–6 months	Over 6 months
Persistent lateness	33%	33%	33%
Poor worker	28%	33%	37%

- These figures varied considerably according to job level, with 15%–20% of professionals expecting dismissal to follow within a month in the case of persistent lateness, as against 40%–50% of manual workers.

Source: Employee Commitment and the Skills Revolution, Policy Studies Institute, 1993

TRAINING

Details of training in health and safety, IT, and foreign
language skills are included in the section relating to the
subject matter

INVESTMENT IN TRAINING

■ *Is investment in training growing?*

Training is only one section of personnel management. It has many competitors for a larger slice of the annual budget pie. Yet we are often told how important training is for a successful organisation. How many organisations are actually increasing the amount of training that they provide for their staff? It turns out that the majority are – 68% say they have increased levels of training over the last two years.

Source: 'Training Climbs the Corporate Agenda', *Personnel Management*, July 1994

- Another survey found that 40% of companies were expecting to spend more on training in 1995 than they did in 1994.

- Only 4% of companies surveyed were expecting to spend less in 1995.

Source: Training Video Survey, Benchmark Research Ltd, 1995

■ *How many companies have a board member responsible for training?*

One way to gauge the significance of any area of company policy is to find out whether there is a board member responsible for it. So how many companies take training seriously enough to take it to the highest level?

- According to one survey, 58% of companies have a board member with a specific responsibility for training.

Source: 'Training Climbs the Corporate Agenda', *Personnel Management*, July 1994

■ *How many companies have references to training in their business plan?*

A company's business plan is another good gauge of how concerned it is with different issues. Training does seem to be of significant importance to the majority of companies. Is this borne out by the contents of their business plan?

- It is – 68% of respondents said that their company has explicit references to training implications in its business plan.

Source: 'Training Climbs the Corporate Agenda', *Personnel Management*, July 1994

■ *How many companies have a training plan?*

Of course, training can simply be given ad hoc, as and when the need arises. But some companies prefer to take a longer-term view of the situation and actually develop a training plan for their organisation. So if you do not have a training plan, or only an informal one, then are you being sloppy, or are you in line with common practice?

Companies with a training budget	67%
Companies with a formal training plan	66%
Percentage of organisations with 500+ employees with a training plan	89%
Percentage of organisations with 25–49 employees with a training plan	57%

- Training plans (formal or informal) are more prevalent in larger companies.

Source: Skill Needs In Britain 1996, Public Attitude Surveys Ltd research for the Department for Education and Employment

■ *What are the main triggers for training initiatives?*

Increasing training in your organisation can have many benefits, and the impetus to review or improve training standards can come from a variety of sources. But some of the potential reasons for updating training strategies may not have as much impact as some would like to think, and there may well be more unexpected factors at work. The *Personnel Management* survey asked respondents to indicate which of the following influences had triggered their training initiatives. Respondents were allowed to indicate more than one factor, and the number indicating each option is shown overleaf.

TRAINING

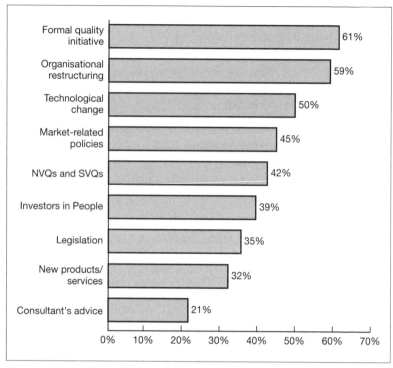

Formal quality initiative — 61%
Organisational restructuring — 59%
Technological change — 50%
Market-related policies — 45%
NVQs and SVQs — 42%
Investors in People — 39%
Legislation — 35%
New products/services — 32%
Consultant's advice — 21%

Source: 'Training Climbs the Corporate Agenda', *Personnel Management,* July 1994

■ *How much training does the average employee receive?*

- Employees given training received an average of 11.4 days, equivalent to an average of 5.3 days for every employee.
- Two-thirds of employees (66%) had a formal training plan.
- A similar number (67%) had a formal training budget.

Source: Skill Needs in Britain, 1996. Public Attitudes Surveys Ltd research for the Department for Education and Employment

■ *Who receives training?*

How do you decide who in the company to train? You are unlikely to be able to give all your staff all the training that they want, so at some point you will have to decide who comes top of the list. This can be a tough decision, and it may help you to find out who receives most training in other companies.

- Training was most common among managers and professionals, then gradually less common through lower non-manual workers, technicians and supervisors, and skilled manual workers, with semi- and unskilled manual workers receiving the least training.

- 71% of managers and professionals with supervisors had received training during the three years prior to the survey.

- Only 45% of skilled manual workers had received training during this time.

- Of semi- and unskilled manual workers, only 34% had been trained in the last three years.

Source: Employee Commitment and the Skills Revolution, Policy Studies Institute, 1993

■ *Who gets the benefit of increased training?*

Of course, it is all very well to say that training is increasing, but that does not mean that it is increasing equally for all levels of staff. Training will always be increasing for some groups faster than for others. So when firms say that they are increasing training, who are they really increasing it for, and are their priorities the same as yours? The figures below show what percentage of firms say that training has increased over the last two years for each grade of staff.

TRAINING

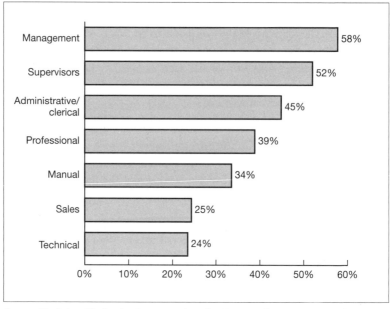

Source: 'Training Climbs the Corporate Agenda', *Personnel Management*, July 1994

■ *What types of training are most commonly provided?*

What areas of training should receive the most concentration? Of course, specific needs may be identified at any time, but without this impetus it can be hard to decide what topics should top the priority list. If this is a decision that you have to make, then it may interest you to know what areas of training are most commonly provided in the business community in general. This is the percentage of organisations providing each type of training:

Health and safety/first aid	84%
Induction training	49%
Management training	47%
New technology training	47%
Supervisory training	41%

Source: Skill Needs in Britain 1994, IFF research for Employment Department

■ *What areas of training are being increased most?*

But current training levels are not the whole story. Some topics will always be becoming more fashionable, while others are likely to be left some way behind. If you are distributing your company's training budget, you may want to know what topic areas most managers say that they are increasing their training in. The chart below shows what proportion of trainers say that they are increasing their training in each area.

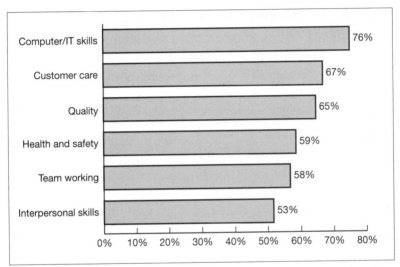

Source: 'Training Climbs the Corporate Agenda', *Personnel Management,* July 1994

■ *How many companies provide off-the-job training?*

Employers seem to be taking off-the-job training increasingly seriously. In a recent survey, 84% are now providing off-the-job training for at least some of their employees, compared with 78% in 1994.

- Off-the-job training was provided for 44% of employees in 1996.
- 71% of employers provided this type of training for new employees.
- 80% of employers funded off-the-job training for existing employees in a 12 month period.
- The most likely training providers were private sector companies (61%) and Further Education establishments (53%).

- 65% of employers who had provided off-the-job training reported that at least some of it was leading to formal qualifications, particularly in the larger firms.

Off-the-job training is defined in this survey as 'all training away from the immediate work position'.

Source: Skill Needs in Britain, 1996. Public Attitudes Surveys Ltd research for the Department of Education and Employment

■ Do larger employers undertake more training than smaller ones?

The amount of training that a company does depends on many factors. If you want to benchmark your activities effectively, then you will have to take these into account. One major difference in training is between small and large companies. But how big a difference is this?

- 72% of companies with 25–49 employees have provided some off-the-job training in the last 12 months.

- But an overwhelming 94% of companies with 500+ employees have done so.

Source: Skill Needs in Britain 1994, IFF research for Employment Department

■ What proportion of experienced employees receive training?

Obviously new recruits need to be trained in how to do their job, but what about employees who have already had time to settle in? Should they be left to get on with their jobs, or do most companies still consider it necessary to give them further instruction? In 1996, off-the-job training was arranged by 80% of all employers for employees who had been employed for over 12 months.

Source: Skill Needs in Britain 1996, Public Attitudes Surveys Ltd research for the Department for Education and Employment

■ What is the average amount of training provided for employees?

The preceding figures give some idea of how many companies provide off-the-job training, but they do not indicate how much training they give. So how can you tell if the amount of training that you provide for your employees is greater or less than the average? In 1994, employers provided an average of 2.7 days' off-the-job training for each employee, and an average 6.4 days for each employee trained.

Source: Skill Needs in Britain 1994, IFF research for Employment Department

■ How many companies have a training budget?

Many training providers see themselves as fighting for a piece of their customers' training budgets. But how many companies actually have such budgets? If your training expenses are decided on a different basis from the standard budget, is this a peculiarity of your company, or there many others who operate in the same way?

- 67% of companies have a training budget.
- Large companies are much more likely to have training budgets (formal or informal) than small ones.

Source: Skill Needs in Britain 1996, Public Attitudes Surveys Ltd research for the Department for Education and Employment

■ How often is the budget reviewed?

If you do have a training budget, then you may want to review it, or you may just want to leave it alone. But is this latter choice a popular one, or does a budget usually come with reviews as part of the package?

- 90% of companies with a training budget do review it at some time.
- In 88% of cases, this is done formally.
- 79% of organisations that review the budget do so annually.
- Larger employers are more likely to review their budget than smaller ones.
- 97% of companies with 500+ employees make such reviews.
- This compares with 90% for companies with 25–49 employees.

Source: Skill Needs in Britain 1994, IFF research for Employment Department

■ How are training needs evaluated?

Evaluating the need for training is an important part of a training manager's job, and it is not just a question of reading through training catalogues. So how do most people with this responsibility actually evaluate the training needs of their company? One survey asked this question, and allowed respondents the option of giving more than one answer.

- It found that 38% of employers rely on management to evaluate training needs.
- Individual appraisals were used by another 34%.

Source: Skill Needs in Britain 1994, IFF research for Employment Department

■ To what extent is training subsequently evaluated?

If you are providing training for your employees, then you may want to know to what extent, if any, it was worth the money that you spent on it. If you want to find this out, you will have to evaluate the training in some way. But how common is it to evaluate the training that you have provided for your staff, and what methods are used for such an evaluation?

- 65% of the companies who had provided training in the last 12 months had evaluated the training in some way.
- The most common methods used were:

Method	Proportion of companies
Informal feedback from employees	58%
Assessing the impact on employees' performance	54%
Management assessment	53%
Formal feedback from employees	51%

Source: Skill Needs in Britain 1994, IFF research for Employment Department

■ How much training leads to formal qualifications?

When deciding what training to provide for your staff, you will need to consider whether this training should lead to some sort of qualification or not. How many other companies are helping their employees towards a qualification?

- 65% of employers who had provided training over the last 12 months said that at least some of this was leading to formal qualifications.

Source: Skill Needs in Britain 1996, Public Attitudes Surveys Ltd research for Department for Education and Employment

■ How many employers have on-site training facilities or training staff?

Of course, if you are doing a significant amount of training, then it may be cheaper and easier for you to provide the facilities for training staff yourself. But this can be quite a commitment of time and resources, and before you go ahead you will want to decide whether it is really necessary. Naturally this depends on your circumstances, but one factor that might influence your decision is whether having on-site training provisions is a standard procedure for many companies, or whether most other organisations manage to do without. The figures below take 'on-site' to mean at the particular location, rather than in the organisation as a whole.

- By this definition, 20% of employers who had provided training in the last 12 months had an on-site training facility.
- Also, 17% had full-time training staff on site.

Source: Skill Needs in Britain 1994, IFF research for Employment Department

■ To what extent are external training providers used?

Another possible option is to go to an external provider. But before making a decision like this, it may again help to know how common this solution to training issues is, and which providers are most often used.

- 77% of companies who provided training in 1994 used an external provider.
- The most common providers were further education colleges, used by 51% of companies.

- The next most common were private sector companies, which were used by 45% (multiple answers were allowed).

- In 23% of cases where an outside provider had been used, a TEC/LEC had facilitated the process.

Source: Skill Needs in Britain 1994, IFF research for Employment Department

■ How important is training for managers?

It's not easy being a good manager. There are many skills involved, and training can help the learning process. If you are overseeing the management training practices of your organisation, then you may want to know how your managerial employees perceive training. So how do managers feel about being trained?

- 89% agreed that 'the business environment is changing so rapidly that managers need more training than in the past'.

- 83% said that 'organisations ought to require all of their managers to undertake some training every year'.

- 81% also said that they 'would be a more effective manager if [they] received more training'.

Source: Training for Managers, Institute of Management, 1991

■ How many managers receive training for their job?

How many managers actually get the chance to use the many management training products and services available? If your training practice does not extend to include managers, or only occasionally, then you might like to know whether this is the usual state of play, or whether managers in other companies are likely to be receiving more training than yours.

- One survey found that 88% of managers received some sort of training.

- For 82% of managers, this was work-time training.

- 49% took part in training in their own time.

- 43% of managers were trained both in their own time and during working time.

Source: Training for Managers, Institute of Management, 1991

■ What are the most popular training media?

Training can be given in many forms, each with different advantages and disadvantages. If you have the job of selecting what sort of training to provide for your managers, it may help you to know what forms of training are most often used. Naturally, this differs between training that takes place in work time and training that managers undertake in their own time.

Time of training	Preferred methods
Work-time	Courses; conferences; seminars
Own-time	Professional meetings; conferences; home-study programmes

Source: *Training for Managers*, Institute of Management, 1991

■ Do older managers need less training than younger ones?

So, now you know something about the usual provision of training for managers. But this is not the whole story. Some might say that, because of their experience and previous training, older managers do not need as much training as their younger counterparts, but is this the general consensus of opinion? Apparently not – a resounding 87% of managers agreed that 'managers over 50 should receive as much training as younger managers'.

Source: *Training for Managers*, Institute of Management, 1991

■ Do older managers receive the training they need?

Most managers seem to think that their age should have no bearing on the amount of training that they receive, but how often is this actually the case? If your training favours the younger members of your managerial staff, then is this an oversight on your part, or is it often the way that the training cookie crumbles?

- 34% of managers said that 'managers over 50 in my organisation are less likely than younger managers to receive any training'.

- Managers under 40 received an average of 10 days training of any type (as against 8 days for all managers).

Source: Training for Managers, Institute of Management, 1991

■ *How does the type of training received vary with the age of the trainee?*

It seems that management training is not an ageless society. Older managers do often receive less training than their younger counterparts. But what about the style of training that these groups receive? Should your approach to training be the same for everyone, or is there a precedent for using different styles for managers of different age groups? Not surprisingly, there are several variations between older and younger managers.

- Younger managers were more likely to take correspondence courses and evening classes.

- Older managers more often took part in study visits, professional meetings and conferences, seminars or workshops.

- Older managers were less likely to take training outside that provided by the organisation (although they generally took no worse a view of the importance of training).

Source: Training for Managers, Institute of Management, 1991

■ *How much training do managers receive?*

There are enough management training courses around for any manager to spend their whole time training and never come into the office. This rarely happens, however, but if you are in charge of management training in your organisation, then you may want to know what the usual level of training is, so that you can keep up with Jones plc. So how many days do managers actually spend in training? The median averages are:

- 5 days a year for work-time training.
- 8 days a year for all training.

Source: Training for Managers, Institute of Management, 1991

■ Who pays for own-time training?

If managers decide that they want to receive training in their own time, who is it who normally has to foot the bill? In 50% of cases, managers who undertook training in their own time paid some or all of the costs involved.

Source: Training for Managers, Institute of Management, 1991

■ Are managers happy with the training they receive?

Managers obviously value training, and we have seen how much they receive. But even if you are providing an average (or even above average) amount of training for them, they will not necessarily consider this to be sufficient. So, do most managers think that their organisation gives them enough training, and that it is the training that they really need?

- 51% said that they had received too little training in the last year.

- Around 60% of managers said that their most recent training had been very helpful.

- The other 40%, however, were unhappy with the training that they had received.

Source: Training for Managers, Institute of Management, 1991

■ What forms of training are most valued?

Not all management training, it seems, really meets the needs of the managers concerned. If you are controlling the training provided by your organisation, you will no doubt want to feel that the training you are providing is useful. This means getting it right, not only in terms of subject matter, but also how that subject matter is put across. So which of the many training formats are most likely to leave managers feeling satisfied? The most valuable training formats were considered to be:

- Guided learning schemes
- Project work
- Special assignments
- Study visits.

Source: Training for Managers, Institute of Management, 1991

219

■ *What other factors increase satisfaction with training?*

Some formats are perceived by managers as being more useful than others. If you want to give your trainees what they want, and leave them feeling contented with their training, it is worth considering how much influence your managers have on decisions about their own training.

- It was found that training which was partially or wholly the trainee's own idea was generally rated more highly than training that was simply prescribed for them.

Source: Training for Managers, Institute of Management, 1991

■ *How many companies have formal management training policies?*

A high proportion of managers, it seems, receive some form of training. But how often is that actually part of an organised scheme within the company? If your management training is somewhat ad hoc, then is this the same for many companies or is your level of organisation possibly below the average? In 1991, 31% of managers agreed with the statement that 'my company does not have a formal management training policy'.

Source: Training for Managers, Institute of Management, 1991

■ *How long do training programmes last?*

If you are planning a training programme for some of your staff, then one of the major decisions you will have to make is how long it will last. If so, then you might want to know what length of time training usually takes. One survey asked respondents who had been trained in the last three years how long this training had taken. If they had had more than one period of training then the longest period was taken. The chart below shows what proportion gave responses in each time range.

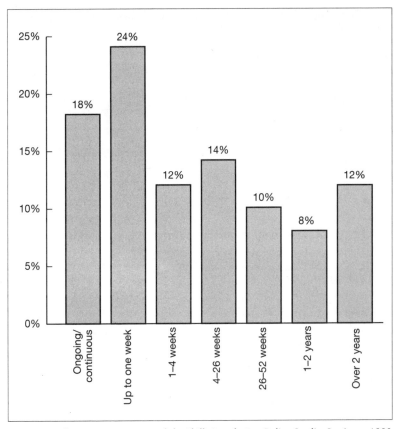

Source: Employee Commitment and the Skills Revolution, Policy Studies Institute, 1993

TRAINING

■ *What are the benefits of training for the trainee?*

If you are providing training for your staff, then their reaction to it may well depend on what they actually thought the point of it was. You may well know what you wanted to be the result, but what do employees actually perceive as the benefits of their training? The list overleaf shows how many employees who had been trained in the last three years cited each suggestion as an actual benefit of their training:

A qualification	36%
A promotion/better job	22%
An increase in earnings	20%
A job	10%
Some other benefit	46%
No real benefit	12%

Source: Employee Commitment and the Skills Revolution, Policy Studies Institute, 1993

Skills gap

■ Is there a training gap?

Everyone wants to have well-trained employees working for them. What about the employees themselves? If you want to benchmark your employees' feelings about the training they receive, or make an informed decision about the levels of training that you provide, then you will no doubt want to know what general perceptions of current levels of training are. So do most people feel that they are getting all the training that they would want? Or are some more keen on receiving training than their employers are on supplying it?

- 65% of those surveyed said that they wanted to receive more training either 'very much' or 'a fair amount'.

- Only 56% of those surveyed, however, considered themselves very or fairly likely to receive training in future.

- Of this group, some were not even keen on being trained. In fact, 20% of those questioned were very or fairly interested in receiving training but considered themselves unlikely to receive it.

- The gap between the desire for training and the expectation of receiving it increased from managers and professionals through lower non-manual staff and technicians and supervisors to skilled manual staff.

Source: Employee Commitment and the Skills Revolution, Policy Studies Institute, 1993

■ *Which employee groups are least well trained at recruitment?*

The easiest way to answer this question is to find out which employee groups are hardest to recruit. Technological and organisational changes in industry mean that new skill needs are always emerging. Is the skills gap worse in some spheres than others?

- Incidences of hard-to-fill vacancies are highest in associate professional and technical operations.

- Personal and protective service occupations have the next highest incidence.

- There is a longer lead time in developing the skills required in higher-skilled occupations.

Source: Skill Needs in Britain, 1996, Public Attitudes Surveys Ltd research for the Department for Education and Employment

■ *Do employees need more skills now than a few years ago?*

- 74% of employers feel that the need for skills in their 'average' employee is increasing.

- The most common reasons given for this rise are changes in processes or technology, and changes in work practices.

Source: Skill Needs in Britain, 1996, Public Attitudes Surveys Ltd research for the Department for Education and Employment

■ *Is there a gap between the skills of your current employees and those needed to meet your business objectives?*

- 20% of employers feel that there is a gap between the skills of their current employees and those needed to meet their business objectives.

- 40% of firms employing 16–19 year olds feel that a skills gap exists.

Source: Skill Needs in Britain, 1996, Public Attitudes Surveys Ltd research for the Department for Education and Employment

TRAINING

223

■ *What skills do your employees most lack?*

Over 4,000 employers with establishments employing at least 25 identified the following lack of skills:

Management skills	66%
General communication skills	65%
Computer literacy	64%

Source: Skill Needs in Britain, 1996, Public Attitudes Surveys Ltd research for the Department for Education and Employment

Training temporary and part-time employees

■ *How many companies train part-time and temporary employees?*

Training is an important investment in all your staff, but with only a limited training budget, doesn't it make sense to invest more in those employees who spend more time at work – the full-time rather than the part-time staff? Well, a lot of companies seem to think so. The figures below show how many employers said it was likely, possible or unlikely that they would train full-time and part-time staff.

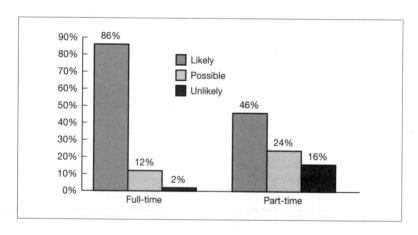

Of course, the same reasoning also applies to temporary employees, but do the results bear this out? It turns out to be even truer for temporary staff than for part-timers.

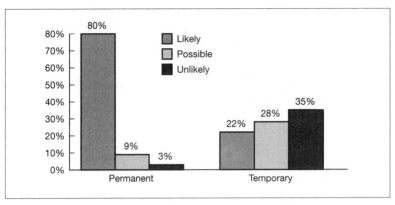

Source: *Flexible Labour Markets; Who Pays for Training?*, Confederation of British Industry, 1994

Induction training

■ *What proportion of employers provide induction training?*

Of course, all new employees need to learn the ropes somehow, but much of this can happen at their work station, learning as they go along. So how necessary is it to provide off-the-job training for recent recruits? And if you do not provide any induction training, are you giving less support than most?

- 63% of employers said that they provided off-the-job training for employees who have been taken on in the last 12 months.
- However, only 47% said that they had actually provided induction training.
- Off-the-job training was arranged for 57% of all employees who had been employed in the last 12 months.

Source: *Skill Needs in Britain 1994*, IFF research for Employment Department

BASIC SKILLS PROBLEMS

■ Are people with basic skills problems less likely to undertake learning?

If there are people with basic skills problems in your company, this may affect more than just their job performance. Problems, such as difficulties with reading, writing, numeracy and oral communication, might also deter employees from taking part in training or educational programmes that could increase their value as an employee. But if some of your staff do have basic skills problems, are they really less likely to engage in learning programmes? The chart below shows what proportion of workers with and without such problems were learning at the time of the survey, had learnt previously, or had never taken part in learning outside standard education.

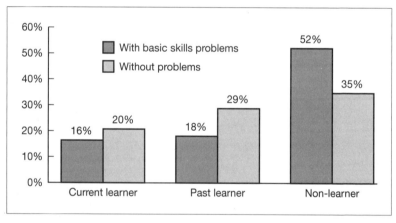

Source: *Individual Commitment to Learning*, Social and Community Planning Research for the Employment Department, 1995

■ What attitudes to learning are characteristic of people with basic skills problems?

People with basic skills problems are less likely to engage in learning than those without problems. If you want to encourage these people to take advantage of learning opportunities, then it might help to know what sort of factors deter them from taking part.

- 55% of individuals with basic skills problems felt that there was not enough information available about learning opportunities, as against 43% of those without problems.

- Those with problems were more likely to feel that there was not enough help or advice available – 48% as against 41%.

- Such people were also less likely to feel that they had a lot of choice open to them – only 31% felt they had a lot of choice, as against 47% of others.

- Those with problems were less likely to feel that they had ample opportunities for learning – only 63% felt this way, as opposed to 75% of those without problems.

- Only 15% of individuals without basic skills problems said they would feel out of place going to evening classes in a college or school, but 44% of people with problems said that they would feel this way.

Source: Individual Commitment to Learning, Social and Community Planning Research for the Employment Department, 1995

■ *What jobs are employees with basic skills problems most likely to be in?*

If you want to take action on a possible problem with basic skills in your organisation, then you will first have to find out where this problem is most prevalent. This may vary from company to company, but it might help to have a rough guideline. The chart overleaf shows the distribution of people with basic skills problems between the Standard Occupational Classifications, as a percentage of those people in each occupation.

TRAINING

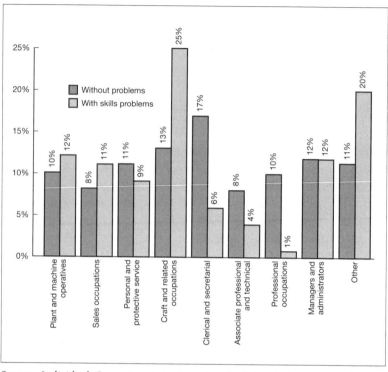

Source: Individual Commitment to Learning, Social and Community Planning Research for the Employment Department, 1995

■ *How greatly do basic skills shortages affect the jobs staff perform?*

You may assume that all your employees have good enough basic skills (reading, writing, numeracy and oral communication) to fulfil their jobs. But, on closer inspection, this may not actually turn out to be the case. One survey, conducted by The Basic Skills Agency, asked employers to what extent, if any, they thought that basic skills problems among their staff affected how well they did their jobs. The percentages of employers saying, for each of several grades of staff, that such shortages 'greatly' or 'somewhat' affected how well employees undertake the duties expected of them, are shown below.

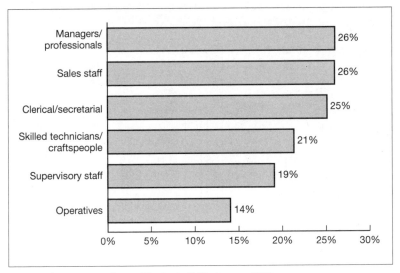

Source: The Cost to Industry, The Basic Skills Agency, 1993

■ *How important are basic skills?*

Whilst employees with poor basic skills can obviously be an issue, this does not necessarily mean that many companies actually consider basic skills to be an important issue for them. So is this a subject that is often glossed over or ignored? Or is there a growing awareness of the importance of basic skills? In this survey, managers were asked how much importance their company places on basic skills. The chart overleaf shows what percentage of managers gave each of the most common responses (a great deal, a little, it depends on the grade of staff) for each skill area (reading, writing, numeracy, oral communication).

TRAINING

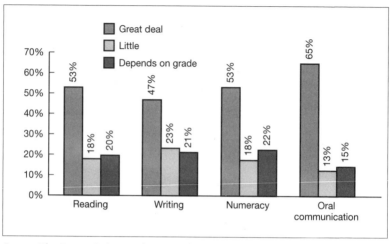

Source: The Cost to Industry, The Basic Skills Agency, 1993

■ *How many companies have a formal policy concerning basic skills?*

There seems to be a general admission that basic skills are an important issue. But how many companies have actually taken action on this to the extent of developing a formal policy?

- If you have no formal policy, you are one of many companies that have not addressed the issue in this way – 71% of those surveyed, in fact.

Source: The Cost to Industry, The Basic Skills Agency, 1993

■ *How many companies offer basic skills training?*

Again, this seems to be an area where concern over basic skills does not show to its full extent in practice. However, if you are considering offering such training, then you will not be the first to think of this – 39% of companies do provide some basic skills training for their staff.

- This training most commonly deals with oral communication skills (in 74% of cases).

- Numeracy is the next most popular area, addressed in 61% of cases.

- 56% of such training is aimed at writing skills.

- Only 41% of basic skills training programmes cover reading skills.

- 68% of companies offering basic skills training offer it to all staff – only 32% limit the training to certain grades.

Source: The Cost to Industry, The Basic Skills Agency, 1993

■ *What are the effects of basic skills deficiencies?*

Basic skills shortages would not be much of an issue if they did not actually affect the running of the company. At first it may seem that so long as staff have the skills required to do their jobs, then there is no problem. But is it really that simple? In the Basic Skills Agency survey, managers were asked which effects they thought basic skills shortages had on their company (they were allowed to indicate more than one effect).

- 57% said that they thought that basic skills shortages had no effect on their company.

- 25%, however, said that basic skills deficiencies ment that they had to recruit externally, rather than internally, for some positions.

- 21% said that such shortages led to a lack of flexibility among workers.

- And 5% felt that basic skills shortages made many staff leave because they could not cope, and hence increased staff turnover.

The survey also asked respondents to indicate whether they agreed or disagreed, strongly or somewhat, with several statements concerning the effects of basic skills shortages. These statements were: 'Poor basic skills contribute to reduced efficiency', 'Poor basic skills contribute to poor image with customers', 'Poor basic skills mean the workforce is unable to adapt quickly to changes in technology', and 'Poor basic skills contribute to higher costs'. The percentage of managers responding in each way to each statement is shown overleaf.

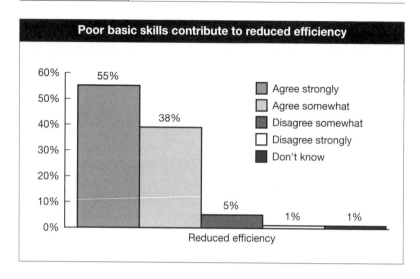

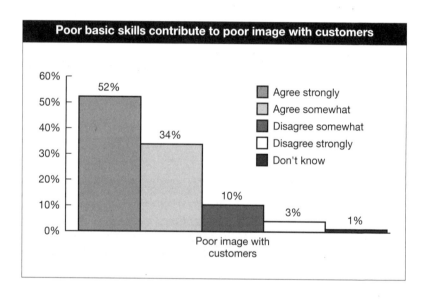

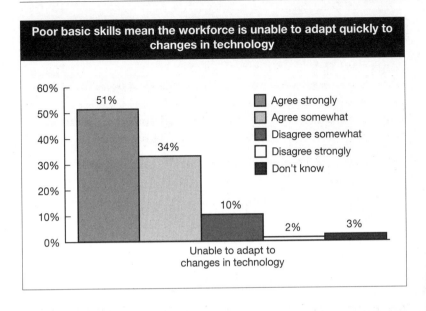

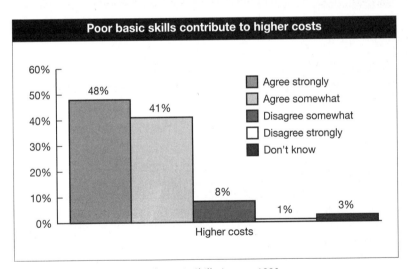

Source: The Cost to Industry, The Basic Skills Agency, 1993

■ *Is the lack of basic skills any greater in Britain than elsewhere?*

People aged 16 to 60 in seven different countries were asked 12 basic maths questions by researchers. Respondents were allowed to use pencil and paper, but not calculators. Questions were kept fairly simple – examples were 'what is left over if you take 2.43 from 5?', and 'what is five-sixths of 300?'. Britain came bottom of the class:

- Only 20% of those questioned in the UK got all 12 answers right; 24% scored 5 or less.

- This compares with Japan, where 43% scored a perfect 12, and only 5% scored 5 or less.

- Australia came next to bottom – but still put Britain to shame with 33% scoring 12, and 15% scoring 5 or less.

- The other four countries – Holland, France, Sweden and Denmark – all had fewer than 10% in the 5 or less category.

Source: International Numeracy Survey, The Basic Skills Agency, January 1997

APPROACHES TO TRAINING

■ *How much unofficial training do people usually receive?*

Aside from formal training schemes and induction procedures, there are often areas of work in which some employees may find they need a little extra guidance, or some brief explanation to clarify aspects of what they are doing. But is this an area which normally takes care of itself, or is there room for improvement? One survey asked respondents how true it was that their supervisor 'helps employees to learn to do their job better'.

- This statement was said to be very true by 24% of those surveyed.
- Another 35% said that it was true.
- For 41% of employees, however, their supervisor did not help them to learn in this way.

Source: Employee Commitment and the Skills Revolution, Policy Studies Institute, 1993

■ How much training do young people receive?

Training for adult workers is a well-researched area, but what if you employ younger workers? What levels of training do under-18s normally receive from their place of work (if they have one)? The chart below shows what proportion of young workers in each group (13–15, 16–18 in full-time education, 16–18 not in full-time education) received training for their job.

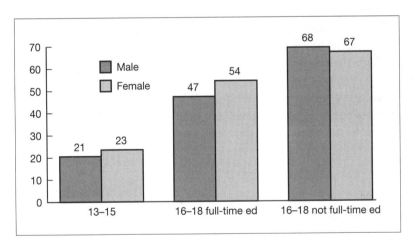

Source: Employment Gazette, April 1995

■ How many companies are aware of the various training initiatives?

Do you know about all the main initiatives to encourage training? Awareness has grown substantially in the last few years. However, some initiatives are better known than others:

235

Awareness of initiatives		
Training initiative	Percentage aware 1996	Percentage aware 1995
Youth credits	85%	37%
GNVQs	82%	72%
NVQs and SVQs	93%	88%
Investors in People	78%	66%
National Targets for Education and Training	31%	–

Source: Skill Needs in Britain, 1996, Public Attitudes Surveys Ltd research for the Department for Education and Employment

■ *What are the key managerial skills?*

If you are involved in assessing managerial ability, then you will know how complex a task it can be. One report attempted to find a path through this maze by discovering what language is most commonly used in relation to managerial skills. In particular, its authors conducted a survey of documents relating to managerial skills assessment and looked for the most commonly used words or phrases. If you are interested to know what defines a manager, here is a list of those words and phrases which were used in 25% of documents or more.

- Oral communication
- Leadership
- Judgement
- Initiative
- Organising
- Communication
- Motivation
- Analytical skills.

Source: What Makes a Manager?, Institute of Manpower Studies, 1988

16-18 year olds

■ *Is the pattern of training for 16-18 year olds changing?*

Rising participation in full-time education has led 16 year olds to swap work-based vocational training for academic study, according to research from the Policy Studies Institute. This examined a series of national cohort studies, to provide for the first time an overall picture of the choices young people make after the age of 16. It found that:

- Between 1989 and 1992, the overall proportion of young people in vocational training fell by 5%.

- Despite the growth of vocational qualifications, the proportion of young people getting formal work-based training from employers or government schemes shrank from 32% to 20% between 1989 and 1992.

- This 12% fall was off-set by a growth of only 7% in the proportion taking vocational courses in schools and colleges, producing a net reduction of 5% of the age group receiving vocational education or training.

Source: Education and Training for 16–18 Year Olds, Joan Payne, Yuan Cheng and Sharon Witherspoon, Policy Studies Institute, 1997

■ *Are more young people taking mathematics and the physical sciences?*

There is still a gender gap in these subjects:

- In 1991, only 40% of young women in their first year of A-level studies took at least one maths or science subject, compared with 56% of young men.

- Even with the science, there was a marked divide between the 'masculine' physical sciences and the 'feminine' life sciences.

- Single-sex schools helped reduce gender types: 26% of girls from all-girl schools took mathematics compared with only 21% of female candidates from mixed schools. Girls from single-sex schools also got better grades in GCSE physical sciences and maths than their counterparts in mixed schools.

Source: Education and Training for 16–18 Year Olds, Joan Payne, Yuan Cheng and Sharon Witherspoon, Policy Studies Institute, 1997

TRAINING

■ Which training initiatives provide the most formal job training?

By 1992, Youth Training (YT) provided three quarters of all formal job training received by 16–17 year olds, although the number of places on YT fell in step with the proportion of 16 year olds entering the labour market.

Source: Education and Training for 16–18 Year Olds, Joan Payne, Yuan Cheng and Sharon Witherspoon, Policy Studies Institute, 1997

NVQs and SVQs

■ Who assesses S/NVQ candidates?

If you are considering using SVQs or NVQs in your training scheme, then you will have to decide whether to have the assessment made by one of your own employees or whether to use an external assessor. One factor that may influence your decision here is which is the most common approach to S/NVQ assessment.

- Of employers who are aware of NVQs/SVQs, 19% said that some of their employees were training to become workplace assessors.

- 22% said that they had engaged an outside organisation to assess their employees.

Source: Skill Needs in Britain 1994, IFF research for Employment Department

■ How often are S/NVQs used in recruitment procedures or for appraisals?

One advantage of using formal qualifications in your training procedures is that you have an objective criterion by which to judge staff. So if you are an NVQ-friendly company then you can use these qualifications for more than just training. And if you do decide to do this, then you certainly will not be going out on a limb.

- Of employers who are aware of NVQs and SVQs, 60% use them either during recruitment or during staff appraisal, or both.

- Of all employers aware of S/NVQs, 56% use them in recruitment.
- 34% use them for staff assessment.
- This mean that 30% use them in both of these procedures.

Source: Skill Needs in Britain 1994, IFF research for Employment Department

■ To what extent are S/NVQs used for selecting candidates?

The Scottish and National Vocational Qualifications have received quite a lot of publicity, but when it comes to recruitment and selection how much currency do they really have? One survey of senior managers asked whether they or their companies use S/NVQs in the selection procedure. The table below shows the responses obtained.

Use of S/NVQs	Senior managers	Companies
Not used in selection	53%	39%
Used in some job applications	29%	34%
Used for all job applications	3%	4%

Source: Training for Recovery? Institute of Management, 1993

■ Why are S/NVQs not used?

S/NVQs are becoming quite popular. Yet there are still many companies which do not use them. To get a clear picture of the situation, you will also have to hear their side of the story. So what are the main reasons for not using S/NVQs?

- 23% of companies who do not use them said that this was because they did not match companies' requirements.
- Another 24% said they did not match individuals' needs.

Source: Skill Needs in Britain 1996, Public Attitudes Surveys Ltd research for the Department for Education and Employment

■ *What are the main advantages of implementing S/NVQs for your business?*

Many employers report significant benefits in using S/NVQs. But if you are considering adopting this practice, then you will probably want a clearer idea of the sort of benefits that you can expect from doing so. One report found that the use of NVQs provides a framework for:

Auditing the skills already possessed by the workforce
Targeting the training needed
Evaluating completed training in terms of its contribution towards defined business objectives
Recruiting, retaining and motivating staff.

Source: Training – The Business Case, Confederation of British Industry, 1993

■ *How well-known are S/NVQs?*

NVQs and SVQs have been well publicised through many channels, but a system like this depends, to some extent, on being a universal currency. So how many companies know about S/NVQs, and how much do they know? One survey conducted in 1993 asked senior managers whether they were familiar with S/NVQs, had only heard of them, or were not sure.

- 41% of managers said that they were familiar with NVQs and SVQs.

- A further 43% had heard of them.

- 14% had not heard of them, and 2% were not sure if they knew what they were.

Source: Training for Recovery? Institute of Management, 1993

■ *How widely used are S/NVQs?*

So, by 1993 most managers had heard of S/NVQs. But this is a long way from actually using them, and creating the universal currency that is required. So, to what extent are these qualifications actually used by businesses?

● S/NVQs seem very popular with large businesses, but less so with smaller organisations.

● At the time of this survey (1994), 44% of large companies (over 500 employees) were using S/NVQs.

● A further 34% of companies of this size anticipated using them.

● On the other hand, only 6% of small companies (under 50 employees) were using S/NVQs.

● Only another 14% of such companies anticipated using them.

● In the country as a whole, it was estimated that 28% of employees were in a company that used S/NVQs.

Source: National and Scottish Vocational Qualifications: Early Indications of Employers' Take-Up and Use, Institute of Manpower Studies, 1994

In an earlier survey, this time specifically covering senior managers, respondents were asked if their organisation used S/NVQs as part of its training programme.

● 61% of senior managers said that their company did not use S/NVQs as part of its training programme.

● 28% said that they did use S/NVQs.

● 11% did not know or were not sure about the use of S/NVQs.

Source: Training for Recovery? Institute of Management, 1993

■ *For what level of staff are S/NVQs used?*

S/NVQs are available for every grade of employee, but not surprisingly some of them are more widely used than others. So what grades of staff are most likely to use S/NVQs? The graph below shows what percentage of organisations using S/NVQs use them at the specified staff level.

TRAINING

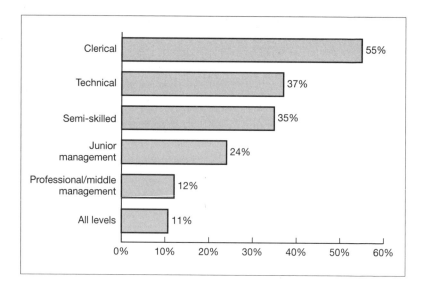

- Despite this imbalance in the use of S/NVQs, 42% of senior managers believed that they are suitable for training at all levels.
- Only 13% said that they are only suitable for low skill jobs.

Source: Training for Recovery? Institute of Management, 1993

■ *What do the participants think of S/NVQs?*

Between March and May 1996 the Policy Studies Institute surveyed 800 individuals who had completed a vocational qualification. The research aimed to explore individuals' knowledge and understanding of S/NVQs and their motivation and incentive to take them up. The study showed that there is now a high level of awareness of S/NVQs as they have become more widespread:

- 99% of respondents had heard of S/NVQs.
- 89% knew what the initials stood for.
- A sizeable majority were satisfied with the training they received, what they learnt and the relevance of them for their job requirements.

Source: Individual Take-up of N/SVQs – Stimuli and Obstacles, Policy Studies Institute research for the Department for Education and Employment, 1996

■ *Do participants understand the purpose, structure and assessment arrangements of S/NVQs?*

The extent and nature of individuals' knowledge about S/NVQs varied:

- Individuals who were or had been pursuing an S/NVQ were significantly more knowledgeable than those involved with another type of qualification.

- Despite this, two out of three respondents either did not know or were confused about the fact that S/NVQs can be attained without doing a taught course.

Source: Individual Take-up of N/SVQs – Stimuli and Obstacles, Policy Studies Institute research for the Department for Education and Employment, 1996

■ *Why do people take S/NVQs?*

Individuals had a very wide range of reasons for deciding to do a qualification. Most often quoted were interest in the subject area and the desire to improve their labour market prospects and opportunities. These remained popular despite people's employment status. The other reasons varied by employment status:

- 57% of the unemployed respondents embarked on their qualification to help get a job, compared with only 11% of the employed.

- 28% of the employed were hoping the qualification would lead to a better job, compared with 12% of the unemployed.

- 19% of the employed hoped the qualification would enable them to perform their job better, compared with 9% of the unemployed.

Source: Individual Take-up of N/SVQs – Stimuli and Obstacles, Policy Studies Institute research for the Department for Education and Employment, 1996

■ *Who chooses which qualification each individual takes?*

Do you tell trainees which qualification to take, or do you let them choose for themselves? The employee appears to have considerable control over the original decision to take a qualification:

- One third of employees chose their qualification by themselves.
- A further quarter had their qualification chosen for them by their employers.

For the remainder, the decision was taken jointly.

However, when it comes to subsequent qualifications, it would appear that employers are in the driving seat:

- Almost three out of four respondents stated that they had no choice over which qualification they subsequently took.
- Very few individuals (4%) were in a position to choose between an S/NVQ and some other sort of vocational qualification.

Source: *Individual Take-up of N/SVQs – Stimuli and Obstacles*, Policy Studies Institute research for the Department for Education and Employment, 1996

Investors In People

■ *How well known is the Investors In People initiative?*

Investors In People (IIP) is a national standard for employers, and as such could well be used as a goal for your organisation. But there is no point boasting about an award that no one has heard of. So, how many senior managers have actually heard of it?

- 29% of senior managers were familiar with the IIP initiative.
- 31% had heard of it.
- 38% had not heard of it at all, and 2% were not sure whether they had.

Source: *Training for Recovery?* Institute of Management, 1993

■ *How many organisations are trying to achieve the Investors In People standard?*

Having a national standard, of course, does not count for very much if no one is trying to meet the standard. If your company is thinking of dedicating itself to achieving this award, then you will probably want to know how many other companies are doing the same. So how many companies are aiming to become Investors In People? The Institute of Management asked this question of the senior managers it surveyed.

Already achieved the IIP standard	1%
Committed to achieving the IIP standard	13%
Planning to achieve the IIP award at some time	15%
No plans to achieve the IIP award	42%
Not sure of where they stood on the subject	28%

Source: Training for Recovery? Institute of Management, 1993

■ *What are the main advantages of achieving the Investors In People award?*

If you are considering your position on the IIP award, then you will also want to know what sort of benefit you might achieve from acquiring it. The following figures show what are perceived to be the top three benefits of the award, with percentages showing what proportion of respondents considered this to be the main benefit:

Benefit	Percentage of companies
Enables structured evaluation of training	30%
Provides a coherent approach for employee development	15%
Ensures a more stable and motivated workforce	11%

Source: Training – The Business Case, Confederation of British Industry, 1993

Competencies

In 1994, Benchmark Research performed a survey for The Coverdale Organisation on the subject of competencies. The survey covered 200 companies each with over 200 staff, all of whom who were already using the competencies approach, as are some 50% of large organisations. The definition of a competency provided by the survey was: 'The application of skills, knowledge, attitudes or behaviour which distinguish SUPERIOR performance from AVERAGE performance'. A total of 89% of respondents agreed with this definition. This section presents some of the main findings of the report. It is worth noting that the report was commissioned by Coverdale, a consultancy which promotes the use of the competencies approach, and it is therefore unlikely that the results of the survey will have been presented in a way which undermines the value of this system.

■ *What are the benefits of a competencies approach?*

Before undertaking any new initiative, it helps to know what the outcome of it is likely to be, and whether this corresponds to what you are hoping to achieve. So the first thing you will want to know about competencies is what effects they have had on organisations that have adopted this approach to personnel management. The survey asked respondents to identify the main benefits achieved through this approach. The percentage of respondents indicating each advantage is shown below.

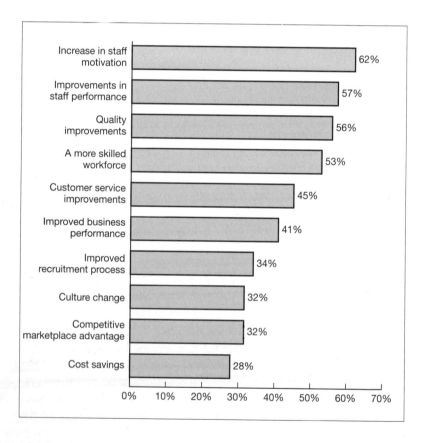

- Only 7% of respondents did not indicate any benefits.

Source: Competencies: The Current State of Play, Benchmark Research Ltd, 1994

■ *Do competencies really work?*

It is easy for personnel managers who have introduced a new system to say that any improvement in staff relations or performance is due to this initiative. This doesn't mean that it is necessarily the case. If you are considering this approach, then you will no doubt want to know how reliable these opinions are. So what evidence did the respondents to the survey have?

- 37% of respondents knew of no evidence to prove that the benefits experienced were directly linked to competencies.
- However, 63% of those surveyed said that they did have direct evidence of the benefits of the new approach.

Source: Competencies: The Current State of Play, Benchmark Research Ltd, 1994

TRAINING

■ *What are the main difficulties with competencies?*

Before converting your entire approach to personnel management it would, naturally, help to know what problems you can expect when you move over to the new system. The graph overleaf shows what percentage of respondents, when prompted, cited each difficulty as being one that they encountered when switching to a competencies approach.

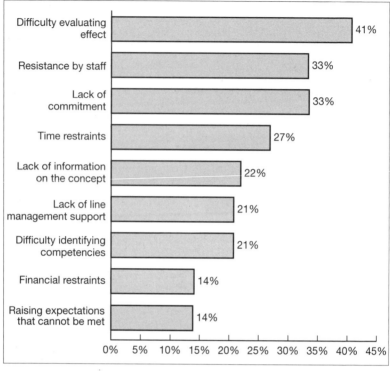

Source: *Competencies: The Current State of Play*, Benchmark Research Ltd, 1994

■ *What factors make a competencies programme successful?*

So, if you know the potential benefits of the system you may be introducing, and also some of the pitfalls that you will want to avoid, the next question is how you can achieve the former and prevent the latter. The Benchmark survey asked what factors were considered to be most important in contributing to the success of a competencies programme. The five most common responses are shown below, together with the percentage of respondents citing each one.

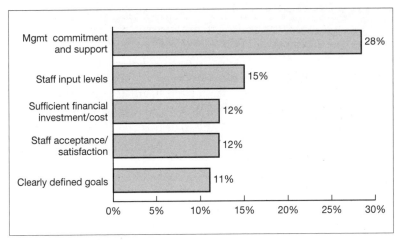

Source: Competencies: The Current State of Play, Benchmark Research Ltd, 1994

■ *How are competencies used?*

A new system such as the competencies approach can be used in many ways – for performance appraisal or during recruitment, for instance. But if you are planning to take on this initiative, then it might help to know how it is most often used by companies which are already using it. The list below indicates what percentage of companies surveyed use competencies for each application.

To help individual development	84%
Part of performance appraisal system	75%
To improve business performance	69%
To encourage team development	64%
Part of the promotion process	58%
To align personnel practice with business needs	55%
During the recruitment process	47%
To bring about a culture change	40%
As part of the remuneration process	31%

Source: Competencies: The Current State of Play, Benchmark Research Ltd, 1994

■ *At what grade are competencies being used?*

Of course, a system such as the competencies approach does not have to be introduced at every level of your company; it could be used solely for managers, or for shopfloor staff. However, most systems like this are more relevant to certain occupational groups than others. One way to gauge this relevance is to look at what groups the competencies approach is normally used for. The chart below shows what percentage of companies using competencies use them for each occupation group.

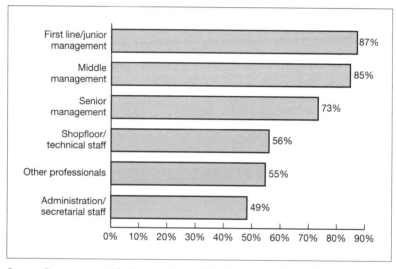

Source: Competencies: The Current State of Play, Benchmark Research Ltd, 1994

■ *How are competencies identified?*

One of the fundamental aspects of developing a competencies pro-gramme is to define the competencies that you are identifying and evaluating. There are, naturally, several well-established competencies, but since every company uses competencies in a different way, it can also be helpful to define competencies in a way that is specific to your needs. But are such definitions usually developed specifically for the company, or do most companies simply go along with the standard formula?

- 15% of companies identify competencies on the basis of a well-established, pre-defined list.

- 58% of companies develop an entirely bespoke set of competencies specific to their own needs.

- 26% of companies favour a combination of these two approaches.

Source: Competencies: The Current State of Play, Benchmark Research Ltd, 1994

TRAINING FORMATS

Training materials

■ *Where do training materials come from?*

There is an extremely large market for training materials, but it is also possible to produce training materials in-house. But how real is this alternative? How many companies do actually use some externally provided training materials? According to one survey, 91% of companies use at least some materials supplied by external training organisations or consultancies.

Source: Training Video Survey, Benchmark Research Ltd, 1995

Video

■ *How widely are training videos used?*

Videos have been one of the most popular training products for many years, and they are still widely used, but to what extent? If you use training videos a few times a year, are you spending more than most, or are you making less use of this medium than others?

- 40% of companies use training videos every week.
- Videos are used on a monthly basis by 30% of companies.
- Only 20% of organisations use training videos less than once a month.

Source: Training Video Survey, Benchmark Research Ltd, 1995

■ *How many organisations have a training video library?*

Training videos can be used over and over again, and if this is what you are intending to do, then it may be cheaper to buy the videos than rent them. But how common is this in practise?

- Over 50% of companies have a central/corporate video library.
- One third of these libraries (17% of all companies) have more than 100 videos on their shelves.

Source: Training Video Survey, Benchmark Research Ltd, 1995

Computer-based training

■ *How widely is computer-based training used?*

The rapid development of computer technology has had an effect on many things, including training programmes. With the ever-expanding base of CD-Rom and CDi machines, more and more computer-based training packages are becoming available. If you haven't tried any of these yet, are you behind the times?

- Over 50% of companies use, or have used, computer-based delivery technologies.
- More than 25% of companies feel that these are now competing with videos for training spend.
- Only 20% of companies, however, say that videos are an outdated delivery format.

Source: Training Video Survey, Benchmark Research Ltd, 1995

CAREER DEVELOPMENT

■ *How many organisations offer career guidance?*

Career guidance can be a valuable resource for staff. How many companies actually provide this service for their employees? If you have no such facility in your organisation, is there a strong enough precedent to justify reviewing this situation? According to one survey, only 32% of organisations offer formal career guidance.

Source: Skill Needs in Britain 1994, IFF research for Employment Department

■ *How much training is part of a long-term development plan?*

Training and career development are very different things. It may be worth considering whether you would like to be giving training that is part of a longer-term plan. But is career development common practice, or is it only really available to a select few? One survey of supervisors found that not only had 50% received no training in the last year, but that only 41% of the training received had been given as part of a longer-term development programme.

Source: People, Supervision and Profit, Confederation of British Industry, 1992

■ *To what extent should individuals be responsible for their own development?*

It used to be the case that when you joined a company, you were stepping on to the first rung of a career ladder. The training and pro-motion system within the company would then slowly lead you to the top. But in today's business world, with so much emphasis on personal development and transferable skills, this is happening for fewer and fewer people. So does this mean that people need to look out for their own interests in being trained, rather than expecting their company to fulfil all their requirements? A total of 84% of senior managers think so, saying that 'individuals will increasingly need to take responsibility for their own development'.

Source: Management Development to the Millennium, Institute of Management, 1993

TRAINING

253

■ How can individuals be encouraged to take responsibility for their own development?

Personal development can be an important issue for companies, but without individual initiative there is only so much that you can do. This is especially relevant for those who are not permanent, full-time staff. So if you want flexible staff to take care of their own personal development, what steps can be taken to encourage them? One survey asked employers what were the most effective steps that could be taken to encourage flexible workers to take more responsibility for their own training. Respondents ranked the suggestions from 1 to 5, with 1 as the most effective, and the average ranking is shown in the following chart.

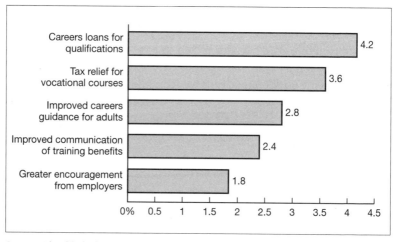

Source: Flexible Labour Markets; Who Pays for Training?, Confederation of British Industry, 1994

■ *What are the main reasons for individuals engaging in learning?*

Many individuals take part in learning programmes other than their company's standard training. But what are the main motivators for doing this? If your employees are taking this option, are they likely to be fighting for promotion, or is it more probable that they are doing it to improve their enjoyment of their jobs? The chart below shows the most commonly given reasons for engaging in learning, together with the percentage of learners who cite each reason.

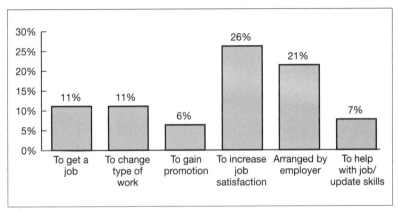

Source: Individual Commitment to Learning, Social and Community Planning Research for the Employment Department, 1995

TRAINING

255

HEALTH AND SAFETY

ACCIDENTS

■ *Are most accidents investigated?*

The law requires that major injuries are reported to the Health and Safety Executive (HSE). Yet the HSE does not necessarily investigate all accidents reported to them. So what proportion of accidents are investigated?

	1994–1995	1996–1997
Major injuries reported	24,214	50,000
Major injuries investigated	3,713	2,158
Percentage investigated	15.3%	4%

So 96% of serious workplace accidents in 1996–97 were not investigated – including 75% of amputations and 94% of blindings.

Source: Health and Safety Executive figures, published by the Institute for Employment Rights

■ *Is the number of workplace accidents increasing or decreasing?*

We all aim to reduce accidents at work, but we don't always succeed. Accidents and deaths at work increased significantly in 1996–97. Frequently, those affected were self-employed, with little or no experience, and with little health and safety training.

- Deaths rose by 25%.

- Serious accidents doubled in number.

- Violence in the workplace accounted for 2 deaths, 697 major injuries, and 3,980 injuries of sufficient seriousness to keep the victims away from work.

Source: Institute for Employment Rights

■ *Do prosecutions for workplace accidents lead to convictions?*

A total of 1,600 prosecutions in 1996–97 resulted in 80% convictions. However, sentences varied. A construction company was fined only £345 and £50 costs when a new recruit to the firm fell to his death from an unprotected ledge.

Source: Health and Safety Executive figures, published by the Institute for Employment Rights

WORK-RELATED ILLNESSES

■ *How many people are affected by work-related illnesses?*

If you are finding that an increasing number of your absentees claim that work has made them ill, are you alone? It would appear not:

● Each year an estimated 2.2 million people record that their ill health has been caused, or made worse by, work.

Source: Good Health is Good Business, HSE Books, 1996

Stress

■ *What proportion of workers are highly stressed?*

Before taking action on a problem such as stress, it is worth finding out how large a concern it really is. One way to do this is to find out if it is a concern in a wider context than just your company – in the country as a whole, for example. Such nation-wide figures are also useful for benchmarking the results of a stress audit, should you ever undertake one. In one survey, workers were given four statements and asked to rate how frequently they applied, using a six point scale ranging from 'all the time' to 'never'. The statements were:

After I leave my work I keep worrying about job problems.

I find it difficult to unwind at the end of a workday.

I feel used up at the end of a workday.

My job makes me feel quite exhausted by the end of a workday.

The survey analysis classed a highly stressed person as any respondent who responded to one or more questions with 'most of the time' or more frequently:

- Overall, 31% of employees were considered to be highly stressed on this measure.

- This figure was virtually identical for men and women.

- Managers and professionals were the most highly stressed group, with 39% of them falling into this category.

Source: Employee Commitment and The Skills Revolution, Policy Studies Institute, 1993

■ *What actions are most often taken to deal with the problem of stress?*

Stress can be a very real problem for many workers in today's business environment. It cannot be dealt with by sending round memos telling staff to 'chill out'. However, many companies do take some action on this issue. If you are also considering taking such action, then you may want to know what the most common approaches are.

- 60% of companies give consideration to job design, training and communication as ways of preventing a stressful workplace.

- Counselling, employee assistance programmes or stress helplines are provided by 44% of companies.

- 24% of companies follow some procedures for detecting stress among their employees.

Source: Working for your Health, Confederation of British Industry, 1993

■ What problems do you face in dealing with stress at work?

Organisations face various 'problem areas' as they attempt to deal with stress at work, according to a recent survey. Jill Earnshaw is a lecturer in employment law at UMIST, and she comments that:

- Personnel professionals have to make difficult decisions about the stage at which they dismiss those who cannot cope, and about how people deal with inherently stressful jobs.

- If a company sends personnel to visit, then it could be accused of harassment and making the stress worse, but if the company does not keep the stressed employee in the picture, then there could also be problems.

Source: 'Managing Stress', Jill Earnshaw's speech at the IPD National Conference, 23 October 1997

■ What can you do to reduce the risk of stress-related illness?

Jill Earnshaw suggests a list of preventive measures, starting with changing the employer's approach to recruitment. Although refusing to take an employee on the grounds of stress-related illness might breach the new Disability Discrimination Act, it is perfectly reasonable for an employer to ask what caused the problem in the past. Jill Earnshaw also recommends:

1 Restructuring jobs

2 Effective policies against bullying and harassment

3 Training for line managers

4 Matching people to jobs

5 Reviewing security arrangements

6 Examining the corporate structure.

In general there needs to be a shift away from the attitude which says 'It's your problem, but we'll help you with a bit of counselling' towards an approach which says 'It's our problem as an organisation, and we should do something to tackle it before it lands on your shoulders'.

Source: 'Managing Stress', Jill Earnshaw's speech at the IPD National Conference, 23 October 1997

HEALTH AND SAFETY

■ *How many companies undertake health initiatives to reduce the risk of coronary heart disease in their staff?*

Coronary heart disease is one of the major causes of death in Britain. Many companies see it as part of their job to help reduce the risk of coronary heart disease in their employees. If you want to take action on this issue, you will be far from alone – 28% of companies undertake such initiatives. But if you are thinking of undertaking such an initiative, it helps to know what are the most common ways to promote this issue in the workplace.

Companies undertaking initiatives to promote healthy diets	29%
Companies undertaking initiatives to reduce high blood pressure	29%
Companies undertaking initiatives to promote exercise	24%
Companies placing some restrictions on the availability of alcohol in the workplace	78%

Source: Working for your Health, Confederation of British Industry, 1993

■ *To what extent does stress contribute to sickness absence?*

Stress has been shown to have many physiological effects, some of which could contribute to absence from work due to sickness. But if your staff are experiencing a lot of stress, to what extent does this actually affect their time off work? It is impossible to measure this relationship accurately, but 65% of employers do think that stress contributes to the absence levels for white collar workers.

Source: Counting Costs to Keep Competitive, Confederation of British Industry, 1994

Noise

■ *Are many employees exposed to excessive noise?*

Sadly, yes – and the number suffering is growing. If your employees have to put up with a lot of noise, it could do them permanent damage.

- The 1990 labour force survey showed that 100,000 suffered hearing damage due to excessive noise in the workplace.

- By 1994, civil liability claims had risen dramatically; 80% of occupational health claims and 50% of awards were hearing-related.

This is despite the HSE limit of noise levels, and stringent regulations on ear-protection.

Source: Good Health is Good Business, HSE Books, 1996

Other illnesses

■ *What other work-related illnesses cause problems?*

Musculoskeletal disorders are the largest problem:

- In 1990, 5.4 million working days were lost in England and Wales alone as a result of musculoskeletal disorders.

- 600,000 cases a year are caused by work.

Source: Good Health is Good Business, HSE Books, 1996

■ *What is the cost of work-related illness?*

A CBI survey looked at the overall costs of sickness, and the costs of work-related illnesses. It found that:

- Sickness accounts for 3.5% of working time a year – so costs £13 billion a year.

- Inefficiencies arising from stress cost up to 10% of GNP – thus £3.7 billion.

HEALTH AND SAFETY

- Back pain in the UK accounts for 106 million lost working days – so £5.2 billion loss. This figure has increased five fold since 1987.

- Absence due to alcohol- and tobacco-related illnesses costs £5 billion a year.

Source: Confederation of British Industry Employment Survey, CBI, 1996

There is, of course, another potential cost of work-related illness. Workers increasingly sue employers for the personal cost of the illness:

- In a survey of affiliated members in 1994, the TUC found that members had been awarded £335 million in damages.

Source: TUC Members Survey, 1995

SMOKING

■ *How many companies have non-smoking policies?*

Smoking can be a hard-fought issue, both on health and safety grounds, and by non-smokers who simply want to breathe relatively clean air. Smokers, on the other hand, often do not take too kindly to being forced to indulge their habit only in certain specified places. But if you are thinking of introducing smoking restrictions in your workplace, then it seems that you will be joining the majority. One survey found that 85% of companies have at least some smoking restrictions in force at their workplace.

Source: Working for your Health, Confederation of British Industry, 1993

■ *How are smoking policies designed?*

Of course, smokers may not take it kindly if complaints by non-smokers are greeted with an outright ban on cigarettes anywhere in the building. This is something that most companies seem to appreciate, and smokers are usually given a say. The same survey found that 67% of companies with smoking restrictions agreed these in consultation with staff or staff representatives.

Source: Working for your Health, Confederation of British Industry, 1993

■ *How many companies have a helpline for quitters?*

There are already national helplines for people who are trying to quit smoking but cannot break the addiction. Could you take such action into your own hands? Some dedicated companies have set up their own helpline or counselling service for smokers trying to quit. In fact, this is not as rare as one might think, with 33% of companies offering these services.

Source: Working for your Health, Confederation of British Industry, 1993

ALCOHOL

■ *Is alcohol consumption really a problem?*

Alcohol consumption at work can be a serious problem, but before you launch any costly initiatives, you will want to consider whether it really is, or could be, a problem for you. So how many companies do actually have a problem with alcohol in the workplace? One survey asked senior directors, personnel directors, and workers in general how significant a problem they thought alcohol was in their workplace. The following chart shows what proportion of each group thought that the problem was widespread, moderate, only applied to a few employees, or was not a problem at all.

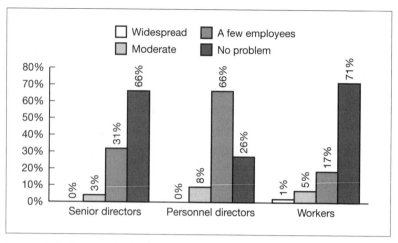

Source: Attitudes towards Alcohol in the Workplace, MORI for the Health Education Authority, 1995

■ *What problems can alcohol consumption create?*

If you want to act upon the issue of alcohol in your workplace, or if you have not yet decided whether to do so, then it might help you know what sort of problems alcohol can cause in your workplace. The next chart shows a list of such problems, together with the proportion of personnel directors who said that their organisation encountered some alcohol problems, and who also said that they had encountered this particular problem.

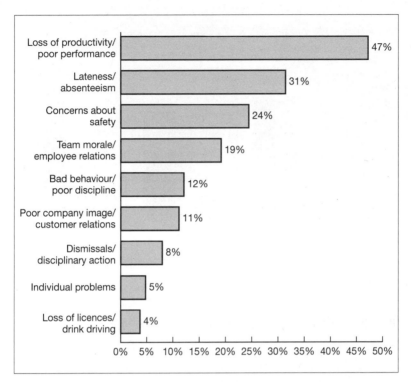

Loss of productivity/ poor performance	47%
Lateness/ absenteeism	31%
Concerns about safety	24%
Team morale/ employee relations	19%
Bad behaviour/ poor discipline	12%
Poor company image/ customer relations	11%
Dismissals/ disciplinary action	8%
Individual problems	5%
Loss of licences/ drink driving	4%

0% 5% 10% 15% 20% 25% 30% 35% 40% 45% 50%

Source: Attitudes towards Alcohol in the Workplace, MORI for the Health Education Authority, 1995

HEALTH AND SAFETY

■ What attitude do most companies have to alcohol issues?

If you are reviewing your alcohol policy, then you might like to know what sort of policy most companies have in this area. The figures below show, for senior directors, personnel managers and all workers, what proportion say that there is a formal written policy on alcohol in their company, what proportion say that there is no policy but that drinking during working hours is discouraged, and what proportion say that their company has no clear policy on these issues. The figures also reveal discrepancies in perceptions of alcohol policies between these groups.

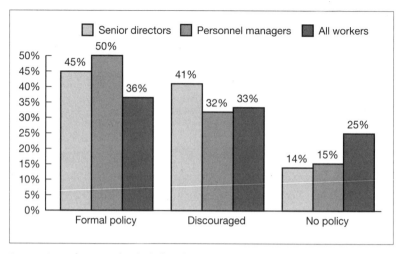

Source: *Attitudes towards Alcohol in the Workplace*, MORI for the Health Education Authority, 1995

■ What alcohol issues do formal policies cover?

If you are introducing or reviewing an alcohol policy in your company, then you will have to decide what aspects of drinking this policy will deal with. The figures below might help you in this task. They show the percentage of personnel directors with formal alcohol policies saying that this policy covers disciplinary issues, safety, and health concerns.

Issue	Percentage of personnel managers
Discipline	97%
Safety	87%
Health	90%
All three	79%

Source: *Attitudes towards Alcohol in the Workplace*, MORI for the Health Education Authority, 1995

■ *How effective are alcohol policies?*

It is one thing to have a formal policy on alcohol, but it is quite another for that policy to have a significant effect on staff behaviour. So what are the chances that introducing an alcohol policy will actually be an effective way of dealing with the issues?

● Overall, 37% of personnel directors consider their policy to be very effective, and another 52% consider it to be fairly effective. Only 8% consider it to be not very effective.

● Senior directors are much more optimistic, with 67% feeling that their policy is very effective and the other 33% considering it fairly effective.

● Workers in general seem to concur, with 66% saying that their company's policy is very effective, 22% describing it as fairly effective, and only 7% saying it is not very or not at all effective.

● Personnel directors in manufacturing companies are more optimistic than those in services – 57% consider their policies very effective, and 32% consider them fairly effective, as against 21% and 68% respectively for their service industry counterparts.

Source: Attitudes towards Alcohol in the Workplace, MORI for the Health Education Authority, 1995

■ *How many companies have bans on alcohol in the workplace?*

One measure that you could take to reduce the chance of encountering alcohol-related problems in your company is to ban alcohol either totally or partially from the workplace. But is this an extreme measure, or is there a significant precedent for such a ban? The next chart shows what proportion of senior directors, personnel directors and general workers reported a total or partial ban on alcohol in their workplace, or no ban at all.

HEALTH AND SAFETY

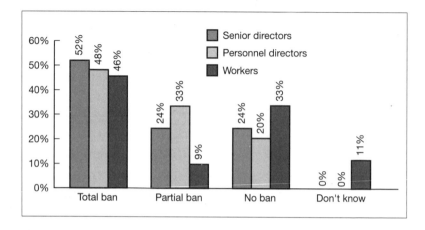

- Bans appear to be more common in larger companies, with 51% of personnel directors in organisations with over 10,000 employees reporting a total ban and 37% reporting a partial ban, as against 46% and 29% respectively for those in smaller companies.

- Also, 60% of personnel directors in the manufacturing sector report total bans and 37% report partial bans, whereas in the service sector only 39% report total bans and 30% report partial bans.

- 95% of personnel directors in companies operating such a ban said that it applied to all workers.

Source: Attitudes towards Alcohol in the Workplace, MORI for the Health Education Authority, 1995

■ *What proportion of companies provide information about alcohol?*

Another form of action that you can take on alcohol and related issues is simply to make information on the subject available to all your staff to make them aware of the issues involved. But is this really a measure worth taking, or is it generally not considered worthwhile? One way to gauge this is by seeing how many companies make such a provision. The next chart shows what proportion of senior directors, personnel directors and general workers reported that their company provides such information, or does not provide it, or that they did not know.

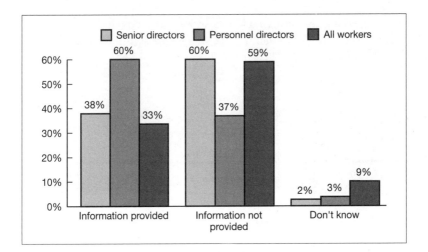

- This information seemed to be more widely available in the manufacturing sector, with 46% of senior directors and 63% of personnel directors saying that it was provided, as against 31% and 58% respectively in the service sector.

Source: Attitudes towards Alcohol in the Workplace, MORI for the Health Education Authority, 1995

■ How widely available are counselling services which deal with alcohol-related problems?

If your employees do have alcohol-related problems, then it might help them to go and see a counsellor. This is a service which your company could provide. But are such services commonly available, or would this be a very generous provision?

- 20% of personnel directors said that their company did not provide such a counselling service, and a further 1% were unsure.

- This means that 79% reported that their company did have such a service.

- 2% of respondents said that there was such a service available, but that they did not know whether it was internal or external.

- 55% of respondents said that they had an internal counselling service for this kind of problem, and 37% said that they had an external service.

HEALTH AND SAFETY

- This implies that at least 15% of those surveyed had both an internal and external counselling service dealing with these issues.

Source: Attitudes towards Alcohol in the Workplace, MORI for the Health Education Authority, 1995

HEALTH AND SAFETY MANAGEMENT

■ *Do companies pay enough attention to health and safety issues?*

It is all very well benchmarking your standards against those for the country as a whole, but whose standards are they? If you do meet these standards, does that mean that you are really doing enough? One survey asked senior directors and personnel managers, separately, whether they thought that their company paid too much, too little or the right amount of attention to health and safety issues.

- Only 1% of each group said that their company paid too much attention to health and safety.

- 90% of senior directors thought that they paid about the right amount of attention, but only 65% of personnel managers concurred with this.

- This means that while only 9% of senior directors felt that they paid too little attention to health and safety, one third (33%) of personnel managers were unsatisfied with their companies' policies.

Source: Attitudes towards Alcohol in the Workplace, MORI for the Health Education Authority, 1995

■ *How much do companies spend, on average, on health and safety management?*

If health and safety laws are copious and confusing, then what can be said about the guidelines that are laid out by the government and other organisations? Health and safety management can be time-consuming and expensive, so how much do companies usually spend in this area?

- The mean average spend on health and safety management is £262 per employee per year.
- The median average spend is only £117 per employee.
- This means that many companies do not spend as much as the 'average' amount of £262.

Source: Survey of Health and Safety Management in the UK, Performance Support International, 1994

■ What is the health and safety budget spent on?

If it is your job to oversee health and safety costs, then you may be interested to know how the average budget is distributed. One survey divided the costs into three areas – 'Personnel costs' of staff involved in health and safety (including salary, pension schemes, etc.); 'External invoiced costs' for equipment, materials, consultancy, external training etc.; 'Training costs' for personnel receiving internal training.

- Personnel costs were largest, accounting for 56% of the average health and safety budget.
- External invoiced costs took up 37% of the budget.
- Training costs were on average only 7% of the total.

Source: Survey of Health and Safety Management in the UK, Performance Support International, 1994

■ What are the major factors affecting health and safety costs?

So many things can make health and safety much more expensive, or much cheaper, than might be expected. In the Performance Support International survey, managers were asked how important they considered various factors to be. Each was rated on a scale from 0 (not important) to 5 (very important). The average scores were:

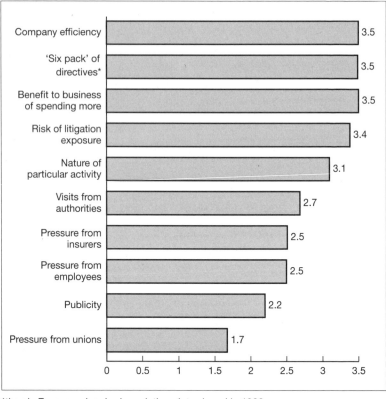

*the six European-inspired regulations introduced in 1993

Source: Survey of Health and Safety Management in the UK, Performance Support International, 1994

■ *What are the major problems confronting health and safety managers?*

Many things can obstruct efficient health and safety management, but some problems just will not go away. Performance Support International asked their respondents what they felt were their key concerns in this area. The answers were again on a scale of 0 (not a problem) to 5 (a key concern).

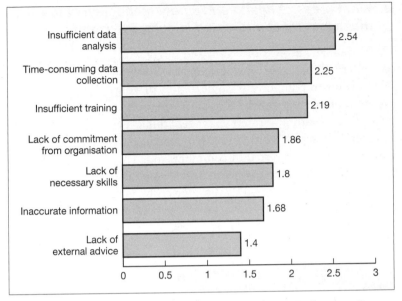

Source: Survey of Health and Safety Management in the UK, Performance Support International, 1994

■ To what extent are computer-based systems used for health and safety management?

Computers are taking over in many parts of the office environment, and there is a lot of health and safety software available. But before you computerise your entire health and safety system, you will probably want to know how many other companies have taken advantage of these technological developments.

- Only 37% of companies used any sort of computerised system for health and safety management.

- This figure was, not surprisingly, even lower in smaller companies – only 26% of companies under 200 employees used a computer-based system.

- Even in companies with over 1,500 employees, however, only 49% used computers for health and safety.

- Despite this, 93% of health and safety managers said that they would consider using a computer-based system for at least some aspect of their work.

Source: Survey of Health and Safety Management in the UK, Performance Support International, 1994

275

■ *What areas of health and safety management are managers most interested in computerising?*

There are many aspects of health and safety which can be effectively computerised, but some obviously have a higher priority than others. If you want to computerise some aspect of your health and safety system, but are unsure where to start, then you may want to know what other health and safety managers think. Performance Support International asked health and safety managers which areas of their work they were interested in computerising. The results show what proportion of managers were interested in computerising that area, and they are broken down as those given by large companies (over 1,500 employees) and those given by medium sized companies (200–1,500 employees).

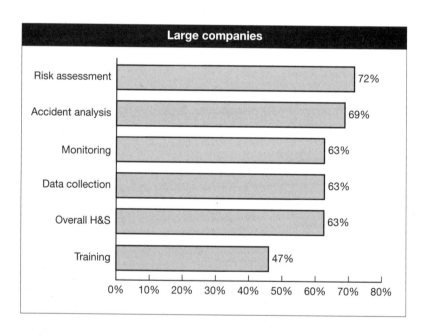

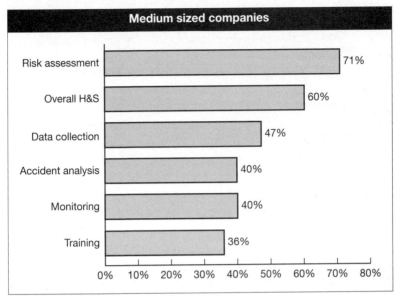

Source: Survey of Health and Safety Management in the UK, Performance Support International, 1994

■ *What are the most common reasons for improving the health and safety system in an organisation?*

Many health and safety systems do not work at optimum efficiency, but what will it actually take for the system to be reviewed and revised? If you are concerned about the need for a review, but are unsure what would spark this off, then these figures might give you a clearer picture of the situation. Managers were asked to rate the potential factors on a scale from 0 (not important) to 5 (very important). These were the average ratings:

Legal requirement	3.93
Internal health and safety review	3.39
Ease of use of alternative system	3.28
Dealing with a variety of health and safety regulations	3.26
Price of improvements	3.22
Flexibility of an alternative system	2.9
Cost savings	2.79

Source: Survey of Health and Safety Management in the UK, Performance Support International, 1994

■ Why are companies concerned about health and safety issues?

It would be nice to think that all companies are caring, concerned parents who protect their employees out of love. Few business truths, however, are actually this simple. There are, in fact, many reasons for improving health and safety in the workplace. If you want to know which factors to take into consideration in your health and safety plan, it is helpful to know which are the prime motivators. One survey asked employers which factors most motivated their concern for their employees. Respondents ranked the factors from 1 (high) to 7 (low), and the average ranking is shown in the next chart.

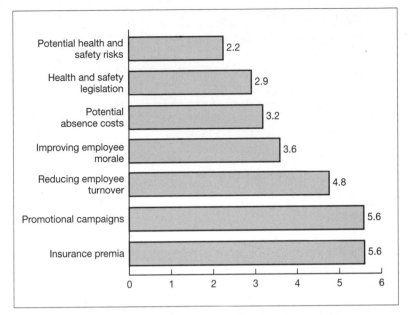

Potential health and safety risks	2.2
Health and safety legislation	2.9
Potential absence costs	3.2
Improving employee morale	3.6
Reducing employee turnover	4.8
Promotional campaigns	5.6
Insurance premia	5.6

Source: Working for your Health, Confederation of British Industry, 1993

HEALTH AND SAFETY

■ *Where do companies get advice on health and safety issues?*

Of course, before undertaking any health and safety initiatives, it helps to know what areas of health and safety you need to work on, and what you should do about them. But if you don't know the answers to these questions, then who is going to tell you? The next chart shows what percentages of companies get health and safety advice from different sources.

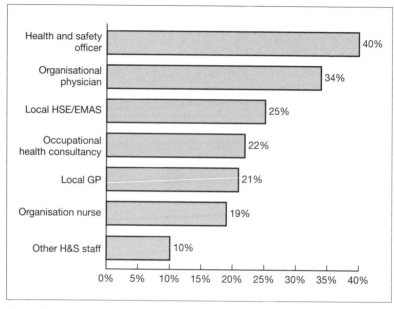

Source: Working for your Health, Confederation of British Industry, 1993

Health and safety law

■ *What level of legal action does the Health and Safety Commission take?*

The legal aspects of health and safety may be only one aspect of this area of management, but if you are concerned about where you stand with regard to certain rules and regulations, then you may want to know a little more about the level of action that the Health and Safety Commission takes. These are the Health and Safety Executive's figures for 1993/94:

- 29,442 accidents or complaints were investigated.
- 10,523 improvement and prohibition notices were issued.
- There were 1,507 convictions with an average fine of £3,061.

Source: Health and Safety Commission Annual Report 1993/94

- The conviction rate in 1992/93 for informations laid by HSE inspectorates and HSC agencies was 86%.

Source: Health and Safety Statistics, HSE, Supplement to 1993/94 annual report

Health and safety training

■ *How many employers provide health and safety training?*

Health and safety issues can be fairly straightforward, but there may be certain areas in which you feel that staff might need some training. But if you do not provide any training at all in health and safety matters, then are you overlooking an important part of health and safety procedure, or is this form of training only provided by a few companies anyway?

- In 1994, 64% of employers provided some form of health and safety or first aid training.
- This figure rose to 86% in organisations with 500+ employees.
- Of organisations with 25–49 employees, however, only 58% provided such training.

Source: Skill Needs in Britain 1994 IFF research for Employment Department

■ *Are health and safety personnel receiving enough training?*

We have seen what sort of level of health and safety training is normally provided, but just because this is the usual level does not mean that it is sufficient. So, how many health and safety managers feel that their company is providing enough training for them to do their jobs properly?

- Overall, 46% of those surveyed agreed or strongly agreed with the statement that 'training currently provided is insufficient'.

Source: Survey of Health and Safety Management in the UK, Performance Support International, 1994

HEALTH AND SAFETY

HEALTH

■ **What aspects of health are personnel managers most concerned about?**

If you do not know which health issues should come at the top of your priority list, then it might help you to know how others in your position feel. One survey asked personnel managers whether each of the issues below was a major concern, a minor concern, or no concern at all.

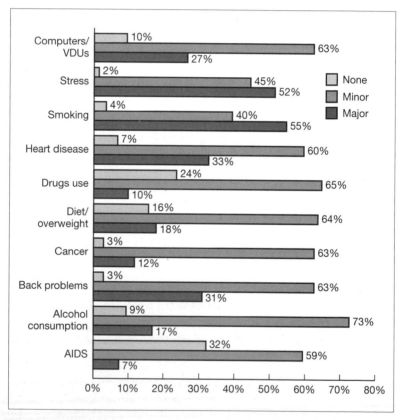

Source: *Attitudes towards Alcohol in the Workplace*, MORI for the Health Education Authority, 1995

■ *What steps do companies take to encourage their staff to be healthy?*

Some companies only take an interest in health and safety in as much as they are legally obliged to. Others actively encourage their staff to look after their health. Such strategies can be achieved through company newsletters, posters or management statements. But how many companies are actually only doing the bare minimum, and how much over and above this are other companies doing? In one survey, respondents were given these options to describe their influence on employee health: 'No influence other than basic workplace safety', 'Minimum influence to ensure that employees are fit for work', 'Encourage employees to take initiatives to improve their health', and 'Actively try to change employees' behaviour'. The responses broke down like this:

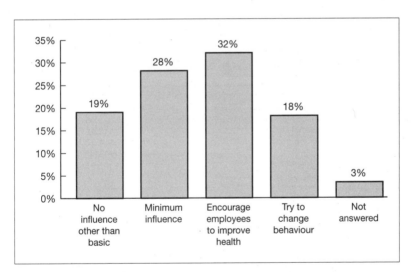

Source: Working for your Health, Confederation of British Industry, 1993

■ *How do companies undertake health education?*

As we can see, many companies do take steps to encourage their employees to improve or maintain their health. But if you wanted to start such an initiative, how would you go about it? The next chart indicates the most common methods of health education in companies, and shows the percentage of companies that use each method.

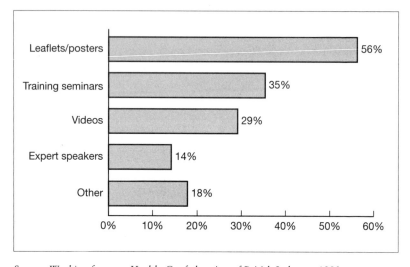

Source: Working for your Health, Confederation of British Industry, 1993

■ How do companies monitor employee health?

Health and safety officers cannot just stand in the door of their office and watch staff walk by to tell whether they are healthy or not. So are measures to gauge employees' health rare occurrences in a few paranoid organisations, or are they a common health and safety practice? Not surprisingly, the frequency of such tests varies between manufacturing and non-manufacturing companies, but the Confederation of British Industry survey kindly gives figures in both categories for the percentage of companies running each kind of test on employees.

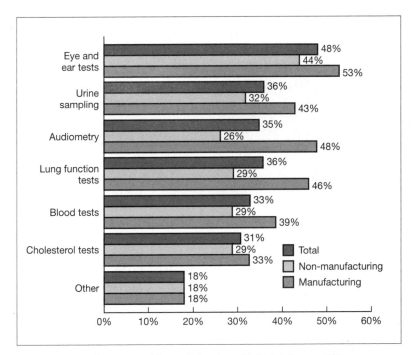

Source: Working for your Health, Confederation of British Industry, 1993

■ *What are employers' main physical health concerns?*

What should employers focus on amongst the myriad of possible complaints? Repetitive strain injury has had a lot of press in recent years, but how much of a problem is this relative to old, well-known concerns such as back problems and stress? Some health problems are more relevant in certain occupations, such as manufacturing, but if you want to know what health problems may be afflicting your employees, here is a graph of the major concerns of companies in the Confederation of British Industry survey. The figures show the percentage of respondents who rated each affliction as a concern.

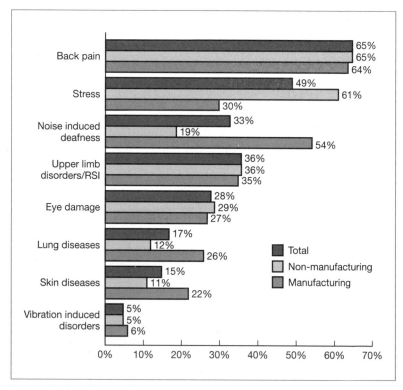

Source: *Working for your Health*, Confederation of British Industry, 1993

286

TOWARDS THE MILLENNIUM

TRENDS AND ISSUES

Development

■ What are the main issues in development?

As we hurtle towards the new millennium, are there trends we should be aware of when attempting to motivate ourselves and others? Both the American Society for Training and Development (ASTD) and Britain's Association of Management Education and Development (AMED) have tried to identify the significant issues facing development. AMED's list is shorter:

1. Humanising work
2. Globalisation
3. Sustainable development
4. Stakeholder relationships
5. Ethics and values in development.

Training trends defined by the ASTD

1 Skill requirements will continue to increase in response to rapid technological change
2 The workforce will be more educated and diverse
3 Corporate restructuring will continue to reshape the business environment
4 Corporate training departments will change dramatically in size and composition
5 Advances in technology will revolutionise the way training is delivered
6 Training departments will find new ways to deliver services
7 Training professionals will focus more on interventions in performance improvement
8 Integrated high-performance work systems will proliferate
9 Companies will transform into learning organisations
10 Organisational emphasis on human performance management will accelerate

Source: Wake up to the End of the Anti-People Trends, Andrew Leigh, Maynard Leigh Associates, 1997

Human resource management

■ *How can human resource professionals make the right decisions?*

Management is all about asking the right questions – and having the data available to generate action-oriented answers. Peter Kingsbury has written a powerful new introduction to harnessing IT to HR decision making. He argues that we can no longer just collect relevant information – this information has to be part of a flexible and dynamic electronic datastore. Only then can it streamline all the key personnel processes and feed into robust and reliable reports.

There are legitimate concerns – a reluctance to reduce individual employees to a set of figures, doubts about the ability of computers to make people decisions. Yet the potential contribution of databases is 'limited only by the imagination of the user or application builder'. Relational databases hold the key.

Source: I.T. Answers to H.R. Questions, Peter Kingsbury, IPD, 1997

TOWARDS THE MILLENNIUM

■ *What personnel functions are most often run on technology-based systems?*

IT is taking over many areas of business, and the human resources department is not immune to the steady advance of computerisation. But converting to a technology-based system can be expensive and time-consuming, and you may well not want to put all your personnel functions on to a computer system. But which functions should be the first to reap the benefits of new technology, and which should be left behind? One survey aimed to find out which applications are most commonly run on human resources systems. The results below show what proportion of companies operate each of the systems that was run by at least half of the organisations contacted.

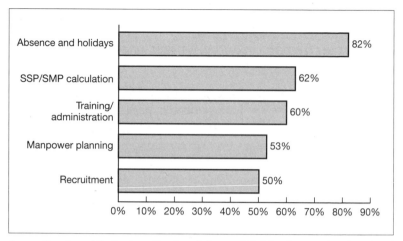

Source: *People and Technology*, Benchmark Research Ltd for Coopers & Lybrand and Oracle, 1994

■ What are the advantages of introducing a technology-based human resources system?

If you are thinking of introducing a computer system for dealing with part of your personnel management function, it might help to know what benefits can be expected from such a system. Should you want to know what the potential advantages of introducing such a system are, then these are the main advantages indicated by respondents to the Benchmark survey, along with the percentage of companies indicating each one.

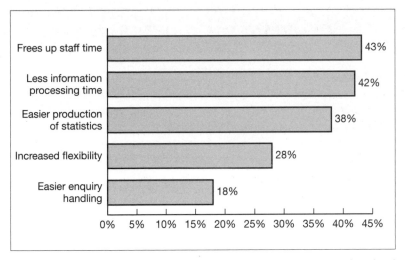

Source: People and Technology, Benchmark Research Ltd for Coopers & Lybrand and Oracle, 1994

■ Who has access to human resources/payroll computer systems?

Once a technology-based system is in place, then the question of who has access to this system arises. Should the board have access to it, or should it be restricted solely to the personnel function? And what about line managers? Naturally these decisions are very important when considering the actual use of a new system, and different companies approach the issue in different ways. The list below shows what proportion of companies grant access to personnel and/or payroll systems to each category.

Payroll function	78%
Personnel function	63%
IT function	18%
Line management	11%
Finance department	9%
Pension function	8%
Directors/partners	2%

Source: People and Technology, Benchmark Research Ltd for Coopers & Lybrand and Oracle, 1994

INFORMATION TECHNOLOGY

If the technology of a Rolls Royce had improved at the same rate over the same period as the PC, it could now circle the globe on half a gallon of petrol at some 50,000 miles per hour, and would cost the same as a Fiat Uno. In terms of precision, if the technology of the aerospace industry had improved at the same rate as computer storage, a jumbo jet could fly around the M25 six inches off the ground and in perfect safety.

Source: Garry Veale, Marketing and Strategy Manager, IBM

■ *To what extent has IT made life easier for managers?*

There is so much that can be done with IT these days, but how much use does it actually prove to be in the day-to-day office? If you are continually updating your office, you will no doubt want to know whether the consensus of opinion is that this is all worth it.

- 67% of managers said that IT has speeded up communications and improved their access to information.

- Only 40%, however, feel that IT has made information any more relevant to its target audience.

Source: *Are Managers Getting the Message?* Institute of Management, 1992

■ *How many employers feel that there is an IT 'skills gap'?*

'Skills gaps' are talked about in many areas of business, but how applicable is this concept to the fast-moving world of IT? Of all employers who felt that there was a 'skills gap', 53% said they felt that there was one in computer literacy and knowledge of information technology (the most commonly mentioned area).

Source: *Skill Needs in Britain 1994*, IFF research for Employment Department

■ *How effective are technology-based forms of communication?*

New technology always receives a lot of hype, and it doesn't always live up to the claims that are made by its marketing team. So before you set about buying every gadget available, you will no doubt want to know whether the newest forms of telecommunication are useful tools, or just gizmos.

● Faxes were judged to be the most useful 'technology-based' communication system.

● Electronic mail systems were also judged to be useful, although 20% of managers thought their e-mail systems were overburdened with junk mail.

● More sophisticated systems were less likely to be used, however – video conferencing was used by 25% of managers.

Source: Are Managers Getting the Message? Institute of Management, 1992

■ *Do managers make the most of IT?*

Information technology certainly has a lot to offer business, but there is a big difference between having a sophisticated computer system installed and knowing how to use it. Before you kit out your office with all the latest computer gear, you may want to pause for a while to consider how much of it is likely to be used. So, are managers in general getting everything they can from their IT systems, or is the truth a little less techno-utopian than that?

● Just over 50% of managers said that IT had been installed on a coherent basis in their organisation.

● Less than 25% of managers felt that their current IT system was being exploited to its full potential.

● Only 15% of managers claimed to understand fully the capabilities of the system in place.

Source: Are Managers Getting the Message? Institute of Management, 1992

Computers

■ *How widespread is the use of computers?*

The IT Skills Forum is a non-profit making consortium of 70 businesses and other organisations whose aim is to share knowledge and promote the research and education of IT throughout the UK. Their recent research shows that:

- Three quarters of the general workforce are not using IT to their maximum advantage.
- 7 out of 10 users believe their IT systems are not providing any return on their investment.
- Around 20% of IT spend is wasted.

Source: Information Technology, Barclays Review, 1996

■ *Does using computers entail an increase in skills?*

Computers are supposed to make jobs easier for us, but to what extent is this case? If certain jobs have been affected by computerisation, does this mean that people doing them will now need more skills than they did before?

- 73% of people using computers in their job said that they had increased their skills.
- Only 49% of those not using such equipment, however, said the same of their skills levels.

Source: Employee Commitment and the Skills Revolution, Policy Studies Institute, 1993

■ *Are word processors a benefit to employees?*

Word processors can be difficult to master, and make a significant change to the way that work is done, but is this all worthwhile for the final result of introducing such machines?

- 34% of employees in organisations that had recently introduced word processors thought that staff had benefited a great deal from their introduction.
- Another 40% said that staff had benefited a fair amount from this change.

Source: Employee Commitment and the Skills Revolution, Policy Studies Institute, 1993

IT solutions

■ *Are the benefits of IT well understood?*

The immense impact of the personal computer on business life over recent years is undeniable. Yet many small businesses feel that they have been let down by the IT industry.

- Only 10% of small businesses say that the IT industry is very good at explaining the benefits of IT to the business community.

- Many feel that the industry has often become caught up in developing increasingly powerful and sophisticated information technologies at the expense of addressing basic business needs.

- Nearly one third of small businesses say that they learn of developments in IT through their friends and family.

Source: Information Technology, Barclays Review, 1996

■ *How can you make sure that money spent on IT is well spent?*

Barclays Review of Information Technology and small businesses gives the following tips:

Top tips for buying IT

1 **Evaluate your business needs.** Discuss the ambitions of your business with your supplier so that they can provide solutions for the future as well as for the current state of your business.
2 **Be systematic.** Compile a list of prospective suppliers
3 **Don't buy equipment that might soon be outdated.** Consider leasing.
4 **Plan ahead.** Think beyond initial low prices and consider the ongoing maintenance and upgrading costs.
5 **Check service agreements.** Look for on-site service agreements and compare each supplier's arrangements.
6 **Train staff.** This will maximise your return on investment.
7 **Look for ways in which computers can add real value to your business.** Don't see computers simply as a way of replicating a manual process.

Source: Information Technology, Barclays Review, 1996

TOWARDS THE MILLENNIUM

■ What are the benefits of electronic networks?

Simple technologies mean that you and your PC can link quickly and cheaply to other PCs. In the United States, an estimated 25% of small and medium sized enterprises use external mail, yet the percentage in the UK is much smaller – a mere 9%. So what are the benefits of electronic networking?

- IT can make internal and external communications much more effective. You don't need to post letters to suppliers and customers when you can communicate instantly with them via e-mail.

- The spread of electronic networks is creating an international electronic marketplace. Electronic networks can mean more efficient working practices, new products and new customers.

Source: Information Technology, Barclays Review, 1996

■ How do you use the Internet effectively?

The Internet provides businesses with a unique opportunity – cheap access to a vast global market. In the UK alone, there are over 100,000 company websites; private users have already topped 1.5 million. Barclays research shows that 8 out of 10 UK companies see the Internet as a business opportunity; only 1% see it as a threat. So how do you use the Internet effectively?

Top tips for getting connected

1 **Match your needs and your budget with your Internet provider.** Prices vary from £3 to over £20 per month. The amount of free access time also varies. Make sure that the access number is a local one, or your costs will soar.

2 **Consider a server with an on-line information service.** For first-time users, this is a must – the information service will stop you getting tangled in the Web!

3 **Subscribe to an Internet magazine or visit a Cybercafé.** Magazines provide vital information; cybercafés allow you to practise surfing until you are confident.

4 **Consider an adaptable software package.** There are several available off-the-shelf which allow you to design your own site.

5 **Don't forget to check your electronic mail regularly.** This way you won't miss out on orders. Make sure that you can process the transaction speedily and efficiently.

6 **Include your electronic address on all your stationery.** Put it on your promotional literature, too, so that all your customers can find you easily.

Source: Information Technology, Barclays Review, 1996

■ *How can you make the best use of your phone?*

Virtually every business has a telephone. Yet the use of telecommunications remains relatively unsophisticated in many businesses. Tim Harrabin, Marketing Director of Talkland, says:

> *In the 1990s, small businesses need to be exploiting the benefits of new telecommunications products and services. The difficulty they face is keeping pace with technological change and understanding how it can be harnessed to create competitive advantage, not to mention keeping track of new tariffs which often lower call charges.*

A wide range of services is now on offer, and the cost of telecommunications continues to fall as the market becomes increasingly competitive. So how do you make the most of your phone?

TOWARDS THE MILLENNIUM

Making the most of your phone

1 **Consider a personalised message service.** Voice-mail systems allow you to receive calls in your absence, and forward messages to your colleagues in or out of the office.

2 **Subscribe to a personalised phone number.** You keep this for life. It means that you will receive all your calls from anyone who dials your number, no matter which phone you are using.

3 **Use a call forwarding service.** Then you can redirect calls to the most appropriate telephone number – perhaps your mobile phone, or the number in a different office.

4 **Consider all telephone suppliers.** Each one has a different tariff – there is likely to be one which is particularly suitable to your business needs.

5 **Consider a freephone sales number.** This tells your customers that you value their custom. Speak to your telephone provider, who will explain the costs and billing arrangements to you. The cost may not be as great as you think.

Source: Information Technology, Barclays Review, 1996

IT training

■ *How many employers provide IT training?*

If you are deciding whether to provide training for your staff in various aspects of IT, then one factor that you may want to take into account is whether such a provision is standard procedure within most companies, or whether it usually falls by the wayside.

● 47% of employers said that they had provided 'new technology' training in the last 12 months.

● The figure for employers with 500+ employees was 83%.

● However, only 38% of employers with 25–49 employees provided such training.

Source: Skill Needs in Britain 1994, IFF research for Employment Department

■ *What are the main reasons for providing IT training?*

No one would provide any sort of training without an expectation of
the outcome and a reason for doing it. This is as true of IT training
as of any other area. But what would induce you to provide training
in IT? One survey asked respondents what their key reason was for
providing training.

- 62% of interviewees said that the key driver for their use of IT
  training was the improvement of computer literacy.

- Improving the standing of IT in the company was the next most
  commonly cited reason, given by 17% of respondents.

- 7% said that their main reason was to standardise working practices.

Source: Benchmark Research Ltd Survey for Hewlett Packard, IBM and Oracle, 1995

■ *What organisational factors have most effect on IT training?*

If you want to know where your IT training will be in a year's time,
what factors do you need to consider? The Benchmark survey asked
respondents to rate the importance of various factors from 1 (not
important) to 5 (extremely important). The average rating for each
factor is shown overleaf.

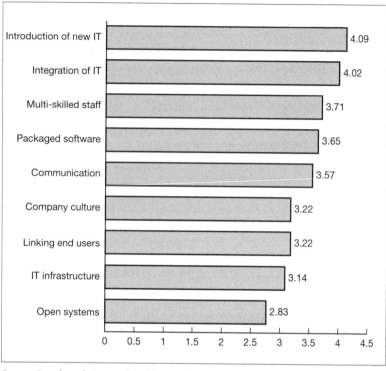

Source: Benchmark Research Ltd Survey for Hewlett Packard, IBM and Oracle, 1995

■ How important is IT training for different occupations?

Another factor to consider when planning an IT training programme is which staff most need to be trained in this area. There is no point ploughing all your training resources into training sales assistants who will never have to operate anything more technologically advanced than a till. But how does this priority system actually work out in practice? The same survey asked respondents to rate the importance of IT training for various occupational groups from 1 (not important) to 5 (extremely important). The average ratings are shown next for two groups – departments and levels of managers.

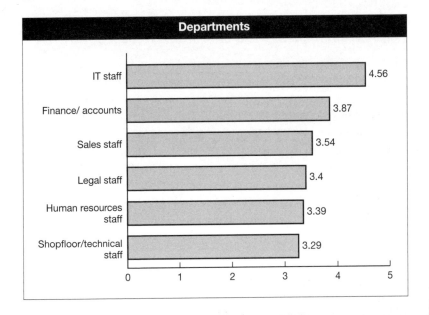

Departments

IT staff	4.56
Finance/ accounts	3.87
Sales staff	3.54
Legal staff	3.4
Human resources staff	3.39
Shopfloor/technical staff	3.29

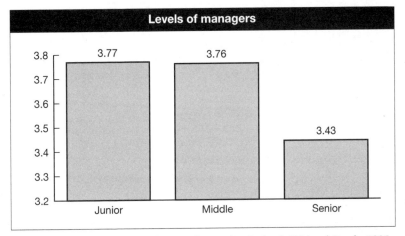

Levels of managers

Junior	3.77
Middle	3.76
Senior	3.43

Source: Benchmark Research Ltd Survey for Hewlett Packard, IBM and Oracle, 1995

TOWARDS THE
MILLENNIUM

■ How many companies have a formal IT training programme, and what time-frame does it cover?

Companies often develop formal policies or programmes for areas of business that are particularly important to them. So, is IT important enough to warrant such a formal programme? For 56% of the companies covered by the Benchmark survey, it is. Of course, such programmes may be long-term strategies covering the next two years, or they could only be applicable for the next six months. If you are thinking of developing a formal programme for IT training, it might help to know what sort of time-span is usually considered most appropriate. The chart below shows what proportion of those companies with a formal programme use each of the given time-frames.

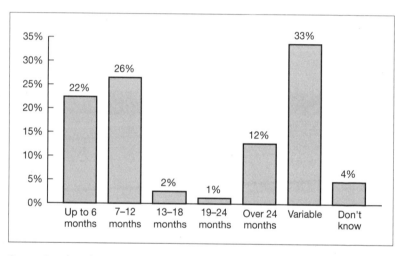

Source: Benchmark Research Ltd Survey for Hewlett Packard, IBM and Oracle, 1995

■ Which functions does your business use computers for?

Efficient use of computers will require simultaneous, not singular work functions. Yet IT training will not hit the mark unless you understand how computers are used in your business. So how do other businesses use their computers?

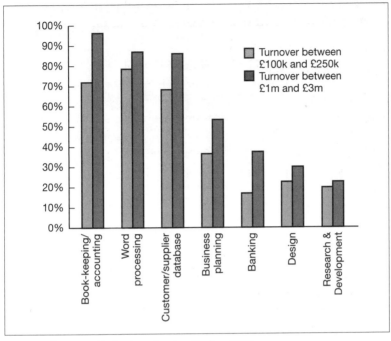

Source: Information Technology, Barclays Review, 1996

■ What are the main areas of IT training?

As it is not always possible to cater to every need, there must be some priority system for which areas of IT most need the limited training that you can provide. Information about the extent to which most companies train in the various areas of IT might help establish priorities. The next chart shows what proportion of companies provide training in each area of IT.

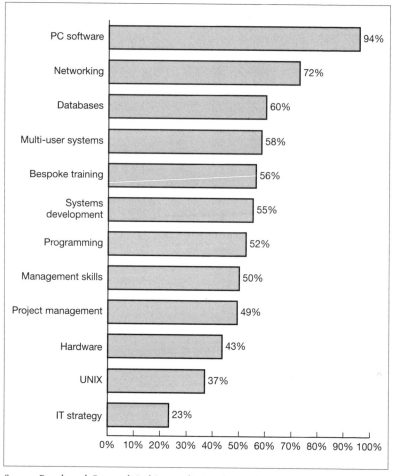

Source: Benchmark Research Ltd Survey for Hewlett Packard, IBM and Oracle, 1995

■ *What are the best ways to select IT training suppliers?*

Trade magazines, sales representatives and trade fairs can all be used to find an IT training supplier, but how reliable are they? Is the method that you are currently using one of the best? The Benchmark survey asked respondents what source they thought was best for choosing a training supplier for IT.

- 52% of those contacted said that they thought that word of mouth was the best way to find a training supplier.
- The next most popular method was direct mail, which was favoured by 12% of respondents.
- Catalogues were considered the best route by 9%.
- There was no other method cited as best by more than 4% of respondents.

Source: Benchmark Research Ltd Survey for Hewlett Packard, IBM and Oracle, 1995

■ *What proportion of the IT budget is spent on training?*

IT can be a very expensive area of business, and training can have a lot of competition for its slice of the budget pie. But what is a reasonable proportion of the budget to be spending on training? Well, that naturally varies according to many factors, especially whether there have been any other major outlays. For the companies covered by the Benchmark survey who revealed their IT training expenditure, it accounted for an average of 13% of the IT budget. The chart below shows what proportion of the budget went on training for what proportion of companies.

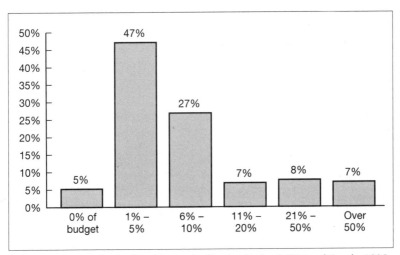

Source: Benchmark Research Ltd Survey for Hewlett Packard, IBM and Oracle, 1995

Small businesses

■ *How important is IT to the small business?*

David Lavarack, Small Business Services Director, Barclays Bank plc, reckons that IT is a fundamental tool for developing a business. He says:

> *Small businesses that use their IT more effectively will benefit from freeing up valuable time that can be used to plan and market the business more effectively ... Small businesses recognise that they need to embrace IT more fully in order to gain its full benefit ... Ever decreasing purchase costs and continuous improvements in speed and power now enable even the smallest businesses to compete against their larger counterparts on a level footing.*

- 9 out of 10 small businesses feel that IT has a positive benefit for their businesses.

- Yet only 7% say they are using it efficiently – half of the small businesses in the survey who had recently invested over £10,000 in IT had not undertaken any training in how to use the new equipment.

Source: Information Technology, Barclays Review, 1996

HOMEWORKING

■ *What are the main reasons for introducing homeworking?*

Working from home is certainly a growing practice, but what are the reasons for its popularity? If you are thinking of introducing homeworking practices in your company, then it might help to know what factors most often prompt its introduction. The following graph shows what percentage of companies that have introduced homeworking schemes cite each of the given reasons for doing so.

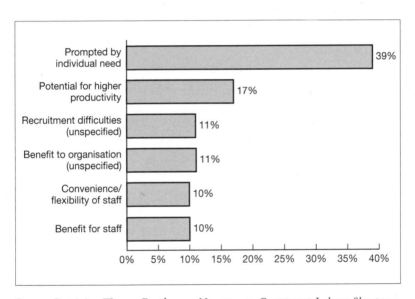

Source: Retaining Women Employees: Measures to Counteract Labour Shortages, Institute of Manpower Studies, 1990 (crown copyright)

307

FOREIGN LANGUAGE SKILLS

■ *How well can companies handle calls in a foreign language?*

Many companies do at least some business with overseas clients, especially those in Europe. But do they have the necessary language skills within their organisation to deal with calls in their clients' languages? Do you know how well your staff could deal with a phone call from a French speaker? One survey aimed to find out, by phoning the UK's top 100 exporting companies, and the results are quite startling.

Of French language enquiries to the top 100 UK exporters, 14% of calls were handled well, 12% were handled reasonably, 12% were barely managed, and 62% were abandoned with no resolution.

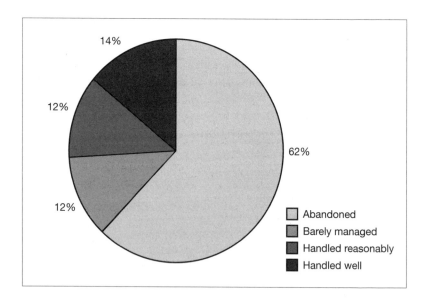

Of German language enquiries, 10% were handled well, 10% handled reasonably, 10% barely managed, and 70% were abandoned.

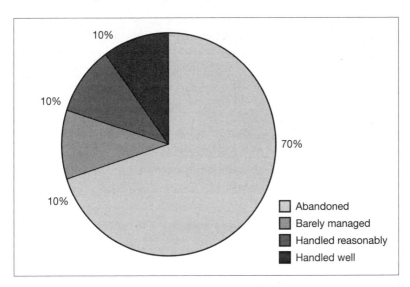

Of Italian enquiries, 7% were handled well, 7% were handled reasonably, 9% were barely managed, and 77% were abandoned.

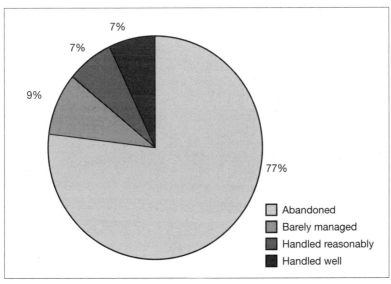

Source: Survey of the UK's Top 100 Exporting Companies, LinguaTel, 1995

■ How important is foreign business and therefore languages to British companies?

The Foreign Language Needs of Business Survey, 1991, makes interesting reading. This survey, conducted by the Institute of Manpower Studies (now the IES), covered nearly 2,000 companies. A total of 41% of these said that foreign business was of major importance to them, 17% said it was of some importance, and 3% said it was of little importance.

- In total, over 60% of these companies conducted business with foreigners whose first language was not English.

- Approximately 30% of companies surveyed provided some language training for their staff.

- 23% of companies who conducted some foreign business said that a lack of a particular language created a barrier to business in certain countries.

Source: The Foreign Language Needs of Business Survey, Institute of Manpower Studies, 1991

■ Is it always necessary to speak your customer's language?

It may be polite to speak your customer's or client's native tongue, but to what extent is it necessary? English is a very widely spoken language, and it may be that you can do quite a lot of business overseas just by speaking it slowly and loudly. But this is truer in some countries than others. So which countries can you deal with in English, and which will you need to communicate with on their terms? The next chart shows the percentage of companies whose most important foreign business was of the specified nationality who said that they could conduct all their business in English.

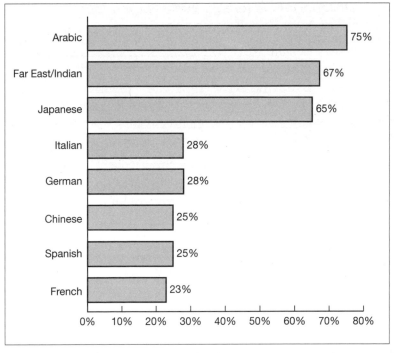

Source: The Foreign Language Needs of Business Survey, Institute of Manpower Studies, 1991

TOWARDS THE MILLENNIUM

■ For what foreign clients are foreign language skills really needed?

If you are expanding your business to deal with more foreign customers, then you will have to decide what language needs are your top priorities. You may decide this on the basis of what languages are already spoken by your staff, or what foreign contacts you have, but if you have a particular country that you want to deal with in mind, then it would help you to know how likely you are to need someone who can speak that particular language. The next chart shows what proportion of establishments whose main foreign business was with a given nation thought that their staff needed to know that language. For example, 88% of establishments whose main foreign business was with the French thought their staff needed some ability in French.

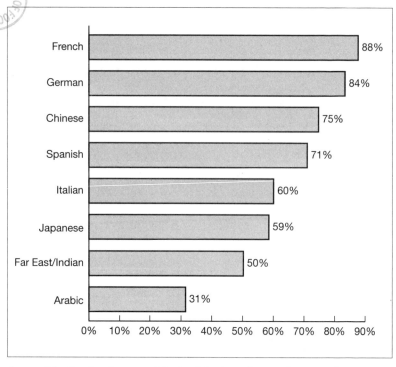

French — 88%

German — 84%

Chinese — 75%

Spanish — 71%

Italian — 60%

Japanese — 59%

Far East/Indian — 50%

Arabic — 31%

Source: The Foreign Language Needs of Business Survey, Institute of Manpower Studies, 1991

■ *Who needs to be able to speak a foreign language?*

Of course, not everyone in your company will be in contact with foreign customers, and hence not everyone will need to be able to speak their language. But where are your real language needs likely to be? Respondents to *The Foreign Language Needs of Business Survey* were asked whether they thought staff at each of these levels needed to be able to speak a foreign language. The percentages who answered 'yes' were:

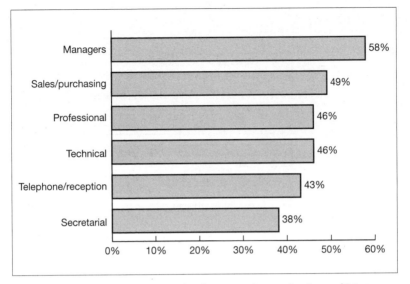

Source: *The Foreign Language Needs of Business Survey*, Institute of Manpower Studies, 1991

■ *How are language needs most commonly met?*

Of course, sometimes you will be able to get by simply by using English. But how often is this the case, and how many companies have to ensure that their staff have the necessary foreign language skills? Companies who considered their language needs met were asked in what way they were met – by having foreign language speakers in the organisation, or by not needing a foreign language for their business contacts? More than one answer was allowed. They gave answers for each of these six job categories:

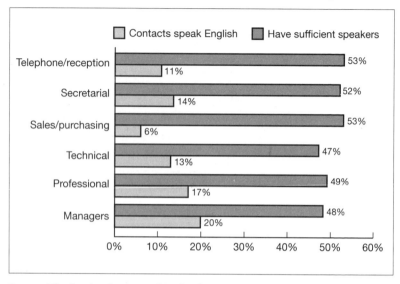

Source: The Foreign Language Needs of Business Survey, Institute of Manpower Studies, 1991

■ *How do people cope with unmet language needs?*

If you do encounter a customer or client who does not speak English, and their contact in your company does not speak their language either, then there are various options open to you, other than simply hanging up the phone. But how often are these options used? Will your foreign counterpart expect you to turn immediately to an external translation service, or is it perfectly normal for a stilted conversation to ensue which manages to perform the necessary communication in English? The figures given in the next chart are the percentage of companies responding.

● that they get by in English or an inadequately spoken foreign language;

● that they use an internal translator;

● that they use an external translator;

● that they use inappropriate staff who can speak the language.

Again, more than one answer was allowed.

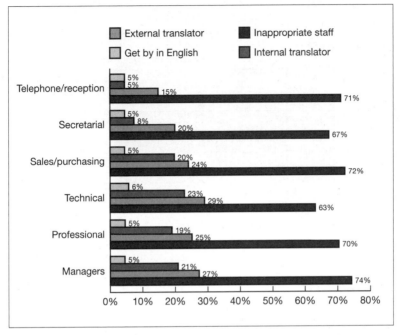

Legend:
- External translator
- Get by in English
- Inappropriate staff
- Internal translator

Telephone/reception: 5%, 5%, 15%, 71%

Secretarial: 5%, 8%, 20%, 67%

Sales/purchasing: 5%, 20%, 24%, 72%

Technical: 6%, 23%, 29%, 63%

Professional: 5%, 19%, 25%, 70%

Managers: 5%, 21%, 27%, 74%

Source: *The Foreign Language Needs of Business Survey*, Institute of Manpower Studies, 1991

■ Which languages create a genuine barrier to business?

Perhaps you do not have specific intentions to deal with any particular country, but still want to improve your overseas contacts in general. If so, the decision over which languages to cater for may be based on those which are the greatest barrier to business if you do not have them. But which languages are these? The Institute of Manpower Studies questionnaire asked which languages created a barrier to foreign business. The next chart shows the percentages of all respondents to the questionnaire who indicated each language.

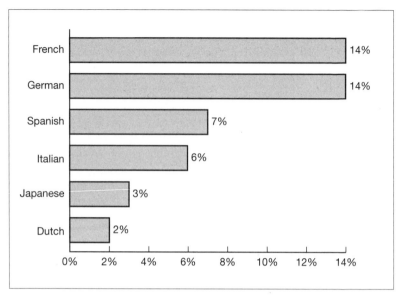

Source: The Foreign Language Needs of Business Survey, Institute of Manpower Studies, 1991

■ *How many companies provide language training for staff who need to speak that language for their work?*

If you need to have certain staff who speak a foreign language, then one option is to provide training for them in that language yourself. But how often is this used as a solution to the language problem? The following figures are the percentage of companies who provide language training for those staff at each grade who have a business need for languages.

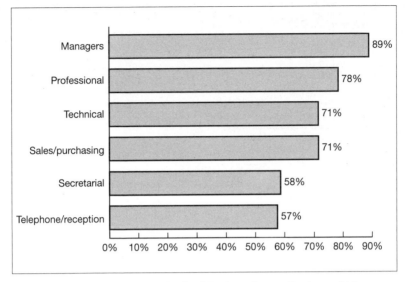

Source: The Foreign Language Needs of Business Survey, Institute of Manpower Studies, 1991

■ *What are the most popular methods of language training?*

If you decide to provide foreign language training for some of your staff, then you will also have to decide what format to provide this training in. The staff involved may have their own opinions, and you may have yours. You may also want to know what formats are generally preferred for this sort of training:

● The most preferred method of training, by quite a long way, was found to be intensive private tuition.

● After that came in-house non-intensive tuition.

● In-house intensive tuition came a close third.

Source: The Foreign Language Needs of Business Survey, Institute of Manpower Studies, 1991

Appendix 1
HOW TO READ STATISTICS

This book is packed with statistical figures – percentages, average marks out of ten, tables, graphs, charts – and after a while it can become hard to take in so much information in this form. There are also various conventions and standard formulae that are used to analyse and present such statistics. It seemed worthwhile to give brief descriptions and explanations of these in case you haven't come across them before, or not for a long time, and might benefit from some clarification of what it all actually means.

This appendix, then, is intended to clarify some of the types of statistical data that can be found in *The Essential Personnel Sourcebook*, and *The Essential Marketing Sourcebook*. Of course, it may come in handy any time that you are presented with some statistics and would like to refresh your memory of what exactly they are telling you, or not telling you. It is also intended to clear up some of the confusions that can easily be caused by the use of technical terms, particular formats and so on.

CHARTS, GRAPHS AND MATRICES

There are many charts included in this book, and each has been picked to present the data in the most convenient way. It is therefore worth mentioning the particular properties and uses of each chart, so that you will know at a glance what is being presented. The easiest way to do this is to go through the different types of chart and give a brief explanation of each one.

Bar chart

This is one of the most common types of chart. It shows figures (usually quantity or percentage) for various different items. For example, it might show what percentage of people in an office have each of the following items of fruit in their fruit bowl at home:

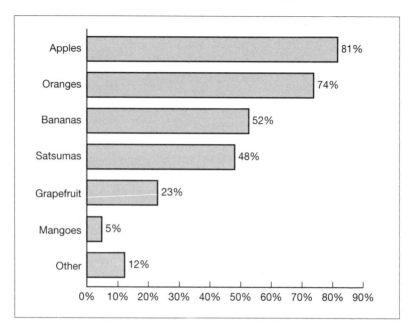

As with this chart, the highest number (and hence longest bar) should come at the top, with the others decreasing in order. Certain categories are exceptions to this rule, by always coming at the end. The most common of these are 'other' and 'none' (which may occur, for instance, in a survey of what the people in the office had for breakfast). The figures in this example do not add up to 100%, of course, since many people have more than one type of fruit in their fruit bowl.

Column chart

This looks very similar to a bar graph, but the blocks go up rather than across. Despite this similarity, it is used in a significantly different way from a bar chart. It is used in instances where the different columns progress along a sequence. Typical examples of this are when the figures apply to different times (1990, 1991, 1992, etc), different scores (strongly agree, agree, not sure, disagree, strongly disagree), and different age groups (16–19, 20–23, 24–35, 36–39). This last example is important since the groupings given are not equal. The column for people age 24–35 is likely to be much larger than for the other groupings, since it covers a much wider range of people. This sort of distortion is worth looking out for in general (although in this series we have avoided it wherever possible), and has a certain amount of effect every time there is an open-ended group (e.g. age 40+).

Since the different categories in a column chart follow a sequence, the relative heights become much more important. For instance, let's see a graph of the number of people in the office with apples in their fruit bowls for each of the last 4 weeks.

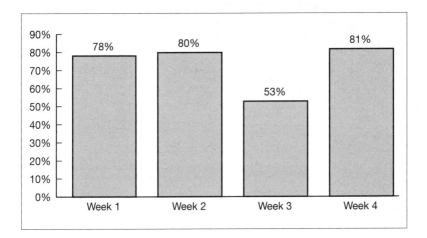

Perhaps there was a major deadline at work at the end of Week 3 and no-one had time to go shopping. It is variations like this that are the main point of information in most column charts.

Pie chart

A pie chart is used in similar cases to a bar chart, but there is one special property of a pie chart. This is that the figures in it must add up to 100%. Of course, the figures may be given as quantities rather than percentages, but there are no overlaps or omissions – the total sample is divided up completely between the various sections of the chart. For example, let's look at one fruit bowl, and see how many pieces of each type of fruit there are in it:

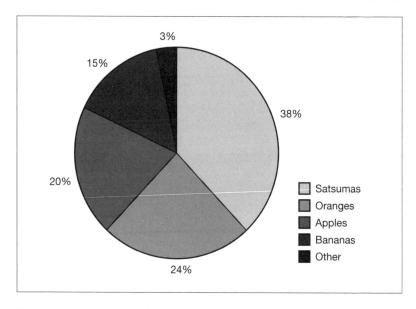

The largest segment should start at 12 o'clock and be measured clockwise from there, with subsequent segments being progressively smaller. In this way, the chart not only shows which figure is largest, but also visually conveys the relative sizes of the sections very effectively. Of course, it can be confusing if you try to fit 18 segments into a pie chart, so these are generally only used when there are 6 sections or fewer. Also, since the main strength of a pie chart is to convey relative sizes, there may be times when a bar chart is used instead, since this is not the main significance of the figures.

Line graph

These are used almost exclusively to show changes over time, and also sometimes to show changes according to age group. As we have seen, column charts can also be used for this purpose. The main differences between these two charts are:

- Column charts are only useful when there are relatively few figures – otherwise you end up with too many columns and it is hard to read.

- Column charts tend to be used to show specific variations rather than general trends.

So a line graph is used for time-series comparisons when there are many figures, and usually when there is a general trend rather than a horizontal line with a few kinks in it. An example would be an analysis of the number of apples I have eaten each week for the last 3 months.

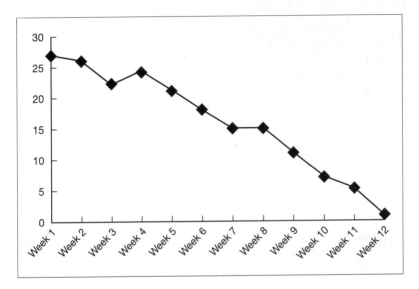

I am now completely sick of apples. What this chart conveys most effectively is the rapid decline in my apple addiction, rather than the number of apples that I ate in any given week.

Scatter chart

Scatter charts are used to show correlation – that is, the relationship between two factors. In this way, they could be used to show the relationship between the value of the pound and my tendency to eat apples. There is unlikely to be any real relationship here – both of these factors will vary without having any effect on each other. However, the relationship between the number of apples I eat and the number of bananas I eat may be very strong.

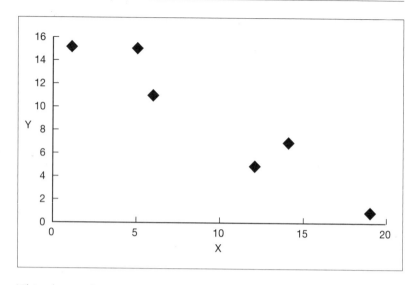

This shows that as my consumption of apples decreased (as shown by the values on the vertical Y-axis) my consumption of bananas increased (as shown by the value on the horizontal X-axis). So when I eat 15 apples, I eat one banana; when I eat one apple I eat 19 bananas. This can be seen from the fact that the points on the graph go in something approximating to a straight line from the top left to bottom right of the chart. If I tend to eat as many apples as bananas on any day, then the line would go from the bottom left to top right. If there were no correlation then they would not form any noticeable line. Scatter charts are quite uncommon, but are the most appropriate chart for showing this sort of correlation.

Matrix

Matrices vary from the other charts described here in that they are not necessarily dependent on numerical figures. The axes are normally shown crossed, giving a dead centre at the point where they cross. This divides the chart into four quarters, and the main information given is which quarter each item is in. In some matrices, items are not positioned any more specifically than this, while in others they are given a precise place on the chart.

Suppose, for instance, that I generally eat fruit either because it tastes nice, or because it is filling, and I want to know how well each type of fruit fills each of these criteria. If I were only interested in taste then I might give marks out of ten and show the results on a bar chart, but I want a chart that will show me both figures at once.

The chart I want is this one:

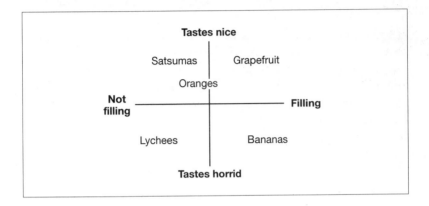

This chart tells me that if I want something filling, and I don't care about the taste, I should have a banana (the most filling item), or if I want it to taste nice as well, then I should have a grapefruit (not as filling, but much nicer). It also tells everyone exactly what I think of lychees. I could have given marks out of ten on each axis, which would have given each fruit a precise point on the graph, or I could have simply put each fruit in one of the four quarters and not been any more specific than this. The matrix above is a compromise between the two.

So matrices are useful for showing how a variety of items rate according to two different variables (e.g. taste and fillingness).

INDEXING

One particular statistical convention that may be used occasionally in these books is indexing. This is a relatively uncommon way of quantifying information, so it is probably worth giving a brief explanation of it for anyone who may not have come across it before.

Indexing is used when there are no absolute figures available, only relative ones. The information therefore shows the relationships between these figures. However, this cannot be done with percentages or quantities, since the data does not exist in this form. So how can the information be presented? The solution is to take an arbitrary figure as the standard, or as the maximum, and then rate other figures relative to this.

Suppose I want to rate how much Alice, Bruce, Cynthia and David enjoy eating apples. I am not asking for scores out of ten from each of them, I am trying to measure their actual enjoyment, so there is no absolute measurement that I can apply. However, I may still have meaningful and useful information to give on this topic. One way that I can present this is to say that Cynthia seems to be fairly ambivalent about eating apples, while the others have stronger feelings one way or the other. So I take 100 as the amount of pleasure Cynthia experiences from eating an apple. Using this, I now have a scale on which to judge the pleasure of my four subjects.

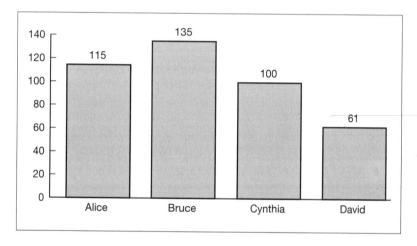

Note that the '100' here does not measure anything specific such as the volume of 'Mmmm' noises or number of endorphins released in the brain. And rather than having 100 as the most neutral point, I could have had it as the maximum enjoyment. This choice was entirely arbitrary, it was simply necessary to provide a way of presenting the data, and the data itself shows only the relationship between these four people's enjoyment of eating apples, and cannot be related to anything beyond this.

AVERAGES

Most of us can remember from school that there are three different kinds of average, even if we can't quite recall what all of them are. Since they are used in these books, it might be wise to recap them. Imagine that 35 of us have fruit bowls, and I want to know the average number of apples in each bowl. My three options are:

1. Mean average: the total number of apples divided by the total number of fruit bowls (this is the most commonly used type of average, and the one that we generally mean when we don't specify which sort of average we are talking about).
2. Median average: the half way point between the highest (9) and lowest (0) number of apples.
3. Mode average: the single number of apples that occurs more frequently than any other.

I'll give you an example. The following line chart shows the number of fruit bowls containing each quantity of apples; 5 bowls have no apples in them, one contains one apple and so on.

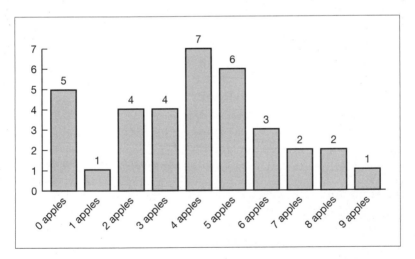

- Mean average number of apples (136 apples divided by 35 fruit bowls): 3.9
- Median average number of apples: 4.5
- Mode average number of apples: 4

FIGURES THAT SEEM TO CONTRADICT EACH OTHER

In books like *The Essential Personnel Sourcebook,* and *The Essential Marketing Sourcebook*, there are many figures which refer to very similar things. In some cases these figures may appear to directly contradict each other. In fact, we have taken great pains to ensure that no contradictory figures are included in any of *The Essential Business Sourcebooks*, but there are often subtle differences between statistics which are easy to overlook, and may give the impression that they cannot both be correct.

For example, suppose we are examining the composition of a particular fruit bowl which contains four satsumas and a grapefruit. We may say that:

- The contents of the fruit bowl is made up of 20% grapefruit.
- It is also made up of 50% grapefruit.

For the sake of this example, these figures are obviously deliberately unhelpful, but they may both be correct. The first, in fact, applies to the composition in numbers of fruits (four satsumas and one grapefruit), and the second applies to the composition in weight (since four satsumas weigh the same as one grapefruit). Naturally, we will explain such differences whenever there are potentially confusing figures like this in any of *The Essential Business Sourcebooks*, but if you are only looking up one piece of information, or if you are in a hurry and concentrating more on the figures than the text, then it is easy to miss such slight but crucial differences.

In order to minimise the likelihood of this happening, and make it easier to spot the reasons for such discrepancies in this book or elsewhere, I will briefly explain some of the main reasons that such apparent contradictions can occur.

Differences in the sample

Even if two surveys ask exactly the same question, it is exceptionally unlikely that they will be asking the same people. For this reason, results will always vary slightly between different surveys. Often surveys will deliberately be asking different people about the same thing – one survey may ask all workers, for instance, and another may be asking only managers. This may produce substantially different results, and these differences may even be the main point of interest in the figures.

The differences are sometimes even more subtle than this; for instance one survey may ask workplaces if they operate a certain policy, and another may workers if their workplace operates the policy. If the policy is most often operated by large workplaces with many employees, then the proportion of workers answering 'yes' is likely to be higher than the proportion of workplaces answering 'yes'.

Differences in survey characteristics

Sometimes differences may be less deliberate. One survey may have covered more large companies than another, for instance, and in many cases this will lead to different results. This does not mean that one was a survey of large companies and the other a survey of small companies, it simply means that their balance of companies of different sizes was not the same. Similarly, one survey may have been conducted by interview and another by postal questionnaire, and this will also have an effect on the results.

Another factor that may lead to differences is the time of the survey. Figures of change over time can be very useful information in its own right, but since any two surveys are likely to vary in many ways (such as what exact question was asked, who was asked and so on) it is often misleading to compare results from two totally different surveys conducted at different times.

To avoid this type of confusion, the figures in this book have been selected as the most reliable ones of all that were available. However, there may be times when two different surveys cover the same topic but ask slightly different questions, in which cases both will be included, in order to provide as much useful information as possible. In such cases, it is worth remembering that the two surveys were very probably conducted at different times and in different ways, and while both are informative and valid, they are unlikely to have produced exactly the same results.

Differences in conceptual structure

Many decisions are made when designing a survey, and this is
another area where surveys can vary. If I am conducting a survey into
how many people eat apples often, then I will have to define 'often'.
Is it once a week, twice a week, or once a fortnight? Naturally, the
choice I make in defining this term will affect what figure I arrive at
at the end of the survey.

Similarly, I may be surveying how many apples people eat in a
week. If I am doing this on a tick-box questionnaire, then I will have
to chose what categories to provide a box for – it may be '0–3',
'4–8', '8–11', '12+', or it may be '0', '1–5', '6–10', '11+'. It will be
very hard to tie together the two sets of figures that I receive, and
each grouping has its own strengths and weaknesses.

Similarly, I may be surveying peoples favourite fruits, and listing
them either by colour, or by price, or in groups such as citrus, tropical and so on. Again, I may not be able to compare the different
results that I receive in any meaningful way. Each set of results will
tell me something that I want to know, but will fail to tell me something else. So each set of results simply has to be taken on its own
merits, and the inherent differences borne in mind when taking the
results together.

NOT ADDING UP TO 100%

In this book, and elsewhere, percentage figures are often given which
do not total 100%. At times this may be confusing, particularly
when you want to be sure that you have complete and reliable information. Of course, there are many legitimate reasons why this can
occur, and it is worth running through these quickly so that, when
such a situation occurs, you will be able to see why it has happened.

More than 100%

Rounding

Some of the figures that are given as whole number percentages may originally have been calculated to one or two decimal places. This level of detail is often unnecessary, and can complicate the information that is being given, and hence the figures have been 'rounded' to the nearest whole number. This process can occasionally produce figures which total 101% or 102%, although it is rare to create any more of a disturbance than this.

For example, the composition of my fruit bowl (by weight) is:

Apples: 30.6%
Oranges: 32.7%
Bananas: 36.6%

This makes a total of 100%. However, I would like to make these statistics easier to read and take in, so I want them as whole numbers. Since the numbers after the decimal places are all greater than 5, this means that all these numbers will be rounded up, giving this composition:

Apples: 31%
Oranges: 33%
Bananas: 37%

This totals 101%. This is an unfortunate, but unavoidable, effect of rounding. Although it can be disconcerting, the only way to treat it is to simply accept that it happens, but that it causes only very minimal distortion of the statistics, since the total of the percentages very rarely comes to more than 102%.

Multiple answers

Let's consider the example given earlier in this section of the proportion of people with each given fruit in their fruit bowl:

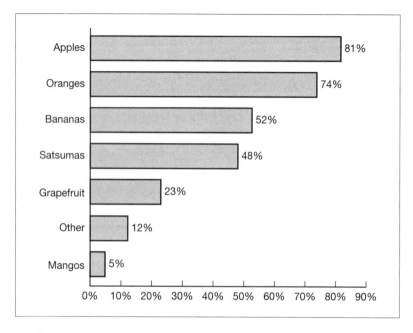

The total here is obviously much greater than 100%. The simple reason for this is that many people have more than one fruit in their bowl. Questions like this, for which each individual can give more than one answer, often end up with figures that total more than 100%. So long as we do not find that 117% of people have apples in their fruit bowl, then the data is perfectly correct.

Overlapping categories

I have found that my fruit bowl contains (by quantity), 50% tropical fruit and 70% citrus fruit. These figures seem hard to reconcile, but of course there is an explanation for this. This explanation involves grapefruit, which I class as a citrus fruit and also as a tropical fruit. My fruit bowl contains 5 satsumas, 3 bananas and 2 grapefruit. Hence there are 7 citrus fruits (satsumas and grapefruit) and 5 tropical fruits (bananas and grapefruit).

It is often useful to collect information in groupings which do not have overlaps, so as to provide a total figure of 100%. However, it may also be that two particular groups are of interest (e.g. tropical and citrus fruits), and that these groups have an overlap. If so, the figures for these groups, when added together, may total more than 100%.

Less than 100%

Rounding

The effects of rounding, as discussed previously, can produce figures which total less than 100%. On re-examining my fruit bowl, I have discovered its composition (by weight) to be:

Apples: 31.3%
Oranges: 32.4%
Bananas: 36.3%

This, again, totals 100%. After rounding, however, the figures are:

Apples: 31%
Oranges: 32%
Bananas: 36%

These figures only add up to 99%. Again, there is nothing that I can do about this rounding error, except to acknowledge that it is unavoidable, and causes only minimal distortion of the statistics.

Omitted categories

The most obvious categories which could be relevant here are 'Not Answered' and 'Don't Know'. If I ask everyone in my office whether they have apples in their fruit bowl at home, I may find that:

- 72% do have apples;
- Only 25% do not have apples.

But what about the other 3%? Well, maybe they didn't know, or maybe they just didn't want to say. Maybe they all, in fact, do have apples at home, and maybe none of them do. We simply can't say, and we have to essentially ignore them.

Sometimes figures for D/K or N/A are given, showing how many people did not respond to the question, and at other times they are not. Many survey questions, however, do not receive a full quota of answers, but the number not responding is usually fairly low and, as with rounding, does not undermine the other data to any appreciable extent.

Of course, other categories can be omitted when data is presented – any category can. If I ask my workmates what their favourite fruit is, I may find that:

● Apples are favourite for 43%.

● Bananas are the next most popular, cited by 31%.

● Oranges are preferred by only 14%.

● 4% did not know or did not answer.

This gives a total of 92%. So what about the other 8%? Well, some of them preferred mangoes, others went for satsumas or guava – there were various answers. However, the proportion who opted for each was so low that it did not seem worth including them. The information that I was trying to convey was how popular the most popular fruits are, not a full breakdown with details of fruits that were favourite with only 0.3% of people.

Although *The Essential Business Sourcebooks* try to be as comprehensive as possible, they are designed for practical use, and hence some figures may have been omitted in this way when they were not significant or relevant, and would serve only to confuse the data provided. Such detail may also have been omitted in the source literature from which the statistics were gathered. For these reasons, categories may sometimes have been omitted, giving figures that add up to less than 100%. In these cases, the data is indeed not comprehensive, but the figures that are given are no less valid for it.

Appendix 2
CONTACT ADDRESSES

ACAS
The Advisory, Conciliation and Arbitration Service
Brandon House, 180 Borough High Street, London SE1 1LW
0171 210 3613, fax 0171 210 3645

Barclays Bank plc Small Business Services
54 Lombard Street, London, EC3P 3AH

The Basic Skills Agency (previously ALBSU)
Commonwealth House, 1–19 New Oxford Street, London WC1A 1NU
0171 405 4071

Benchmark Research Ltd
8 White Oak Square, London Road, Swanley, Kent BR8 7AG
01322 614 050, fax 01322 614562
Email: benchmarkresearch@compuserve.com

Capita Group
71 Victoria Street, Westminster, London SW1H 0XA
0171 799 1525, fax 0171 222 6122
Email: 101511,2716@compuserve.com

Confederation of British Industry
Centre Point, 103 New Oxford Street, London WC1 1DU
0171 379 7400, fax 0171 240 1578
http://www.cbi.org.uk

Department for Education and Employment
Moorfoot, Sheffield
0114 259 4024, fax 0114 259 4624
http://www.open.gov.uk
To order *Skills Needs in Britain 1996*, contact:
Mark Spilsbury, Public Attitude Surveys Ltd Rye Park House, London Road
High Wycombe, Bucks HP11 1EF
01494 532771

John Fenton Training International plc
Clifford Hill Court, Clifford Chambers, Stratford-upon-Avon CV37 8AA
01789 298739, fax 01789 267060

Health and Safety Executive
Rose Court, 2 Southwark Bridge, London SE1 9HS
0171 717 6000 or for publications, contact:
HSE Books, PO Box 1999, Sudbury, Suffolk CO10 6FS
01787 881165, fax: 01781 313995

Health Education Authority
Trevelyan House, 30 Great Peter Street, London SW1P 2HW
0171 413 1988, fax 0171 413 0340
http:\www.hea.org.uk

IFF Research Ltd
26 Whiskin Street, London EC1R 0BP
0171 837 6363, fax 0171 278 9823
Email: iff@technocom.com

Incomes Data Services Ltd
77 Bastwick Street, London EC1V 3TT
0171 250 3434, fax 0171 324 2510
Email: ids@incomesdata.co.uk
http:\\www.incomesdata.co.uk

Inland Revenue
6th Floor, North West Wing, Bush House, Aldwych, London WC2B 4PP
0171 438 6692, fax 0171 438 7428

Institute of Directors
116 Pall Mall, London SW1Y 5ED
0171 836 1233, fax 0171 930 1949

Institute of Employment Studies
Mantell Building, University of Sussex, Falmer, Brighton BN1 9RF
01273 686751, fax 01273 690430

Institute of Management Foundation
Management House, Cottingham Road, Corby, Northamptonshire
NN17 1TT
01536 204222, fax 01536 201651

Institute of Manpower Studies
see 'Institute of Employment Studies'.

Institute of Personnel and Development
IPD House, Camp Road, London SW19 4UX
0181 263 3240, fax 0181 263 3244
Email: comms@ipd.co.uk
For details of speeches at the IPD National Conference, October 1997,
contact The Press Office at the above address.

IRPC Group Ltd
Stockwell House, New Buildings, Hinkley, Leicestershire. LE10 1HW
01455 894205, fax 01455 894209
Email: mktg@irpc.co.uk

IRS
Industrial Relations Services, Eclipse Group Ltd
18–20 Highbury Place, London N5 1QP
0171 354 5858, fax 0171 226 8918
Email: name@eclipsegroup.co.uk

LinguaTel Ltd
351 City Road, London EC1V 1LR
0171 762 6080

London Business School
Sussex Place, Regent's Park, London NW1 4SA
0171 262 5050, fax 0171 724 7875
Email: name@lbs.ac.uk
http:\\www.lbs.ac.uk

Marketing Week
Centaur Communications Ltd, 50 Poland Street, London W1V 4AX
0171 439 4222, fax 0171 970 4298

Media Monitoring Services
Madison House, High Street, Sunninghill, Ascot, Berkshire SL5 9NP
01344 627553, fax 01344 621037
Email: mms-support@lunar.co.uk

People Management
Personnel Publications Ltd, 17 Britton Street, London EC1M 5NQ
0171 880 6200, fax 0171 336 7637
Email: editorial@peoplemanagement.co.uk

Performance Support International
6–16 Huntsworth Mews, London NW1 6DD
0171 724 8599, fax 0171 724 8627
http:\\www.psi2000.com

Personnel Review Magazine
MCB University Press Ltd, 60/62 Toller Lane, Bradford,
West Yorkshire BD8 9BY
01274 777 700

The Policy Studies Institute
100 Park Village East, London NW1 3SR
0171 468 0468, fax 0171 388 0914
Publications to be ordered from:
Grantham Book Services, Issac Newton Way, Alma Park Industrial Estate,
Grantham, Lincs NG31 9SD
01476 541080, fax 01476 541061

Remuneration Economics
Survey House, 51 Portland Road, Kingston upon Thames, Surrey KT1 2SH
0181 549 8726, fax 0181 541 5705

Romtec plc
Vanwall Road, Maidenhead, Berkshire SL6 4UB
01628 770077, fax 01628 785433
http:\\www.romtec.co.uk

Small Business Research Trust
University of Westminster, 35 Marylebone Road, London NW1 5LS
0171 911 5000

Social and Community Planning Research
35 Northampton Square, London EC1V 0AX
0171 250 1866, fax 0171 250 1524

Carolyn Highley
47 Pennine Road, Glossop, Derbyshire SK13 9UL
01457 861445